Voice of the Voiceless

ARCHBISHOP OSCAR ROMERO

Voice of the Voiceless

The Four Pastoral Letters and Other Statements

Introductory Essays by
Ignacio Martín-Baró and Jon Sobrino

Translated from the Spanish by
Michael J. Walsh

ORBIS BOOKS
Maryknoll, New York 10545

Quotations from the Second Vatican Council are taken from *The Sixteen Documents of Vatican II* (N.C. translation; Boston: Daughters of St. Paul, 1967). Quotations from the Medellín General Conference of the Latin American Bishops are taken from *The Church in the Present-Day Transformation of Latin America in the Light of the Council*, vol. 2, *Conclusions*, Louis M. Colonnese, ed. (Washington: United States Catholic Conference, Latin American Bureau, 1970). Quotations from Pope Paul VI, *Evangelii Nuntiandi*, are taken from *On Evangelization in the Modern World* (Washington: United States Catholic Conference, 1976). Quotations from the Puebla General Assembly of the Latin American Bishops are taken from *Puebla and Beyond*, John Eagleson and Philip Scharper, eds. (Maryknoll, N.Y.: Orbis Books, 1979).

The introductory essays and most of the documents of this volume were published as *La voz de los sin voz: La palabra viva de Monseñor Oscar Arnulfo Romero*, introduction, commentary, and selection of texts by R. Cardenal, I. Martín-Baró, and J. Sobrino, copyright © 1980 by UCA Editores, Universidad Centroamericana José Simeón Cañas, Apdo. 668, San Salvador, El Salvador.

The Letter to President Carter and the Last Homily of Archbishop Romero were translated by James Brockman

Manuscript Editor: William E. Jerman

Library of Congress Cataloging in Publication Data

Romero, Oscar A. (Oscar Arnulfo), 1917–1980
   Voice of the voiceless.

   Translation of: La voz de los sin voz.
   Includes bibliographies and index.
   1. Catholic Church—El Salvador—Addresses, essays,
lectures.   2. El Salvador—Church history—Addresses,
essays, lectures.   3. Catholic Church—Doctrines—
Addresses, essays, lectures.   I. Title.
BX1446.2.R6613   1985   252'.02   84-14722
ISBN 0-88344-525-5 (pbk.)

Contents

IGNACIO MARTÍN-BARÓ

Oscar Romero:
Voice of the Downtrodden

Oscar Arnulfo Romero y Galdámez, archbishop of San Salvador, El Salvador, was born on August 15, 1917, in the town of Ciudad Barrios, in the department of San Miguel, El Salvador. He died from an assassin's bullet on March 24, 1980, in San Salvador while celebrating Mass. One well-aimed shot, fired with professional precision, was enough to bring down the small, wiry archbishop. A last mouthful of blood was the final offering of someone who throughout his sixty-three years, but especially during his last three as an archbishop, had given his entire being over to the service of the people of El Salvador, particularly to the service of the poor and the oppressed.

It is important to trace back in Romero's personal history the ultimate basis of his extraordinary apostolate as archbishop. Had one known Father Romero in the church of San Francisco or in the central parish of San Miguel, or had one known Bishop Romero of Santiago de María, it would have been difficult to foresee the role he was later to play as archbishop of San Salvador. All the signs would have pointed in the opposite direction— to a peaceable, spiritually oriented, morally severe apostolate, to a man more likely to be at ease with the powerful than to act in unshakable solidarity with the poor.

Undoubtedly this was the reason why the government of General Molina, and why others in strong economic positions in the country, promoted his candidature for the office, and it is why curial circles in the Vatican preferred his name to that of Bishop Rivera y Damas. Rivera y Damas was the logical candidate both because of his experience and his position, but powerful people in El Salvador had stigmatized him as a "communist Christian Democrat." To the delight of the poor, however, and to the fury of the powerful, to the amazement of the government of El Salvador, the discomfiture of the Vatican, and the disquiet of the United States State Department, Romero became simply *Monseñor* loved and cherished by the masses.

1

This was, without doubt, a transformation, a radical change, a true Christian conversion, and one that deepened as the people of El Salvador gradually awakened to the hope of a kingdom of justice and love.

It will be the task of the archbishop's biographers to delve into the historical background of his personality, the clarity of his moral tranquility, the humility of his intelligence, the spontaneous pleasure of his friendship, to find there—if they can—an explanation for his apostolic conversion—or at least to find the human and Christian basis for that process of radical transformation. I am trying here to do no more than outline that conversion and apostolate, above all as they took shape with a prophetic voice, a voice full of suffering and full of hope.

It is impossible to understand the archbishop's words out of context. That is not to say they were either too difficult or too parochial. In the final months of his apostolate the archbishop's words were heard directly, by means of a series of rebroadcasts, throughout Central America, in Colombia and Venezuela, and even as far away as Argentina and Uruguay. The archbishop received innumerable letters and other messages from these distant places. They thanked him for what he said. They drew attention to the impact his words had on persons who were distant both in space and in spirit. His pastoral letters and homilies have been, and are still being, translated into other languages. Persons of diverse cultures and differing histories are finding in his words inspiration and Christian encouragement. But the archbishop's words cannot be fully understood outside their context, because essentially they were words spoken in history. Their universality, their capacity for uplifting hearts so different and so distant, comes about precisely because they were uttered in a particular place and time, in the here and now of the people of El Salvador in the closing years of the 1970s.

It is this context, this close bond between the archbishop's words and the concrete historical situation in which they were spoken, that I am going to try to outline in this introductory essay. It has to be understood, however, that the archbishop's words took the form of a critical dialogue with the de facto situation, a dialogue that destroyed death and imparted life, a dialogue in which God made himself evident and real to the people of El Salvador. It was a dialogue that those who know only how to dictate terms from a position of strength, backed up by money or weapons, cannot abide. And so they killed the one who asked the questions. They assassinated the archbishop.

APPOINTMENT AND CONVERSION

On February 3, 1977, Romero, at that time bishop of Santiago de María, was appointed to replace Bishop Chávez y González as archbishop of San Salvador. Both ecclesiastically and politically, the circumstances surrounding the appointment were extremely tense. El Salvador was living through the nightmare of a vain attempt to modify very slightly its traditional agrarian structures. The attempt led the way to a wave of repression that drowned in a bloodbath the hopes that had been raised—a bath that also washed away the anxieties of those who, for a short period, had seen their traditional domination threatened.

Ever since its fraudulent election in 1972, General Molina's government had tried to walk the tightrope of a reformism that was intended, by means of a policy of handouts to the masses, to legitimate the maintenance of some fundamentally oppressive structures.[1] In 1975, by which time Molina had already begun to foresee the end of his period in office as president, the Salvadoran Institute of Agrarian Transformation was created. On June 29, 1976, the legislative assembly approved the First Project for Agrarian Transformation. The project was little more than a very timid attempt to modify certain agrarian structures. Wealthy landowners were directly affected, however, and the Salvadoran oligarchy felt that the reform constituted a dangerous precedent, even though it had been sold to it as a form of "life insurance."[2]

President Molina swore repeatedly and in public that he was not prepared to go "even one step backward." Scarcely three months later, however, on October 19, 1976, a new decree from the legislative assembly canceled the project for all practical purposes. The failure of this small, reformist attempt came about through an extremely violent campaign by the Salvadoran oligarchy against the government. It was orchestrated both on the propaganda level and at the level of economic pressure coupled with threats of a coup d'etat.[3] But the disquiet felt by the oligarchy was not completely laid to rest by the simple abandonment of the reformist project. It was necessary to undo the "evil" caused in the country. It was necessary to extirpate entirely the hopes and expectations that had been awakened in certain *campesino* groups. It was necessary to pull out by the roots even the tiniest suspicion that some day the country might change, even in minor ways. So the cancellation of the project for agrarian transformation was followed by a period of violent repression, especially against *campesinos*. The armed forces had publicly committed their honor and prestige to the implementation of the reform. Now they had to turn themselves to carrying out a totally different project: massive repression.

Political repression, and especially repression directed against the rural and urban masses, was nothing new in El Salvador. Ever since 1932 the people of El Salvador had become accustomed to paying, in their blood, the quota of violence needed to keep in existence an almost feudal system of exploitation.[4] But on this occasion the repression unleashed by the government of General Molina, in conjunction with the financiers and the exporters of agricultural produce, included a new element. For the first time it lashed out against the Catholic church.

The persecution campaign against the church, in which both the government and major private businesses were involved, was directed against priests and religious orders, against institutions and organizations linked to the church, and against all lay persons who were committed to working for the church, particularly catechists and lay "ministers of the word." By the time that Romero became archbishop of San Salvador, the archdiocesan printing press, the St. Paul Bookshop, and the Central American University had already been the target of bombs. The campaign of defamation in the press and on radio and television had reached unimaginable heights. Six priests had been expelled from the country, two of them after being tortured. The house of a diocesan priest had been raided by the security forces.[5] Even Archbishop Chávez had been attacked by the media. He was accused of allowing and encouraging "communistic sermons," and of initiating the violence of *campesino* organizations, such as the UTC (*Unión de Trabajadores del Campo,* Farmworkers' Union).

In this climate of generalized repression it was obvious that the naming of a replacement for Archbishop Chávez would have a tremendous political, as well as ecclesiastical, significance. Within church circles the problem came down to fidelity to the pastoral approach outlined by the Second Vatican council, and already applied to Latin America by the Latin American Episcopal Conference in Medellín. This approach implied an understanding of the church as the people of God and, as a consequence, an identification with the sufferings and with the hopes of the people, especially with those of the poor and the oppressed. That made the church's task eminently one of promoting awareness—conscientization—with the aim of forming communities that might begin to make real on earth the salvation proclaimed by Jesus, and to create a society of brothers and sisters, of children of God, in which all injustice, all exploitation, and all oppression would be done away with. This very fact, however, would make the church a subversive influence within a social order that was founded upon the injustice, exploitation, and oppression exercised against the many by the few. Hence, before Chávez's resignation as archbishop of San Salvador, both the government and the Salvadoran oligarchy pressured the Vatican to choose as his successor someone who would have the complete confidence of those in power— someone more concerned to keep the peace than to promote the Christian life of the people of God.

When news came from Rome that Bishop Romero had been chosen to succeed Archbishop Chávez, the Salvadoran government and the oligarchy were jubilant. They were certain they had won a great victory for the conservative cause. As far as right-wing forces were concerned, Bishop Romero was, from every point of view, the ideal candidate. With his penchant for conciliation, his clearly conservative outlook, the links that he had with the Salvadoran oligarchy and with traditionalist groups within the church (with Opus Dei, even!), Romero appeared to be the perfect man to return the church to the sheepfold, the priests to the sacristy, and Catholic teaching back to the Council of Trent and Vatican I. For their part, a good number of the clergy of the archdiocese received the news of his appointment with dejection and apprehension. They regarded it as a sign that Rome seemed more concerned to maintain good relations with the government than to serve the needs of the Christian community in El Salvador.

On February 22, 1977, Romero took over as archbishop of San Salvador in a simple, private ceremony. It was a small detail, but it made a good impression upon the clergy of the archdiocese, especially because the government was not asked to be present at the ceremony. In keeping with the situation of oppression and repression against the Christian people, there was no sign of triumphalism. Two days before, the people of El Salvador had yet again been defrauded in the voting booths. Violence, and even more blatant fraud, had made General Carlos Humberto Romero the country's new president. This new trickery gave rise to considerable unrest, and to a string of protests in San Salvador, including the threat of a general strike.

Against this background Archbishop Romero began to win hearts when, in the course of his first meeting with the clergy of the archdiocese, he introduced himself with great simplicity and asked for the advice and support of everybody. These first words, like all that were to come, were words of truth: he was always ready to accept advice and help. It enabled him to bring together the feelings of the majority of the population, to discern the Spirit in the community, and to unite the clergy and the laity in the common task of achieving salvation in history.

On February 28, scarcely a week after Romero had taken up his office as archbishop of San Salvador, the security forces together with the military spread death and destruction in the Plaza Libertad, where huge numbers of demonstrators were protesting against the fraudulent presidential elections. According to official figures, six civilians were killed. In fact the number of dead was very much higher, and the government declared a state of siege in order to suppress any manifestation of discontent or popular protest. After that massacre a new popular organization sprang up in the political arena: the Popular Leagues of the 28th of February (*Ligas Populares 28 de Febrero*), a class-based organization characterized by its radicalism and fearsome aggressiveness.

Thus, against the background of deception and calumny, of dead and wounded, of oppression and repression, February 1977 saw the arrival upon the Salvadoran stage of three figures of very different quality, who symbolized to perfection the principal forces in the life of the country: General Romero, who had been minister of defense and public security from 1972 to 1976, and who represented the most reactionary elements, the army and the oligarchy; Bishop Romero, a conservative churchman who took over the leadership of the most important, and the most pastorally advanced, Salvadoran diocese; and the Popular Leagues of the 28th of February, which, following in the steps of other, already flourishing, popular organizations, represented the new courage and new determination of the people of El Salvador to fight in defense of their interests regardless of the sacrifices they would have to make.

In the two weeks between February 21 and March 4 the persecution of the church seemed to grow in intensity. One priest was arrested and tortured; there was an attempt to capture another priest; a house of lay collaborators was raided; eight priests were prevented from entering the country. On March 12 Jesuit Fr. Rutilio Grande and two companions, a boy and an old man, were killed while they were on their way to celebrate Mass in the village of El Paisnal, where Fr. Grande was a parish priest and where he had been born.[6]

Both nationally and internationally the killing of Fr. Grande had an enormous impact. He was the first of what was to become a great number of priests murdered by the Salvadoran oligarchy and its armed servants. His murder had been prepared for by a continual campaign of insult and detraction in the media. The murder of Fr. Grande clearly represented more than the elimination of a priest. It represented an attack against the pastoral approach made its own by the Catholic church, against the church's preferential option for the poor. It was an attack against the identification made by priests and religious with the hopes and sufferings of the people of God. Fr. Grande had been one of the key figures in the apostolic renewal in the archdiocese, a pioneer of the application of Vatican II and Medellín to the Salvadoran church, a leader of Christian work for and with the poor and oppressed.

For Romero the assassination of Fr. Grande, as the archbishop was himself to remark many times afterward, was the crucial moment in his conversion: the road from Aguilares was to be his road to Damascus. Fr. Grande had been a great personal friend, a faithful and close collaborator, a man whose stamina and apostolic clarity he had always admired. So for the first time, though it was to become almost a routine, Romero hurried to a distant place to receive the bodies of a priest and two other Christians murdered as witnesses to the faith. With Fr. Grande he began his archiepiscopal way of the cross. "It was my lot to go on claiming dead bodies," he would comment later. "These days I have to walk the roads gathering up dead friends, listening to widows and orphans, and trying to spread hope."[7]

The road to Damascus was, for the archbishop, a road bespattered with the blood of the people, with the blood of his priests, his catechists, of faithful Christians, of so many men and women who were to be sacrificed to the need of the powerful to set up a national security state. Little by little Romero began to change. His voice, more accustomed to proclaiming peace, was now also raised in denunciation of the sinful injustice that brought death. His words, which had hitherto reflected generalities or abstractions, took on the harsh realism of daily life. His voice took over the cry of a crushed people and, in a country where money and power had made a prostitute of words, he gave them back their truth and their force. As the bishops' message of March 5 put it, and as Romero often repeated, "It cannot be denied that the church, and Christians, are passing through a process of conversion, one that is painful but real." This process brought Romero to an integrated, living faith.

THREE YEARS AS ARCHBISHOP

1977: The Persecuted Church

General Romero's formal assumption of power on July 1 marked for the country the consecration of a political program that was purely repressive, one that abandoned even reformist intentions and handed over the country to the most reactionary financial and agro-exporting interests. General Romero's successive cabinets were characterized by a shameful lack of political and technical expertise. Repression would have been even more intensive, had the international situation permitted it. The government's slogan, "For the well-being of all," was a farce that fooled nobody. It did not even convince those of the oligarchy whose power and profits it was trying to preserve and promote.[8] Coffee, the main staple of El Salvador's economy, fetched the highest prices ever on the international market. The country, however, not only did not benefit from this bonanza; it entered a period of quickening capital decline, both because of the bad public administration of funds and because of the flight of private capital toward less hectic political climes.[9]

The repression of the people that followed the collapse of the program of agrarian reform and, above all, that which followed the fraudulent elections that put General Romero into power as president, was the most notable characteristic of life in El Salvador during the first half of 1977. The massacre of supporters of the opposition coalition on February 28, the massacre of workers in the San Salvador Parque Cuscatlán on May 1, the military operation against the village of Aguilares that resulted in the death or disappearance of a great number of persons, are three monuments of the universal repression to which the government systematically subjected the country.

The Catholic church was a major part of this persecuted people. On May 11 the dead body of Mauricio Borgonovo was found. He had been a prominent member of the Salvadoran oligarchy and a foreign minister, and had been kidnapped by guerrillas. In reprisal, that same day a band made up of persons of the extreme right wing entered the house of a diocesan priest, Fr. Alfonso Navarro, and murdered him in cold blood. There was also killed alongside him a young neighbor, no more than a child, who happened to be visiting him at the time. Over and above the horror of the crime itself, this action indicated that the extreme right wing, protected by the government and using as operational bases the installations of the security forces, and even employing members of the security forces, had identified as their principal political enemies members of the church. Marauders began to work systematically through the country's interior, searching out first and foremost anyone linked with church activities. *Campesinos* whom they came across carrying a Bible, or carrying a copy of the Catholic weekly *Orientación,* or simply having with them a photograph of Fr. Grande were molested and beaten up; often their belongings were stolen or destroyed.

Three other Jesuit priests working in the martyr zone of Aguilares were expelled from the country. The parish church of Aguilares was brutally profaned by army troops, and even the archbishop was prevented from going to remove the Eucharist. When he was at last allowed to enter, he found the parish house violated and sacked, the church half destroyed, the tabernacle broken open, and the Blessed Sacrament profaned.

Faced with this progressive intensification of the persecution of the people and the Christian community in El Salvador, the archbishop began to grow in stature as someone who held the church together. In his denunciations from the cathedral he began to speak out ever more clearly. The ruling class found this intolerable. They were doubly irritated. He had been their candidate. Now he not only refused to give their actions his blessing, he had become their chief critic. So there began a campaign of detraction against him, a campaign that was to accompany him throughout the three years of his archiepiscopal ministry, a campaign that was orchestrated by government agencies and could count upon the unstinted economic support of the Salvadoran oligarchy. As well as the campaign of detraction, there were more and more attacks on the archdiocesan radio station and printing works, which were broadcasting and making more widely available the archbishop's denunciations.

General Romero came to power on July 1. It is known that he had formally promised the oligarchy to put an end to "troublesome elements" in the church, the Jesuits in particular. An extreme right-wing group had threatened in June that the Jesuits would either leave the country or be subjected to systematic extermination. But the Jesuits had ignored the threat. Romero made it clear in his inaugural address that he was worried about "the country's image" abroad, and intimated that this image was based on the chaotic situation prevailing in El Salvador. He reaffirmed, however, his determination to see "peace, order, and security" reestablished as a basis for any kind of program of reform. So saying, he affirmed and upheld a short-sighted, ad hoc policy, the sole clear objective of which was repression.[10]

Breaking with a tradition of many years, and despite extremely strong pressures, Archbishop Romero did not attend General Romero's inauguration. In so doing he was adhering firmly to his decision, made public on the occasion of Fr. Grande's murder, "of not taking part in official ceremonies until this situation is cleared up."[11] His absence was the most striking feature of the official ceremonies.[12] No one missed the significance of his symbolic act, which not even the attendance of the papal nuncio and of other prelates could disguise: that there was a fierce conflict between church and state, a conflict that had arisen from the persecution of the church—that is to say, of the people of God. The archbishop explained the reason for his absence in a homily and indicated that the church was open to dialogue—but only under certain conditions. The conditions, basically, were that there should be a demonstration by deeds, and not merely by words, of openness and sincerity.

After the inaugural address given by General Romero, the archbishop put before the Christian community, and before the whole country, his second pastoral letter. In this he spoke of the reality, and of the life, of the church as the people of God. The letter is a deep theological reflection upon what the country had been living through: the awakening of the people to the realization that it was a community of faith and, therefore, a living community called upon to take charge of its own history in a process of salvation that had to begin with its own liberation. The words and the person of the archbishop became a catalyst. He fired consciences and united spirits. As never before in the history of the archdiocese—and, indeed, in the history of El Salvador—the masses began to form a tight-knit ring around their archbishop. They made him their leader and their spokesman.

On November 25 the repressive program of the ruling class took on the force of law with the promulgation of the Law of Defense and Guarantee of Public Order.[13] This law was a miscarriage of justice. Under the camouflage of democratic principles and the defense of human rights, it empowered the government to eliminate any voice, any person or group, that it found troublesome.[14] The law legitimized the arbitrary imprisonment of individuals or groups, it legitimized systematic torture, the suppression of the right to hold meetings, to spread ideas, even to think. It was the perfect symbol of all that the government of General Romero and his right-wing patrons stood for. From the very moment of its promulgation the Law of Defense was roundly condemned by a whole sweep of national and international agencies as juridically aberrant, politically ineffective, and ethically immoral.[15]

The archbishop not only attacked the law and all the abuses protected under it by what he said, he began also to take practical measures to protect—physically, morally, and legally—the growing number of persons who were fleeing from repression and seeking assistance against legalized abuses. From then on the archbishop's house became a haven to which would come, as if to their last hope of safety, those whom oppression was denying even the most elemental of human rights. The constant stream of these afflicted and derided victims became a source of inspiration that fed the archbishop's prophetic words. He saw in them the living countenance of Jesus, crucified anew. From them came the encouragement for him to step forward as the imperturbable defender of a justice that the economically, politically, and militarily powerful were busy daily trampling underfoot.

1978: Organization of the People

The year 1978 began in the same key in which 1977 had ended—that is to say, with complete political ineffectiveness, with the absence of programs for promoting the common good, with the accelerating deterioration of the economic situation (scarcely alleviated by the windfall from world coffee prices), and with the systemization of repression against the people under the shelter of the Law of Defense and Guarantee of Public Order.

The events of March 17 may serve to show what kind of repression it was. On that day a delegation of about one hundred *campesinos* went to the Banco de Fomento Agropecuario to discuss their needs. When they arrived at the bank, they found it closed and guarded by security forces. The *campesinos* staged a nonviolent demonstration, but were then machine-gunned by the soldiers, leaving several dead and wounded.

This event had a twofold significance. The government and the oligarchy were already beginning to concentrate their activities in the countryside, and more specifically in those areas where strong rural organizations had begun to arise. Huge operations were mounted by the army and national guard against selected villages. Operations in the zones of San Pedro Perulapán and San Marcos Lempa, and the military occupation of Cinquera, were particularly bloody.[16] A clearer picture of the size of those repressive military operations is had when one reflects that, by the end of 1978, it was documented that 1,063 persons had been arrested—violently—for political reasons; 147 had been murdered by the security forces; a further 23 had disappeared—and all for political reasons.[17] Among those murdered in 1978 was another priest, Fr. Ernesto Barrera. The policy of repression became even more widely known when a political prisoner, Reynaldo Cruz Menjívar, gave evidence before a notary of his kidnapping and imprisonment by the security forces, and of the savage tortures to which he had been submitted.[18] The systematic practice of torture was also confirmed by a commission from the Organization of American States that visited the country. Its report filtered down to the people toward the end of the year, much to the government's embarrassment and anger.[19]

All this repression was taking place against a background of hastening economic decline. The government's inability to revive the national economy was manifest. Not even the sectors of the oligarchy most closely committed to General Romero hid their unease and dissatisfaction. Private capital fled the country in massive proportions, proving yet again that money knows neither frontiers nor "patriotism." The fabulous coffee prices had no positive effect upon the national economy: profits either did not come back into the country, or they were squandered on luxury goods.

The institutional decline that accompanied the economic crisis and the growth of repressive violence only served to encourage and to speed up the growth of popular organizations. Because of their size, energy, and ability to bring persons together, they began to emerge as a real political alternative for the country's future. This frightened the oligarchy, which saw with increasing clarity the challenge that the people and their representative organizations were posing. Hence its clamor for repression and its connivance with the government despite the fact that it stigmatized the government as "soft" and "not firm enough" in confronting "subversion."

In this socio-political context two events can be seen as characteristic of the archbishop's stance: his public denunciation of the Salvadoran judiciary, and his third pastoral letter, in which he examined, from a Christian perspective, the phenomenon of the popular organizations.

In his homily of April 30 Romero publicly praised a group of lawyers who were battling to win an amnesty for political prisoners and trying to ensure that the law be carried out and justice done despite the corruption in the security forces, despite venal judges, and despite the Supreme Court itself, blind and indifferent as it was to the constant abuse of, and deviation from, the judicial system.[20] This accusation brought a response from the Supreme Court. The archbishop was challenged publicly to name the "venal judges" to whom he had referred in his homily. This was obviously a simplistic maneuver to try either to debunk the archbishop or, at best, to cloak a serious problem of corruption inherent in the system with an accidental failing due to a few faulty individuals. Romero did not step into the trap. His homily of May 14 was a full reply to the Supreme Court. He pointed out that not only was there a series of cases of venality or corruption, but moreover "the fundamental rights of the people of El Salvador day by day are being trodden underfoot, while no [government] agency denounces the outrages or acts sincerely and effectively to improve the situation."[21] He expressly denounced illegal detentions, the impossibility of applying writs of habeas corpus, the increasingly frequent political "disappearances," the exile—against the express provisions of the Constitution—of members of the opposition, the ignoring of demands and denunciations, the violation of the right of association and of the right to strike. "Where," he asked, "is that transcendental role of this authority which, in a democracy, has to be vigilant and demand justice against all who violate it?" Faced with this brave, well-documented riposte, the Supreme Court was silent, thus tacitly conceding the truth of all that the archbishop had charged.

On August 6, El Salvador's national patronal feast, Archbishop Romero and Bishop Rivera y Damas of Santiago de María published a joint pastoral letter on the church and popular organizations. This letter, once again, was a pastoral response to the historical problems and to the unrest of the people of El Salvador, this time focused on the impressive phenomenon of the popular organizations. In the letter the two bishops analyzed the relationship between the popular organizations and the church. The church was not to be identified with them: their formal purposes, and their mode of operation, were, to a great extent, different from those of the church. The church, on the other hand, defended the need for such organizations because they constituted, in the present history of the country, a much-needed channel for building up the kingdom of God as Christianity preached it.[22]

The pastoral reflections of the two bishops were seen to be all the more enlightening when some days later, on August 28, there appeared a declaration from the other four Salvadoran bishops on the same topic.[23] Theirs was a total, simplistic condemnation of the popular organizations. It failed totally to understand their nature and their historical significance. It misrepresented their theological significance by bandying doctrinaire slogans that had more to do with the ideology of social control than with the Christian search for faith, love, and justice within the Salvadoran community. The magazine *ECA* in an editorial note summed up the contrast between the two documents:

> The bishops who signed the declaration have a pre-Vatican II ecclesiology, regarding the church as an institution that ought, before all else, to defend itself. But the bishops who signed the pastoral letter have a post-Vatican II ecclesiology, regarding the church not as something turned in upon itself but as proclaiming that the kingdom of God should come into being among the people. The bishops of the declaration fail to assess adequately the importance of the promotion of justice for the proclamation of the faith, but the bishops of the pastoral letter make of the promotion of justice a fundamental part of their mission of evangelization. The bishops of the declaration have not yet come to understand either what a church of the poor is, or what it requires, but the bishops of the pastoral letter are striving to create—out of the primacy that is due to the poor within the church—a church for everybody.[24]

On February 14, Georgetown University bestowed on Archbishop Romero an honorary doctorate because of his resolute defense of human rights. Toward the end of 1978 various groups in several parts of the world, including 118 British parliamentarians, put him forward as a candidate for the Nobel Peace Prize. Both events were symbolic recognition of the worldwide resonance of the archbishop's words and of his struggle for justice. It is interesting that the Salvadoran press and its journalists, instead of taking pride in these distinctions, unique in the history of El Salvador, chose to interpret them as part of a "Jesuit-communist" conspiracy against the country's prestige. That gives some indication of the depth of the abyss between himself and those established in positions of economic and political power in El Salvador.

1979: Persecution of the People on the Grounds of National Security

The year 1979 falls into two clearly distinct parts: before and after October 15. Before that date the most characteristic aspect of the country was a sharpening of repression and the absolute enthronement of "national security" as the sole policy of General Romero. In its Salvadoran version, the North American doctrine of national security meant the systematic elimination of any person or group that even indirectly represented any sort of opposition to the total power of the oligarchy and to their system of economic exploitation.[25] The number of persons arrested for political reasons prior to October came to 460; the number of those murdered during the same period was 580.[26] In other terms, in the first nine months of 1979, the Salvadoran security forces illegally arrested an average of three persons every two days and, on the average, killed another four. Not even these chilling figures, however, demonstrate adequately the full, inhuman brutality that disguised itself under the cover of a policy of "national security."

The first significant "baptism of blood" in 1979 took place on January 20. A large contingent of national guardsmen, together with other members of the security forces, launched a military operation against El Despertar, a retreat house belonging to the parish of San Antonio Abad, on the outskirts of San Salvador. The operation ended with the shameless murder of Fr. Octavio Cruz, whose head was crushed by an armored car, the deaths of four young persons, the imprisonment of a nun, a teacher, and thirty-three other young persons, some of them not yet fifteen years old, who had been at the house making a retreat. So absurd and so shameful was the assault that even the National Guard tried to hide its embarrassment by putting out a defamatory statement to the effect that the group had been holding a subversive meeting, and that the guardsmen had been shot at while approaching the house. Archbishop Romero immediately contradicted the blatant lie.[27]

Indignation within the church and among the people at large reached such a pitch that a procession of priests and religious marched in silence through the streets of San Salvador carrying an enormous placard declaring "Enough!" The people of the capital city spontaneously gathered about this demonstration, showing their repulsion at, and condemnation of, the national security policy pursued by the Salvadoran government. Such a condemnation, however, was not enough to change the demands of the ruling system, and so two other priests were assassinated in the course of the year, Fr. Rafael Palacios on June 20 and Fr. Alirio Napoleón Macías on August 4. The Catholic clergy continued to pay its quota of blood alongside the people, whose cause, under the leadership of the archbishop, they had embraced.

Internationally, the image of the Salvadoran government went on declining. More and more groups of all kinds and persuasions publicly condemned the lack of respect for human rights in El Salvador, a lack of respect bolstered by the law itself. International indignation forced the legislative assembly to repeal the Law of Defense and Guarantee of Public Order.[28] This gave rise to a brief period of hope, but it was soon negated by the unchanged continuance of repression, by the corruption within the judiciary, and by the permanent lack of respect for the human rights of the majority of Salvadorans.

The year 1979 also saw the worsening, to almost insupportable levels, of the economic, political, and institutional crisis that afflicted the country. Demands for their just rights increased throughout the working-class population. Repressive action was no longer capable of containing the opposition, especially the opposition of the politico-military groups, or of offering even a modicum of security to the ruling class. First individuals, then whole groups, began to leave the country. Their money, of course, had preceded them. The banks went into ill-disguised collapse. Many businesses closed their doors, thus adding to the already intolerably high rate of unemployment. The country was emptied of foreigners. In a few days, for example, the Japanese community declined from 2,400 to 200 persons. Some embassies shut. Others reduced their staffs to the minimum. Skirmishes, occupations of buildings, confrontations on the streets began to be normal occurrences. The rich who had not gone to Miami began to turn their houses into fortresses and organized what amounted to private armies for their personal defense. Bands of extreme right-wing terrorists began to proliferate. Under the shelter both of darkness and of official protection, they spent nights eliminating supposed members of the opposition. El Salvador slid swiftly down the slope of social disintegration. Increasingly there was talk of "civil war."[29]

Out of all these events, two in particular received worldwide coverage. On May 8 troops mercilessly machine-gunned a huge demonstration in front of the cathedral doors. The toll was at least twenty-five dead and several hundred wounded. This macabre spectacle was filmed by several foreign television companies and the world saw, with incredulous astonishment, the inhuman savagery of the Salvadoran security forces. A few days later, May 22, the spectacle was repeated when the security forces machine-gunned a group of students in front of the Venezuelan embassy. The toll this time was fourteen dead, with many others wounded.[30]

Faced with this disintegration, with this crumbling of the social order, Romero raised his prophetic voice not only to denounce the outrages and the injustices, but also to point the way to conversion, to a change in, and reorganization of, the country. With ever increasing clarity the archbishop saw that in some way this road led through the popular organizations, perhaps even through popular insurrection. He faced up to the country's crisis with great honesty in his fourth pastoral letter. Fundamentally, the problem arose out of the complete collapse of the national security policy, a policy that was antipeople and anti-Christian. In this letter the archbishop treated the difficult question of violence. He did so without simplistically condemning it "wheresoever it may come from." He analyzed its specific character, its concrete, historical form, its origins and its consequences. "The church cannot simply state that it condemns every kind of violence," for there are situations, such as that of legitimate defense, in which the use of violence is both necessary and justified. And the archbishop hinted that this might be so in the particular case of El Salvador's popular organizations.

The Sandinista triumph in Nicaragua over the dictatorship of President Somoza was a tremendous confutation of the belief that a people is incapable of overthrowing established authority when that authority is well armed and supported by the United States.[31] The military defeat of Somoza's national guard attracted the attention of the Salvadoran army. It was something they could understand. So despite last-minute efforts by General Romero to redirect his running of the country and of the armed forces, he was deposed on October 15 in a bloodless military coup, led by a large group of reform-minded, democratically-inclined young officers, who could count on the support of the United States. These young officers wanted to break with the corrupt past and with subjugation to the interests of capital, and to begin a new epoch with political and economic reforms.[32]

The young officers, however, had miscalculated their own strength. Above all they had miscalculated the deep-seated, corrupt force of Salvadoran capital. Little by little its devotees came to take over vital positions until they had practically won over control.

The officers set up a government with the aid of sincerely reform-minded politicians, men who were honest and capable, and even open to the popular movements. But it was not enough:

> From the first there was a desire to forget the past without breaking with it. Those who had spread terror were neither imprisoned nor put on trial. From the first there was imposed what was called "order," and to that end high levels of barbarity were reached. From the first there was a desire to maintain, as the fundamental legal instrument, the same Constitution that had been maintained throughout the worst outrages perpetrated under previous administrations. . . . Right-wing interests were still at work within the government, and from their positions they began to undermine what was being undertaken.[33]

After the coup of October 15, in fact, the degree of repression took a new, qualitative leap to even higher levels of mass killings by the security forces, to levels reminiscent of the genocide of 1932. The increasing militancy of the popular organizations—acting as they did as a channel for the people's utter desperation—found expression in an unending series of strikes, in the occupation of buildings, factories, and land, all of which gave the security forces an excuse to behave with a savagery that caused the sincere members of the government considerable disquiet and embarrassment. Military operations were carried out, for example, in Berlín and Opico, and when the *campesinos* were driven out of the farms they had taken over, more than seventy of them were killed. The right wing began to demonstrate against the government in public. The number of demonstrators was small, but they were supplemented by an extraordinary display of luxury cars, of every kind of weaponry, and by very expensive publicity. The political ferment increased daily. Faced with the polarization of the different sectors and social classes, the government showed itself incapable of mediating, or of implementing any sort of sensible policy.

Faced with these events in the political arena, Archbishop Romero's stance was one of critical hopefulness and unshakable demands. At first,

though not without hesitation, he called publicly for a kind of truce between
the different social groups so that the government might have time to show
by its actions that it really meant to carry out what it said. In this context the
archbishop clearly called for justice for both sides: that those who had
yielded to corruption or carried out murders be punished; that the machinery of repression, torture, and institutionalized assassination be dis-
mantled; that organizations or other bodies opposed to the people's good be
disbanded; that political prisoners be freed; that the "disappearances" be
investigated, and responsibility for them determined; that those who had
been defamed and unjustly persecuted have their property, and their good
name, restored to them. Because the government, despite its excellent statements of intentions, showed itself incapable of carrying out these basic
demands, and because repression came once more to dominate, reaching
hitherto unimaginable levels, the archbishop became yet again highly critical of the new rulers.

"The year ended in a nightmare of chaos, with a sense of betrayal and
disillusionment, with the hope that the armed forces might find a way out.
It ended with the rumor that the left wing was unifying. The year closed, as
it had opened, in darkness. One does not know if there will be a dawn."[34]

THE HOLOCAUST

The year 1980 opened with an extremely serious government crisis in El
Salvador. In the space of one week most of the ministers and chief officials
presented their resignations, as did the civilian members of the junta. They
resigned fundamentally because it was impossible in practice to put through
the changes necessary—changes that the young officers had themselves
proposed. They also resigned because of the impossibility of controlling the
repressive activities of the security forces. They were obeying another chain
of command, one that was independent of the government.[35]

The crisis in the government served to draw attention to the increasing
unity of the popular revolutionary forces. In the second week of January
the popular organizations announced that they were to be united under the
CRM (*Coordinadora Revolucionaria de Masas*, Mass Revolutionary Coordinating Committee). The politico-military groups formed a similar united
front. This unity of the people was made manifest on January 22 in a gigan-
tic demonstration, the largest in the entire history of El Salvador. Impartial
observers estimated that some two hundred thousand persons marched
through the streets of San Salvador that day, despite the efforts of the security forces to prevent nonresidents of the capital from entering the city, and
despite a disgraceful publicity campaign intended to deter residents from
joining the demonstration. Unfortunately, threats were carried out. The
security forces fired on the demonstrators from several buildings. They left
at least forty dead and several hundred wounded.[36]

This slaughter was only a small token of the dragnet operation, with human beings as quarry, that was becoming part of Salvadoran life. The assas-- sination statistics under the governments of Molina and Romero, which had hitherto been regarded as extremely high, seemed suddenly very small by comparison. The security forces, now acting with the government's more or less open connivance, and certainly with the blessing of the United States, which was alarmed by the turn events were taking, launched a massive cam- paign of repression and of systematic terror. Extreme right-wing death squads carried out at night the job of "cleaning up." The figures speak for themselves: 265 persons killed in January by the security forces, 236 in Feb- ruary, 514 in March.[37] Many of the murders bore evidence of systematic planning such as the hunting down of teachers. They were being murdered on a systematic basis, averaging one every three days.

The involvement of the Christian Democrats in the second junta and the beginning of some of the reforms that had been promised (agrarian reform and the nationalization of the banking) did not relieve the almost total isola- tion of the group in power. Nor did it alleviate the absurdity of a policy that could not be carried out except at the cost of a torrent of blood. The greatest irony was that the government claimed to be carrying out the re- forms for the benefit of precisely that segment of the population it was daily persecuting, rounding up, and murdering. The isolation of the government was made complete by the abandonment of its ministers as they resigned one by one, as did also other top officials and even some members of the junta. This point was finally reached in the course of the first three months of 1980.

The archbishop faced up to this situation of chaos and of national disin- tegration by what he did and by what he said in his homilies. He had ap- proved of the resignation of the civilian members of the junta because it brought clarity to the political scene, and because it brought moral pressure to bear to bring the crisis to an end and start afresh. But the opportunism of the Christian Democrats prevented this from happening. This distressed the archbishop, who had a great appreciation of, and friendship with, some Christian Democrat politicians. He did not let this friendship and high re- gard get in the way of his critical attitude as he looked on events from the people's point of view. He did not reject the reforms proposed by the sec- ond junta, but he bitterly criticized its basic inhumanity. He regarded it as mistaken to undertake reforms on the people's behalf in opposition to the people and its organizations. It was worse still to put "reforms" into opera- tion at the cost of the people's blood. He believed that the criterion for the validity of reform was to be looked for in an openness to, and sincere con- cern for, the people. And the new junta, for all that it said and promised, could not pass this test. The archbishop therefore stepped up his criticism of the proposed "reforms"—their only obvious consequences being the mili- tary occupation of the countryside and the continued murder of rural and urban workers, of teachers and trade unionists, of students and even of professional persons.

But along with his growing disillusionment with the new rulers, the archbishop could look hopefully toward the growing unity of the popular groups and of left-wing political organizations. He thought the appearance of the Independent Movement of Professional and Technical Personnel a great step forward, in that it made possible the involvement of different sections of the middle class in the popular struggle. He had great hopes for the Programatic Platform of a Revolutionary Democratic Government, put out by a combination of popular groups. Although he was critical of some of its specific activities and plans for government, he had a high regard for the increasing reasonableness and openness of the CRM.

The scale of the repression caused Archbishop Romero very real suffering. Daily he received dozens of persons who had been harassed by violence perpetrated either by the military or by paramilitary forces. They came to him looking for help or protection. They came to complain about harassment or murders, or simply to find some spiritual and human counsel. The archbishop received, and listened to, every one of them. As he learned of the ever increasing torrent of pain, and of the people's blood, his prophetic voice took an angrier tone. His famous letter to President Carter, in which he asked, in the name of the rights of the people of El Salvador, that the president not send armaments, or support any kind of repressive action by the armed forces, is a symbol of his courageous attitude. This letter gained worldwide publicity. It annoyed and embarrassed not only the governments of El Salvador and the United States, but the Vatican as well, which did not seem at all pleased with the archbishop's Christian sincerity, or his disregard of "diplomatic niceties."

His opposition to the repressive violence came to a climax in his Sunday homily on March 23. He called firmly upon the troops and the national guardsmen to obey the law of God and therefore not to obey the orders of officers who might instruct them to kill their brothers and sisters: "In the name of God, then, and in the name of this suffering people whose cries rise daily more loudly to heaven, I plead with you, I beg you, I order you in the name of God: put an end to this repression!"

This call was, it now seems, the last straw. His enemies' anger could tolerate no more. On Monday, March 24, Romero fell victim of an assassin as he was standing at the altar. He had just preached that a life offered for others is a sure token of resurrection and of victory.

Archbishop Romero's funeral was celebrated on March 30. It took place in the square known as Barrios of San Salvador, in front of the cathedral doors. There was an enormous gathering of some one hundred fifty thousand persons, most of them ordinary citizens. It was attended by dozens of prelates, bishops, priests, religious, and other dignitaries from around the world. They wanted to bear witness to the universal appeal of the prophet from El Salvador. Also present was a huge delegation from the popular organizations. Silently, though to the cheers of the crowd, they paid posthumous homage to the archbishop and laid a wreath of flowers before his coffin.

In the middle of the ceremony, just when the papal representative, Cardinal Corripio of Mexico, was preaching, the religious service was blotted out by the fearful noise of a series of enormous explosions. A great number of those present agree that several bombs were thrown into the crowd by persons hidden within the government's National Palace. Snipers, also stationed in the palace, opened fire. The panic and confusion that followed were indescribable. Persons ran in terror, trying to find refuge in the cathedral or to escape as best they could from what was a death trap. The day closed with thirty dead, innumerable wounded, and the profound moral ignominy of the Salvadoran government manifest to the whole world.

In the midst of bombs, shooting, blood, and horror, the archbishop was hurriedly buried. He was interred in the cathedral, the cathedral where the people had listened to his words, the seat of his Christian leadership, and the place of refuge for a persecuted people. He was buried in the midst of the wounded and the dead, the shuddering walls of the cathedral protecting the defenseless from the bullets of the powerful. He was buried as he had lived, in the midst of a downtrodden people, whose cause he had made his own, and to whose aspirations he had given voice.

The archbishop has died. The people of El Salvador, however, the Christian community, men and women throughout the world who love life, know that the archbishop still lives. His word of truth speaks in all who carry on the struggle for justice, in all who strive to unite all human beings before the common Father, in all those who give their lives to bring about here on earth the kingdom of justice, love, and peace proclaimed by Jesus of Nazareth. There were many forces opposed to the archbishop during his life. Many of them today celebrate his death by distorting his message, falsifying his work, prostituting his word. There are many in comfortable living rooms or government offices where English and Spanish are spoken who want the archbishop to be utterly dead and buried. They have money to carry out their wish. They have power, they have weapons. They can make use of authority, pressure, dissuasion, lies, bribery, and blackmail. For them, any means can be regarded as good so long as it buries, once and for all, that for which the archbishop always fought: the seeds of liberation, the only path toward the God of Jesus.

The purpose of this book is to keep alive the words and memory of Archbishop Romero, to prevent, so far as possible, his enemies from burying him in silence and oblivion.[38]

NOTES

1. See J. Hernández-Pico, C. Jerez, I. Ellacuría, E. Baltodano, and R. Mayorga, *El Salvador: año político 1971–72* (San Salvador: UCA José Simeón Cañas, 1973).

2. R. Zamora, "¿Seguro de vida o despojo? Análisis político de la Transformación Agraria," *Estudios Centroamericanos* (San Salvador; hereafter: *ECA*), 335–36 (1977) 511–34.

3. See "A sus ordenes, mi capital," *ECA*, 337 (1976) 637-43.

4. See T. P. Anderson, *Matanza: El Salvador's Communist Revolt of 1932* (University of Nebraska Press, 1971).

5. See Secretariado Social Interdiocesano, *Persecución de la Iglesia en El Salvador* (San Salvador, 1977).

6. See Martin Lange and Reinhold Iblacker, eds., *Witnesses of Hope: The Persecution of Christians in Latin America* (Maryknoll, N.Y.: Orbis, 1981), pp. 27-36.

7. Plácido Erdozaín, *Archbishop Romero: Martyr of Salvador* (Maryknoll, N.Y.: Orbis, 1980), p. 28.

8. See "El plan bienestar para todos," *Boletín de Ciencias Económicas y Sociales*, 1 (San Salvador: UCA, 1978) 1-3.

9. See L. de Sebastián, "Panorama monetario en 1978," *ECA*, 369-70 (1979) 1037-42.

10. See "Mensaje al pueblo salvadoreño del Señor Presidente de la República, General Carlos Humberto Romero (1 de julio de 1977)," *ECA*, 345 (1977) 515-19.

11. "Comunicados del Arzobispo de San Salvador a raíz de la muerte del Padre Rutilio Grande," *ECA*, 341 (1977) 254-57.

12. See G. L., "La presencia de Monseñor Romero el primero de julio," *ECA*, 345 (1977) 495-98.

13. See "Ley de defensa y garantía del orden público," *ECA*, 350 (1977) 935-37.

14. See R. Lara Velado, "Comentarios a la 'Ley de defensa y garantía del orden público,' " *ECA*, 350 (1977) 911-16.

15. See, e.g., "Reporte de la Comisión Internacional de Juristas sobre la 'Ley de defensa y garantía del orden público,' " *ECA*, 359 (1978) 779-86.

16. See "Los sucesos de San Pedro Perulapán," *ECA*, 354 (1978) 223-47.

17. See Secretaría de Comunicación Social del Arzobispado de San Salvador, "Informe sobre la represión en El Salvador," *Boletín Informativo*, 10 (Dec. 12, 1979).

18. See "Testimonio del reo político Reynaldo Cruz Menjívar," *ECA*, 360 (1978) 850-58.

19. See I. E., "La O.E.A. y los derechos humanos en El Salvador," *ECA*, 363-64 (1979) 53-54.

20. See "Las homilías de Monseñor Romero y el poder judicial en El Salvador," *ECA*, 355 (1978) 330-32.

21. Ibid., p. 331.

22. See T. R. Campos, "La Iglesia y las organizaciones populares en El Salvador," *ECA*, 359 (1978) 692-702.

23. "Declaración de cuatro obispos de la Conferencia Episcopal de El Salvador," *ECA*, 359 (1978) 774-75.

24. "División y conflicto en el episcopado salvadoreño," *ECA*, 359 (1978) 687-89.

25. See T. R. Campos, "La seguridad nacional y la Constitución salvadoreña," *ECA*, 369-70 (1979) 477-88.

26. See note 17, above.

27. See "Terror en El Salvador," *ECA*, 363-64 (1979) 85-88.

28. See G.M.U., "La derogatoria de la 'Ley de defensa y garantía del orden público," *ECA*, 366 (1979) 277-78.

29. "Al borde de la guerra civil," *ECA*, 371 (1979) 735-40.

30. See E. C. Anaya, "Crónica del mes: mayo, 1979," *ECA*, 368 (1979) 450-52.

31. See L. E. del Cid, ''¿Por qué cayó la dinastía somocista?,'' *ECA*, 369–70 (1979) 699–708.

32. See ''La insurrección militar del 15 de octubre,'' *ECA*, 371 (1979) 741–44.

33. ''1979: El fracaso de dos modelos,'' *ECA*, 374 (1979) 1037–42; the quotation is from p. 1038.

34. E. C. Anaya, ''Crónica del mes: noviembre-diciembre, 1979,'' *ECA*, 374 (1979) 1088–93; the quotation is from p. 1093.

35. See ''Pronunciamiento de la UCA ante la nueva situación del país (febrero/80),'' *Los Obispos Latinoamericanos entre Medellín y Puebla: Documentos episcopales 1968-1978* (San Salvador: UCA, 1978).

36. F. A. Escobar, ''En la línea de la muerte (La manifestación del 22 de enero de 1980),'' *ECA*, 375–76 (1980) 21–35.

37. ''Comisión de Derechos Humanos de El Salvador, Reporte estadístico,'' *Orientación* (San Salvador), May 11, 1980, p. 4.

38. See also *A Martyr's Message of Hope: Six Homilies by Archbishop Oscar Romero* (Kansas City: Celebration Books, 1981).

JON SOBRINO

A Theologian's View of Oscar Romero

I came to know Archbishop Romero over a period of three years. I saw him first in Aguilares, the night they killed Fr. Rutilio Grande, S.J. The last time I spoke to him was a week before his martyrdom. I brought him a message of solidarity from the participants of the Fourth International Ecumenical Congress of Theology, which had just been held in São Paulo. It is with gratitude that I recall his friendship, the impact of his faith, and the inspiration he gave to theological reflection.

HIS GOSPEL FAITH

Archbishop Romero became a quite exceptional figure, both within the church and within society at large, in Latin America. To understand this, I want to begin by examining something deeper, something of which the social and ecclesial dimensions of his life were the expression, the vehicle. I want to plumb what is the ultimate mystery of every human being, that which is hidden in the depths of the heart, that source from which emanate both our daily lives and the actions we take at crucial moments. I want, in other words, to plumb that most simple yet most sublime thing we call faith.

Perhaps it appears to be saying little, or saying something very obvious, if I begin by describing Romero as a man who believed in God. So little has the word "God" come to mean that it is easily taken for granted that everyone believes in God. On the other hand God can be so readily ignored that no longer does it seem to render particular honor to Romero's memory, or to provide an adequate theological basis upon which to begin, simply to say that he believed in God.

Yet in its Christian fulness, "God" is a far from empty term. It is far from a remote, passive abstraction. Quite the opposite. God is the prime source of all life, justice, love, and truth, and the ultimate horizon to which all these reach out. It is God who lays upon us the absolute demand that we live our lives in a way truly worthy of human beings, that we strive always to make ourselves more human by continually ridding ourselves of that which makes us less than human.

The first thing I want to say of Archbishop Romero, therefore, is that he had a profound faith in God. We know of the devotion, felt not feigned, with which he spoke of God in his homilies. We know of his spirit of meditation and his simple, down-to-earth prayers. For him, to speak with God was something as straightforward and routine as life itself.

I also want to say of Archbishop Romero that he believed in God as did Jesus. That is why I want to examine his following of Jesus precisely from the standpoint of his faith. Like Jesus, to be in communion with God, to speak with God and to speak about God, meant above all making God's will concrete and effective. The measure of Romero's faith can be gauged by the way he utterly and completely defended God's cause. Like Jesus he sought and found God's will as much in the minutiae of everyday life as in life's most profound and significant moments. He never made of God's will something trivial or routine, as all of us Christians—bishops and priests included—do only too often. We—and the church itself—lay down rules and regulations today, just as was done in the time of Jesus. We try to cut God down to size, to manipulate, even to downgrade him. Romero placed no limits to God's will. On the contrary, he sought the will of God where it is in truth to be found: where the lives of men and women hang in the balance, where sin turns human beings into slaves, and where there hence arises a cry for justice, and the hope for society and for the oppressed that is growing in the world. It is this that I shall explain in what follows.

The God of the Kingdom

Archbishop Romero's faith in God made him a defender of life, and especially a defender of the lives of the poor. The anguish of the poor touches the very heart of God. That is why Romero saw in life, and in life at its most basic, the manifestation of God, as did the prophet Isaiah before him. The world of food and work, of health and housing, the world of education—this is God's world. The world God wants is one in which "they will build houses and inhabit them, plant vineyards and eat their fruit" (Isa. 65:21). Poverty and desolation is a denial of God's will, a perverted creation in which God's glory is mocked and scorned. Belief in the fulness of the life to come is no palliative or opiate: faith in God begins with the defense of life here and now. The living person is God's glory. To be absolutely accurate, the living, poor man or woman is God's glory (lecture at the University of Louvain, Feb. 2, 1980).

Because of his faith in God, Archbishop Romero denounced our country's sin with a fierceness that can be likened only to that of the prophets of old, or to that of Bartolomé de Las Casas, or to that of Jesus himself. Hardship, he declared, is not the natural destiny of the people of El Salvador. It is, at root, the outcome of unjust structures. With unequalled ferocity he lashed out at the repression mounted against the people, at the massacres, the genocide.

Romero never ceased in his attack, he never tempered it, he never found prudent reasons for silence. Unlike others, he never put the church's own security before the necessity of attacking repression. He had heard God saying, "You may multiply your prayers, I shall not listen. Your hands are covered with blood" (Isa. 1:15).

Sin for him was an offense against God *because* it is an offense against the people. Sin is indeed something that causes death—that is why it is called mortal. One cannot *see* an offense against God: it becomes visible when one sees blood-stained corpses, when one hears the wailing of the mothers of those who have disappeared, and of the tortured. Because his faith was in the God of life, such sin was utterly counter to his faith. His faith bore him up in his denunciation of sin. It added to the harshness with which he exposed it. It enabled him to ignore the risks, both personal and institutional, that he had to run.

Through his faith in God, Archbishop Romero worked and struggled toward a just solution to his country's problems. He believed in the God of the exodus who today as yesterday looks upon a captive and exploited people, hears their cries, then himself comes to free them, and to promise them a new land.

But Romero also believed that this liberating will of God had to be made effective. He was not content, therefore, simply to speak in favor of life and to denounce all that opposed it. Instead he placed himself clearly on the side of justice—that is to say, on the side of the struggle to win a decent way of life for the poor. He did not rely on purely political considerations, but on his faith in God. That is why he did not stop where others stopped: at conflict and the organization of the poor.

He was a man of peace. He was always in favor of peaceful solutions. But his faith brought him to accept the mystery of the conflict to which sin gives rise. He accepted that sin can be overcome only by a struggle against it. Like Mary he accepted calmly that God "has pulled down princes from their thrones and exalted the lowly" (Luke 1:52). Some pharisaically see a source of scandal in the fact of conflict. For Romero his acceptance of it was a demand made upon him by his faith in God.

And because he believed in a God who wills justice, Romero also embraced that other fact of life from which others hold themselves back—the fact that the poor have to liberate themselves, that they have to take charge of their own destiny, and not simply be passive recipients of benefits that descend from "above." He came to understand that in El Salvador that which is above is made up of the gods of unbridled capitalism and "national security" and that the God of liberation has to be met "below." It was because of that belief that Romero backed all just movements of the people that carried them toward freedom.

Romero believed in the God of the kingdom today in El Salvador just as Jesus had proclaimed it in his own day: a just society for all men and women, and especially for the poor. He also believed that this new society for which battle had to be joined ought to be a society *of* new men and women, *of* men and women of the kingdom. He therefore never lost sight of the moral and spiritual dimensions of the people. He encouraged the view that even in conflict and battle there could be true human values—those of solidarity, generosity, clarity of vision; values, in a word, that Jesus proclaimed in the Sermon on the Mount. And even in just struggle he was critical, as a pastor, of all that might dehumanize human nature.

He was not guided in any way by political calculations, much less by thought of the popularity—or the notoriety—to which his preaching about the values of the kingdom gave rise. He was guided by an unshakable faith in a God who wills a new kind of society and a new kind of human person. Even though the attainment of such a society may have been a lost cause, he time and again urged purity of heart, magnanimity, dialogue, and an openness to one's own conversion. He also spoke for things that few today in El Salvador can mention without cynicism: forgiveness and overcoming the instinct for vengeance.

No one who knew Archbishop Romero would see in his exhortations any naivety or the routine repetition of Christian verities. They would see rather a deep faith in God, a faith that pointed toward the utopia of the kingdom of God and of the people of the kingdom. He was well aware of the problems standing in the way of the achievement of both these utopias, but he never lost heart. He tirelessly proclaimed and promoted them because he believed in God's utopia and because he believed that such a utopia—even though it might never be fully realized—was the best way of bringing about humankind's greater humanity.

The God of Truth

Because of his faith in God, Archbishop Romero associated his struggle for justice with the proclamation of the truth. No one spoke out as much and as clearly about the dire situation in this country. Shortly before his martyrdom he was able to say, as in his own day Jesus too had said, that in more than two years of preaching no one could ever accuse him of lying.

This love for, and ceaseless preaching of, the truth had a profoundly humanizing effect throughout the country. In the first place, it was not that the archbishop merely told the truth: he told the whole truth. In crisis situations it sometimes—if infrequently—happens that the truth is told. It is very rare indeed for the whole truth to be told, because this presupposes not only telling the truth but experiencing the demands that it makes on one. It presupposes that alongside the truth there shall go the struggle for liberation. It also makes the truth a weapon in that struggle. It takes for granted that in the truth there is something that cannot be manipulated, that the effectiveness of the truth lies in its very telling. It is in this sense that Romero was an impassioned teller of the truth.

Secondly, simply by speaking the truth Romero gave its value back to the silenced, manipulated, distorted word. He made the word what it ought to be: the expression of reality. His Sunday sermons were listened to because in them the real situation of the country found expression. In his preaching the daily hopes and griefs that the media usually either ignored or distorted found expression. No Salvadoran can any longer ignore the fact that the word, dialogue, speech have to be at the service of objective reality, not of partisan interests.

That love for the truth, that putting into words of the real state of affairs, was rooted in Romero's faith in God. The phrase used by Christians at the end of Scripture readings, "This is the word of the Lord," was not a mere saying for him. It was an urgent commitment to go on preaching the word and using it to bring before hearers the real situation of the country. "The word of God is not in chains," said St. Paul. For Romero it would have been a fearsome crime to have tied down, or to have ignored, that word both as it is to be found in Scripture and as it is to be found in the events of history. So he spoke, and spoke the truth. He believed that God is also the God of truth. He saw in the truths made manifest in history an indication of God's demands upon us, and a manifestation of God in history.

The God of Change

Because of his faith in God, Romero was not alarmed by changes that took place. Rather he made of change a vehicle for his faith. At a strictly personal level he knew how to grow, to change, even how to undergo conversion. The beginning of his ministry in the archdiocese coincided with the beginning of the persecution of the church and intensified repression of the people. He was changed by this new situation, he was converted. He was fifty-nine years old. Most persons' psychological attitudes and mental patterns have already been formed by that age. He was, moreover, at the head of the church's institutional authority, an authority that, like all others, tends toward establishment and immobility. Yet even from that position and at that age he demonstrated the true humility of those who believe in God. He became someone new. He was driven on by a new and different sense of what it meant to be a Christian. He understood his ministry as a bishop in a wholly new way.

Taking on his new office he began new forms of pastoral activity. He even adopted a new theology, much to the surprise and alarm of those who preferred the old, the known, that with which they felt secure. He was concerned with the new problems that the history of the church and of his country put before him. He did not choose in advance which problems to respond to, feeling safest with traditional ones. Quite the opposite: he faced up to new situations as they arose. To the very end he was concerned with what he called his apostolate of companionship to politically committed Christians, with the changing situation in El Salvador, and with the future—as shown by his keen interest in events in Nicaragua. He was as much surprised as anyone else by the changes that history brought. He was displeased by his feeling of impotence, of being unable to think of an answer immediately. But he was never brought to a dead stop. He was encouraged to go on seeking the will of God in all the twists and turns of history.

His openness to change, his facing up to the challenge of the new, was simply the expression of his faith in a God whose mystery, as John says, is greater than our hearts, greater than any particular situation. Romero readily accepted that God was also present in the old, certainly in his revelation in Scripture and in the traditions of the church. That is why he was so scrupulously faithful to Vatican II, to Medellín, and to Puebla. But the same conviction made him faithful to the Spirit of God, a Spirit not to be encapsulated in the traditions of the church; one that blows when and where it wills. The when and the where have always to be sought out anew. There are no ready-made "traveler's guidebooks."

Because of his faith in the God of change, Archbishop Romero often had to journey alone, misunderstood by many of those around him, even by other bishops. He knew only that, like Abraham, he had to travel a road with trust in the Spirit of God. He knew that God is greater than all the roads already traveled, and that he cannot be localized definitively. Romero heard God's word, "Leave your country, your family and your father's house, for the land I will show you" (Gen. 12:1). To believe in God meant for Romero to take that saying seriously, not reducing it to something manageable but letting God be ever a God of change, following wheresoever the Spirit of God might lead.

The God of the Poor

Because of that faith, Archbishop Romero encountered in the midst of the poor the pathway to belief in God. I am here speaking not so much of the good he did for the poor—I will examine that more closely later—but rather the good the poor did for him, as far as his faith was concerned.

In the first place he found in the poor that which is scandalous in the mystery of God understood in a Christian sense: in those whom history crucifies is made present the crucified God. The kenotic dimension of God—God's emptying himself, in other words—goes on being foolishness, a scandal. It is the dividing line between authentic Christianity and other theistic beliefs. It is made manifest in the poor, in the oppressed and the repressed of his people. In their faces Romero saw the disfigured countenance of God.

And he encountered God from the perspective of the poor. The problem of the locus where God might be found presented itself to him as the problem of finding a perspective from which, afterward, God might always be found no matter what the situation. In hermeneutical theology that question is a matter of complex debate. Romero resolved it very simply. His deep conviction can best be expressed in a sentence from the Puebla documents: "Therefore, because they are poor, God comes to their defense and loves them" (§ 1142). There is stated here a particular relationship between God and the poor, a *preferential* relationship within the overall relationship between God and creation. The beneficiaries of this partiality are those who, in their turn, can point out the locus of the correct relationship with God.

This does not mean that Romero idealized the poor. It means that he had found the locus where something fundamental about God may be learned. He had discovered the perspective from which one can determine in a particular place and time the criteria for building up the kingdom—the place of truth and the direction of change. Precisely from this particular perspective one can overcome the superficial generalization that God can be found everywhere and in whatever manner. Through his partiality for the poor, Romero could be impartial—and find God everywhere.

It is the Christian paradox that the mystery of the great God is first shown in what is tiny, what is least. And it is from that least place that God shows himself ever greater. That is why one can say that the poor preached the gospel to Archbishop Romero. He was preached to by way of those positive values that are very often to be found among the poor. They so situated him that he could correctly hear the good news of God.

The Father of Jesus

In describing the faith that Romero had, I have been describing the Father of Jesus. The God of the kingdom, the God of truth, the God of change, the God of the poor—these are phrases that describe Jesus' God. I should like to bring this short analysis to a close by considering two features of Jesus' attitude to his Father that Romero also shared.

Faith is a gift. But faith was not given to Romero once and for all. Like Jesus he was open to temptation. He had to endure loneliness, ignorance, attack, and persecution. He had to preserve his faith. Like Jesus he had to go on practicing it—through ecclesial and historical tasks that for him were the tasks of the episcopal ministry and a leadership that reached into civil society, as we shall see in greater detail further on.

It is not only that Romero had faith in God, he was also a faithful witness to the end. He became for many Christians what is said of Jesus in the Letter to the Hebrews—though of Jesus in all its plenitude: "[he] leads us in our faith and brings it to perfection" (12:2).

He believed in Jesus' God, and he believed the way Jesus did. Here is the gospel basis for his life and work, the basis of his impressive human qualities. I began this analysis of his life and work with his gospel faith because that is the way that one can most readily come to understand his impact both as archbishop and as a leader in society. In effect it is impossible easily to distinguish between these two dimensions, between his personal faith and his ministry, because they were dialectically linked. His faith was the foundation for his actions, but in turn his actions concretized his faith. There is no doubt that without the gift of faith, and without the quality of his faith, it is impossible fundamentally to comprehend the quality of his public ministry.

HIS EPISCOPAL MINISTRY

Romero was not only a believer, a follower of Jesus. He was in addition an archbishop. It seems to me to be very important indeed to insist that it was through his episcopal ministry that his faith took concrete shape, and not despite that ministry, or in isolation from it.

There is no doubt that episcopacy is one of the crucial aspects of the church as an institution. Equally there is no doubt that the institutional church is going through a serious crisis precisely because of its incapacity to act as an adequate vehicle for a vibrant faith.

Romero knew how to bring faith and episcopacy—personal charism and the institution—together. It was a remarkable gift, and an uncommon one, though he shared it with a number of Latin American bishops of today. I want, in describing Romero as a bishop, to do justice to his work. But indirectly this presentation could also be an aid to the theology of the episcopate, something particularly necessary nowadays.

Confirming the Faith of his Brothers and Sisters

This duty, conferred by Jesus on St. Peter, Archbishop Romero carried out to perfection, and with surprising repercussions. The faith of the archdiocese has undoubtedly grown and deepened. Rural and urban working-class families have made more profound their traditional, popular religion. The middle class, whose faith had been little more than conventional, or whose superficial liberalism had driven them out of the church, has again begun to show its faith in the gospel. At the level of the archdiocesan collective consciousness, the faith has been reevaluated.

This owes a good deal to Archbishop Romero. He learned the lesson well that, as bishop, it was his duty to confirm the faith of his brothers and sisters. And he learned it in a very down-to-earth way. He came to realize that this basic ministry that he had to exercise as bishop is neither identical with, nor can it be adequately fulfilled through, his teaching office. That is to say, it cannot be fulfilled simply by preserving, explaining, and interpreting the formulas of the faith. He did not neglect the teaching office, as we shall see later. But he understood that faith is prior to the magisterium, that the life of faith takes precedence over the *formulations* of faith. In the ministry of confirming others in the faith he saw something that was both deeper than, and prior to, the ministry of teaching. He tried to strengthen the faith of his brothers and sisters in that which is central to, which sums up, the faith: the following of Jesus.

It was the bishop's task, as he understood it, to make the Christian faith "credible" at its deepest level. But he also understood that he should not do this, in the first instance, simply by using the full weight of his authority to proclaim the faith, or to demand it of others. He had to make the faith actual in himself. He had to progress in faith, remain loyal to it, live it out in concrete situations, accept the risks that go along with trying to live it out.

The essential mark of the office of bishop is to be a witness to the faith, truly and deeply. A bishop ought to be such that the faithful believe what he believes, and to believe in such a way that they feel themselves nourished and strengthened in their faith. Every Christian is called upon to be a witness of the faith. But given the prominence of his office, and the opportunities that it provides, it is the special role of the bishop, and his grave responsibility, explicitly to be such a witness.

Defender of the Poor and Oppressed

It was not that he simply imitated Jesus, as do so many other Christians. No, he made the defense of the poor and oppressed a specific and basic function of his episcopal ministry. His pastoral activity clearly put him on their side. He denounced the destitution from which they suffered, and its causes. He identified himself with them. He defended their interests. At the administrative level he had the human and material resources of the archdiocese redistributed to their benefit.

In analyzing his episcopacy it is essential to realize that he made of the defense of the poor his principal ministry. He restored what had been one of the most important aspects of the episcopacy when it was introduced at the time of the colonization, but which was afterward lost. At the time of the colonization the bishop was *ex officio* the "protector of the Indians." On the assumption—very real, as it turned out—that the Indians were going to be marginalized, exploited, and decimated, the bishop had the task of protecting them, defending them from exploitation by either the military or the colonists.

This deeply Christian and ecclesial insight into the role of a bishop, which goes back four centuries, was revived in our day by Romero. The poor, the oppressed, anyone in need knew this, and turned to him for help. They came to the archbishop when they wanted injustices denounced, their rights asserted, missing persons found. They came to him to mediate when lands had been seized or when the security forces had surrounded churches. It was not that they came to him simply as a friend, seeking consolation. They came to him as a protector who was in duty bound to put the full weight of his episcopal authority at the service of the poor and the oppressed.

If the poor came to him spontaneously, it was because he had himself projected that image of what it meant to be a bishop. In doing so he achieved something of the greatest importance—though it may seem, when put down on paper, a little ambiguous. What he succeeded in doing was "institutionalizing" the preferential option for the poor. To "institutionalize," in this instance, does not mean to bureaucratize or trivialize. On the contrary, it means that not only should Christians as individuals make this option for the poor, but so should the church as such, placing at the disposal of the poor the resources that the church, as an institution, has at its own disposal.

Precisely because he was the archbishop and therefore the foremost representative of the institutional church, it became possible to speak of the church of the poor. Because of him the people could judge the various ecclesiastical institutions by that criterion: the defense of the poor and the oppressed.

Evangelist to the Whole Country

Romero fulfilled Jesus' command to his apostles to make a disciple of everyone. He was conscious of the fact that, as archbishop, it was his duty to respond to the "everyone" of the gospel. He had to evangelize the whole population of El Salvador as it then was.

Because both the archdiocese and the nation were small, and their problems similar, the task of evangelizing the whole population was made easier. The archbishop's prestige, and his use of the media, meant that he could reach out into every corner of the land. His evangelization of the whole of El Salvador was based on three principles.

1) It meant, first, to preach the gospel to all, to try to proclaim the good news to everyone, no matter what their personal and social situation. Romero was well aware that even by pastoral, let alone social and economic, criteria, the population was divided into distinct groups. So he undertook his apostolate in different ways, not only as to the means he used, but even in the purpose and direction of his evangelization. In his apostolate among the masses he took into account the need to purify and reinforce popular religion. His apostolate to politically committed Christians took the form of encouragement. Vis-à-vis those Christians in positions of economic or political power, however, his apostolate was to work for their conversion.

2) To preach the gospel to all also meant to evangelize the "structural reality," the country as a whole seen not just as the sum of all those who go to make it up but in terms of the structures that condition the lives of everyone living there. Romero preached the gospel in this sense, denouncing unjust structures, calling attention to the changes—whether social,

economic, or political—that were needed, and promoting the particular projects that seemed most likely to bring about the required changes. He saw clearly that, at the present time, the church has to associate "preaching the gospel to everyone" with "evangelizing the whole of the country in all its social, economic, and political aspects."

3) To evangelize the whole population also meant to understand adequately the ecclesiastical function of small groups within the church, while avoiding the temptation of reducing the church to such groups. Clearly, small groups will always spring up, whether in the traditional forms of religious congregations, or in the form of lay movements, or in the more modern form of basic Christian communities. They should be thought of here in relation to the purpose of preaching the gospel. At bottom, there are two theoretical models of basic Christian communities.

According to one model, the church should promote these groups, take refuge in them, find in them the last stronghold of the faith where the human and Christian needs of a very small number of individuals can be satisfied. This model implies reductionism and, at root, the collapse of the church. It regards these groups as a way of saving all that can be saved of the church.

According to the second model, Christian groups arise out of mass evangelization. Basic communities spring up within the context of local problems and in light of the need to establish the kingdom of God. They arise in response to a need, and as a means of fulfilling it. Hence this model is not so much a "reduction" as a "concentration." The church is concentrated in these groups. The purpose is not so much to better attend to the needs of a few, but to be a better leaven to all.

The fundamental difference between the two models is that, according to the first, the church would go on being turned in on itself, and in the second it would be at the service of the kingdom. In fact, of course, neither model exists in its pure form. I want simply to draw attention to the fact that precisely because Archbishop Romero wanted to evangelize the whole population, he encouraged the second, rather than the first, of the two models of basic communities—a term, incidentally, that can also be used of lay movements or religious congregations. In his heart of hearts, however, he believed that the evangelization of the few, and a form of Christian life that could serve only the needs of a few, profoundly contradicted the word of God addressed to all, and that such a contradiction put in doubt the efficacy of that word.

He understood evangelization to be something that ought to be expressed through every aspect of the church's life, both in its this-wordly and in its transcendental aspects, in personal and in social terms, in its liturgical and educational life, and so on. To the totality there to be evangelized, the church ought to address itself with the totality of its being.

Archbishop Romero did not himself develop a particular theory of evangelization. He was inspired by Paul VI's Apostolic Exhortation

Evangelii Nuntiandi. He put it into practice and, at several points, he added to it. He lived it out in his own apostolate and he impressed upon his pastoral agents that they too should implement it.

He attached great importance to the proclamation of the word. Both through his own Christian conviction and through his personal charism as a preacher, he made the word his most important instrument as an evangelist. He proclaimed the word as the word of God, and in his homilies dwelt long upon explaining it. But it is important to add that he believed the word of God was still manifesting itself today, in "the signs of the times." Moreover he believed that the very proclamation of the word had its own particular efficacy. It is not only a telling of truths, it is truth itself. And that is why it is effective: it makes present that which it proclaims.

He gave high priority to making the word come true, to turning the good news into a good reality. In the third part of this essay I shall show how he turned this proclamation of the word into a force for social transformation. What I want to stress here is that he did not reduce making the word come true simply to the ethical level, so that he fulfilled his evangelizing mission merely by proclaiming the word. He realized that making the word actual is an essential part of evangelization. Hence his insistence that integral liberation is a part of evangelization. There was in his preaching a dialectic between the proclamation and the realization of the good news, in such a way that each helped explain the other.

He also regarded as supremely important the manner of preaching: the testimony of one's own life—in other words, the holiness of the preacher. Just as he believed in the kingdom of God and the people of the kingdom, so too he believed that the efficacy of preaching went hand in hand with the credibility of the preacher. His most valuable contribution here was his concretization of the concept of holiness. A preacher certainly ought to possess the Christian virtues, the marks of a follower of Jesus. But as a preacher he ought to give a yet more fundamental witness: he must not abandon his people, he must travel along with them and, like a good shepherd, be ready to lay down his life for them.

These three aspects of evangelization are to be found in *Evangelii Nuntiandi.* Archbishop Romero emphasized a fourth element: prophetic denunciation. He was renowned in this regard both for his unequalled courage and for his solid incorruptibility. It is important to stress that he even saw denunciation as good news, a sort of gospel *sub specie contrarii.* He proclaimed the good news by negating what was evil. Sin he always denounced with great harshness, but he always managed to keep the accent on good news when speaking to oppressors. They, too, were his brothers and sisters. The good news was intended for them too; it beckoned them to conversion.

For their part the powerful, the ruling elite, the capitalists, reacted violently against him. As they had once said of Jesus that he was mad, that he was a new Beelzebub, that he was a political agitator trying to stir up the masses, so they now spoke of Romero. Money was poured out to belittle and calumniate him. Rarely can there have been so irrational and violent a campaign against a prophet. But Romero saw it all as part of the price a true prophet has to pay. He took it as evidence that what he stood for was the truth. But equally he saw in those who mounted the campaign persons to whom the gospel was also addressed. Like Jesus, he warned them against their unjust wealth. As he so vividly put it: "Pull the rings off your fingers before they cut off your hands." Like Jesus he strove always to hold out to them the promise of true happiness, such as was given to Zacchaeus after his conversion: "Today a blessing has come upon this house."

The overarching of his work of evangelization was the cathedral, "his" cathedral. He had no property of his own, as his will demonstrated, but the cathedral was especially dear to him. He saw in it a symbol of the church and of the nation, in all their nobility and in all their tragedy. He made the cathedral his workplace *par excellence,* the place where the people met, the place that linked hundreds of priests and nuns, the place from which his message went out to the nation, and to the nations of the world. But the cathedral has also been the place where persons have been massacred, the place where they sought sanctuary. It has been a hospital for the wounded, a mortuary for the dead of the church and of the people. Several times the cathedral has been seized by popular organizations, several times closed and opened. It has been a place for the liturgy—and for hunger strikes.

This cathedral, a symbol of sorrow and of hope, a meeting place for the church and for the people, Romero made his own. Before the bodies of the dead he bolstered the hopes of the people. He wanted the cathedral to be what it ought above all to be: the chair from which was proclaimed the good news, the gospel. By nature he was rather shy. But in the cathedral he was transfigured. In it he became aware that the gospel was directed to all Salvadorans, to the whole of the country. He made the cathedral the center both of the church and of the nation. It will never be possible to write the history of the church or of the nation without telling the story of Archbishop Romero's cathedral.

Romero and the Teaching Office of the Bishop

It is obvious that, at the present time, this particular aspect of the episcopal ministry has its problems. Believers are not as ready as they once were to accept the magisterium. But it is also obvious, and especially in Latin America, that many episcopal documents have been issued that are truly inspirational, and are giving a new meaning to the teaching office. As a teacher of the truth, Romero was one of the bishops who helped bring this about. He was well aware of the grave responsibility involved in teaching. He was aware both of the difficulty of, and the need for, this role, and of the need, even for a bishop, of "learning to teach."

He knew how to link the church's general teaching—whether at the Latin American level (Medellín and Puebla) or at the worldwide level (Vatican II and papal encyclicals)—to the situation in El Salvador. He demonstrated this ability both in his four pastoral letters, which were on the whole doctrinal, as well as in his Sunday sermons, which were more catechetical in style. It was not an *a priori* fidelity to the church's documents that brought this about; he achieved it because he looked for, and found, the truths expressed in them. He understood that in what others have taught in the past there is truth to be found—though obviously to different degrees—and that there is still a demand for the truth today. He did not harmonize the church's teaching with conditions in El Salvador simply by applying universally applicable documents to concrete situations. He looked instead for the light that a truth already expressed might shed upon the truth that is to be sought out in a new context. He found illumination in already written documents because he looked for it from within a particular situation.

Romero experienced the demands made upon him by the truth. In other words, it was not he who chose the problems with which he had to deal: he tackled those that history put before him, however novel and difficult they might be. He taught what it made sense to teach, what the situation demanded, and even about matters on which there was no readymade and "safe" doctrine. Objective truth was not the only criterion for his magisterium: relevance was also a criterion. And because his pastoral letters do not simply contain general truths but are relevant as well, they have been widely distributed, and even translated into other languages.

In fulfilling his office of teacher, Romero was pastorally oriented. This was reflected in the manner of his teaching—in his firmness and in his humility. He was firm when he was clear on an issue; he was humble when the solution to a new problem was, by its very nature, provisional: more a search for, than a possession of, the truth. It was for that reason that his pastoral letter on popular organizations was put forward as the first stage in a dialogue, which, in the nature of the case, had to be continued.

He taught with episcopal authority, but not with episcopal exclusivity. He did not shirk ultimate responsibility, but he was in continual consultation with experts in the social sciences, with theologians, with analysts of the national situation and its wider setting. Above all, he took account of the people. He tried to answer the real questions that grassroots Christians asked, and took their opinions into consideration when he replied. Instance the questionnaire he circulated in the basic communities in the archdiocese before setting off for Puebla.

Finally, he taught to the extent that he went on learning. He gave the impression of putting forward a truth that was, of its very nature, always open to further refinement, and even to change, so that he always held himself open to learn. The continual refinement of his teaching was not only the consequence of development in the realm of theory—though that certainly played its part—but also because he kept in touch with the situation in the church and in society. He learned from the context in which he found himself. He learned as a Christian because he truly believed in a God who goes on revealing himself in history. That is why he taught as he learned. It is no paradox to say that Archbishop Romero taught to the extent that he was taught by the world about him. He united in himself the heavy responsibility of teaching with the equally heavy responsibility of learning, and in doing so he exemplified something that is of the greatest importance for the office of bishop.

Head of the Body of the Archdiocese

The archdiocese of San Salvador could not be understood without him—but then neither could he be understood outside the context of the archdiocese. At the theoretical level, the ecclesial reality of the archdiocese can be thought of as a body, with the archbishop at the head. Under Archbishop Romero that theory became a reality.

As he himself confessed, right at the beginning of his archiepiscopal ministry, he was given the very best that the archdiocese could offer. The martyrdom of Fr. Grande, the support of the majority of the clergy and, above all, contact with the sufferings of the people—all these changed him. Over three long years of persecution the courage of Salvadoran Christians, their sufferings and their faith, were molding the archbishop himself. It is in this sense one can say of Romero that he was indeed a symbol, a sign of the best that Christianity had to offer. True though it be that he brought with him to the office those human and Christian qualities already described, in a very real sense the Christian community formed the archbishop.

There was a real link, and not simply a chain of command, between the archbishop and the archdiocese. This link explains both the unity of the church and the creation of a team of evangelists. Romero brought about a rare unity within the archdiocese. Never before had there been such a common sense of purpose among priests, religious, and pastoral workers. But this unity was not all-encompassing.

There was a right-wing minority among pastoral workers in opposition to the archbishop. There were also those who wanted to go further than Romero in involving the church in social and political life. Toward both groups he was understanding but firm. Those on the right almost entirely abandoned him; with those on the left he kept up a dialogue right to the end, listening to them and learning from them.

The unity worked. Tensions were inevitable, but the archbishop managed to make them fruitful tensions, ones that moved forward. The archdiocese was united around its mission—that of evangelization. It was not turned in upon itself and concerned with purely ecclesiastical issues. The unity was, moreover, cemented by suffering and persecution. Yet this mission was also a source of disunity, not only within the archdiocese but even among the country's bishops, some of the clergy, and Christians who belonged to the ruling classes. To give Romero his due, it was not he who dissociated himself from them, but they who cut themselves off from him. It was not his personality that brought it about—he was always kindness and humility itself. Rather it was the mission of the church of which he was the leader. What most deeply saddened him was the division in the hierarchy. Because of the scandal it gave to the faithful it seriously worried him. It impoverished the church's mission in the country and gave support to those who criticized the church. But he put fidelity to his apostolate to the poor, as he saw it, before the anguish of disunion.

This very real unity within the church found expression in Romero's enormous ability for gathering the church together. This was certainly demonstrated when he said Mass, but it was also evident in other church activities. That unity was a real source of strength to the pastoral team made up of priests, nuns, catechists, ministers of the word, and others. Salvadorans understood that the whole of the archdiocese, and Romero himself, was behind all the church's activities.

It is in this sense—a sense that is historical and effective, not simply legal or abstract—that we can say Romero was the head of the archdiocese. He was the expression of all that was best and most Christian among the people. They saw him as their true representative. In this profound sense Romero let himself be made a bishop by his people, and they were grateful to him that he made them truly the body of the church.

Romero and the Institutional Power of the Church

It is clear that, at least in Latin America, the church is still a great social force. But this force can be used in many different ways. At one extreme it would be possible to use politico-ecclesiastical means to influence society, or to impose rules and regulations upon society from above. The other extreme would be to reduce the church to a community that abandons the world to its fate, or merely tries to change the world by the subjective testimony of holiness.

Archbishop Romero exercised an institutional power, but one different from both those extremes. He never wished to become one of the nation's important leaders, but he found himself a mediator, sometimes an arbiter, in a great variety of conflicts within society. Groups of very different tendencies turned to him for help. It is important to examine what Romero thought about this power and, given that he did not reject it, to see how he used it. It is also important to see how he reconciled institutional power with power put to the service of the poor, the majority of the population.

Romero certainly did not understand the church's institutional power in the first sense outlined above. The church's institutional power ought not to be thought of as analogous to state power in such a way that it might be regarded as natural that the church enter into dialogue with the state, the people simply being on the receiving end of power exercised from above by both entities. In terms of this model, the ideal for Christianity would be for the church as institution to be on good terms with the state, avoiding all clashes with it, or resolving all such clashes to the people's cost.

Romero negated this model by the way he lived. The masses were not only not the beneficiaries of state handouts; they were the beneficiaries of no handouts at all. It was neither a power *of* the people, nor a power *for* the people that was exercised over them. The church, therefore, could not make peace with this system. And it had itself been directly persecuted by the state.

Romero broke with the model of church power as analogous to state power in a great number of ways. For example, he took part in no cere-mony, political or ecclesiastical, that would have presented the two powers as being on the same footing and coexisting in supposed harmony. That is why, as he put it so graphically, the church had no problems with the state—only the people had problems. He wanted to make it clear that one should not think of the institutional authority of the church as power "from above," as similar to state power, and as the natural dialogue partner of the state.

But neither did he think of the church as a purely spiritual community, one far removed from any sort of power in society. What he did was to change fundamentally the whole notion of power. The institutional power of the church ought to be exercised through means that are proper to the church, especially through the word that creates a common awareness, and not through politico-ecclesiastical means, always on the lookout for conces-sions from the state. It ought to be exercised for the good of the people, and not for the good of the institution to the detriment of the people.

This change in the understanding of what power meant was not merely theoretical. It changed the church's base. The church found its place, its home, amidst the people. And it was with the people, not with the state, that the church entered into dialogue. From the people he learned what it was to put one's authority at their service. It was his oft-repeated assertion that the church's authority ought to be at the service of the people, and he put this into practice by bringing the church to those it ought to serve. The church's institutional authority was used not only *for* the people but *with* the people as well. It was no longer exercised from above but from within.

This description of Romero's apostolate as bishop does no more than depict—and, indeed, just as Puebla asked (see §§682–84)—the evangelical figure of a pastor, of Jesus. With him, the sheep were safe (John 10:9); his function was to give them life, and life in abundance (John 10:10); he knew his sheep, and his sheep knew him (John 10:14); he was always ready to lay down his life for them (John 10:11).

It is beyond doubt that Romero's faith helped him to make the office of bishop more Christlike. But it is also beyond doubt that his episcopal office helped him to make his faith more real, to make it astoundingly effective. Whatever the theories about the episcopate, Romero demonstrated by his actions that it is possible to live out to the full the Christian understanding of that office. He also demonstrated just how important the office of bishop can be in making the faith effective in Latin America. Romero did not theorize about the various issues currently being debated in the theology of the episcopate. He brought into being a new theology of the episcopate simply by his actions. He did not ignore the traditional characteristics of his office, but in the theology that he lived he made those characteristics more concrete and more complete in a new historical context.

Speaking purely sociologically, one cannot expect many bishops with Romero's humane, Christian qualities to emerge. But speaking theologically we have in him a concrete model of what a bishop, with a gospel faith, ought nowadays to be like, and an example of how important it is for a bishop to make that faith effective for liberation. That is no small merit to his credit.

ROMERO'S JUDGMENT ON EL SALVADOR

Romero truly loved his country. In his apostolate as archbishop he put that love into deeds. Without wanting to do so, he became a national leader. His influence in El Salvador was first of all in the religious sphere but, as he was well aware, it would also be a direct social influence, and an indirect political influence—though in no way did he directly involve himself in politics.

Romero denounced all that disgraced the country; he proclaimed tirelessly the need for a new society; he strove to humanize the processes of change. To record all the positions he took up, all the work that he did during his three years in office, would be an endless task. Instead I am going to attempt to analyze the Christian principles that lay behind his judgment on the nation and go on from there to examine his judgment on the three options with which El Salvador was confronted.

Christian Principles

The principles I refer to arose from Medellín and have been generally accepted in the Latin American church. They have not, however, been accepted in conservative circles, even as broad guidelines.

In my view four fundamental principles guided Romero's judgment:

1) The church is not the same thing as the kingdom of God; it is the servant of the kingdom. It ought, therefore, to practice the love and justice that enable the kingdom to take concrete shape. It ought to be an instrument at the service of the kingdom and in consequence cooperate with those who truly want a more just society, even if they are not explicitly Christians themselves.

2) The poor are those for whom the kingdom is primarily intended. Not that the kingdom ought to be constructed for them: they themselves should be the makers of their own destiny. It follows that they cannot be denied the major part in any process leading to the establishment of the kingdom.

3) As the servant of the kingdom, the church ought also to promote the values of the members of the kingdom, both while the new society is being built up and when it is at length achieved.

4) For the church in any way to impede or thwart either the kingdom of God or the members of the kingdom is sinful. This is true both at the personal and at the structural level, and this sin has degrees of wickedness that will be important to consider when making judgments about de facto situations and courses of action.

These principles can be clearly seen at work in all that Romero did, but he was also well aware that, because they are *general* principles, they have to be put into practice in accordance with the signs of the times. The need to make these principles concrete was an important part of his understanding of them. He therefore gave new importance to a much-neglected canon of pneumatology—that is to say, to the affirmation that the Spirit is constantly at work in history.

In order to understand the judgments that Archbishop Romero made about El Salvador, one has to bear in mind the way in which some key principles were put into practice. Of these principles the following seem to be the most significant:

1) Romero concretized the concept of "the poor." Although recognizing the profound truth in the gospel presentation of spiritual poverty, he went beyond it. In accord with Puebla (§§31–39), he described poverty as it is today in El Salvador. But more than that, he saw in every poor person not just an isolated individual but "the masses." To speak of the poor was to speak of *the* problem in El Salvador. He regarded the masses not just as a sum of individuals but as a collectivity, as a people—however much one would have to nuance this statement sociologically. He saw in this collectivity a social grouping utterly opposed to the ruling group—though as a pastor he was not concerned to analyze the class nature of those groups. In this way he advanced beyond the usual view of a poor person as a peaceable individual who is, at most, the object of an ethical demand upon us. He saw the poor as a collectivity, the very existence of which—and increasingly so as it grows in self-understanding—signals social conflict.

2) Romero concretized what it meant to say that the people ought to be the agent of its own destiny and not simply the beneficiary of real or feigned charity. Hence he understood the logic of moving from "people" to "organized people." He defended, as a Christian principle, the right of a people to organize itself. Though as a pastor he imposed on no one the obligation of joining an organization, he positively encouraged them to do so, though without going so far as to point out which particular organization came closest to fulfilling the ideal of an organized people.

He grew in understanding of the purpose that lay behind a people's banding together. From the very beginning he saw the legitimacy of a people's organizing itself to fight for, or to defend its rights. But he also came to understand, especially in the last months of his life, the importance of a people's organizing itself so as to take over, or to be substantially represented in, political power. He recognized that no political program will successfully benefit the majority of a people unless its own organizations play a major part in the political life of the country.

3) In his promotion of a more just society he introduced the novel idea of the "viability" of theory and practice. The viability of theory prompted him to analyze different political options. He asked himself which was the likeliest to bring about a society most closely resembling the kingdom of God. As a pastor he was concerned with the viability of practice. It was not as a political analyst but as a pastor that he drew attention to the ways that, in his view, were most likely to bring the new society into being. Naturally, there is a tension between the viability of theory and the viability of practice, and Romero understood this. But it is important to emphasize once again that in making actual the kingdom of God he did not concern himself simply with proclaiming it. He thought hard about the viable ways of building the kingdom in El Salvador.

When rooting these Christian judgmental principles in his particular time and place, Romero was deepening his understanding of them. At times he changed his mind. His pastoral letters and his Sunday homilies recount the story of this process. It is important to draw attention to the fact that this rooting in history, with all its complexity and its nuances, even with its changes, had a definite, historical direction. This has to be said because, and especially since his death, he has frequently been presented as someone who was a defender of human rights in the abstract, who loved peace and justice, but who lacked any clear, practical, historical commitment. It is true that he touched on a whole variety of different issues, and that he did so in such changing circumstances that one can always find a quotation to support one's own views. It is possible to play off what he said on different occasions in such a way as to suggest that, having said everything, in the end Romero had said nothing. But that was never his intention, nor is it an objective picture of what happened.

Romero did not apply his general Christian principles to the history of his own time simply on the basis of purely abstract theological reasoning. Nor did he base himself on the evolving magisterium of the church on sociopolitical matters, though undoubtedly both the theology and the social teaching helped him. The principle behind his process of adaptation was the very history of his country or, to put it theologically, the manifestation of the Spirit in that history. That is why his thinking went along fairly clear-cut lines as he himself progressed in discovering, in quite practical terms, the will of God for El Salvador.

As a way of checking on the validity of the development and the direction of his social thinking one ought not to ignore the reaction, both at home and abroad, to his active involvement: the public image that the people as a whole and different social groups had of him. That reaction, that image, are proof enough that his activities led in a definite direction, that his commitment was not merely to the universal values of peace, love, justice, and human rights, but to programs that would best guarantee those values.

The Three Political Options

On the basis of the criteria already cited, their realization and development, Romero passed judgment on the three options confronting El Salvador. He called them the proposals or programs of the oligarchy, of the governing junta, and of the people.

He condemned the policy of the oligarchy—the infamous fourteen families, and their allies, that effectively control the destiny of El Salvador—because it was clearly evil. "When all is said and done, the right wing stands for social injustice. There is no justification for maintaining a right-wing stance," he told *El Diario de Caracas* (March 19, 1980). His fourth pastoral letter denounced its policies as idolatrous—based upon mendacity. It served an idol that, in order to survive, needed more and more victims. It was unacceptable both to Christianity and to history. After fifty years of misery the masses, with their growing political awareness, could tolerate it no longer.

Romero's judgment on the policy of the governing junta changed between the first and the second junta. He was hopeful about the first one. He did not give it his blessing, nor did he give it unconditional support—though he gave it critical support. He saw that there was a chance of implementing the Christian principles outlined above. There were grounds for hope in the fact that the coup had been bloodless, in the honesty and the good intentions of many of the new leaders, and in the promises of radical reform and of dialogue with popular organizations.

But none of this became viable. Repression continued. No one was any the clearer about the fate of all those who had vanished for political reasons. Those who were responsible were not brought to trial—something that Romero regarded as a requirement of simple justice and as a sign that there had been a break with the past. Reforms could not be carried out. There were large-scale resignations by conscientious members of the government, and this convinced him that the policy of the junta would not work.

The second junta had a clearer political program. Romero defined it as "reforms with the big stick"—reforms accompanied by repression. With increased vigor he condemned, as he had always done, the repression of the people. It had become much worse, both in terms of the number of victims involved and the degree of cruelty with which it was carried out. He condemned the final aim of the repression: the destruction of the popular organizations. It was the aim of a faction in the government that, Romero said, acted like a parallel government. He was brought to the point where, with unequalled passion, he called upon the soldiers and other members of the security forces not to obey unjust orders. These were the last words of his last sermon:

In the name of God, and in the name of this suffering people whose cries rise daily more loudly to heaven, I plead with you, I beg you, I order you in the name of God: put an end to this repression! [March 23, 1980].

Because of the repression he became suspicious of the agrarian reform that was announced. Though he stressed its necessity, he foresaw its impossibility because, as Scripture says, land stained with blood will not bear fruit (Gen. 4:12). Agrarian reform ought not to be granted to the people as if it were a gift. It is something they have earned by all the blood they have paid for it. Even in the days of the first junta Romero laid down the real significance that agrarian reform ought to have but that he did not see when it first began to be implemented:

Agrarian reform should not be undertaken simply so as to find a way of salvaging the capitalist economic system, and allowing it to go on developing in such a way that wealth is accumulated and concentrated in the hands of a few, whether they be of the industrial, commercial, or banking sectors of society. Nor should it be done so as to silence the *campesinos*, to prevent them from organizing themselves and so increasing their political, economic, and social involvement. Agrarian reform ought not to make the *campesinos* dependent upon the state. It ought to leave them free in their relationship with the state [sermon, Dec. 16, 1979].

He drew the consequences of his denunciation of this political program. He asked the Christian Democrats to rethink their position in the government. Just five days before his death he gave the following answer to a journalist who was questioning him about it:

I am no expert in politics. I can only repeat what I have heard from prominent analysts. Even though it is true they have the good intention of carrying through structural reforms, the Christian Democrats run a grave risk in being part of a government that is engaged in such fearful repression. In this way the Christian Democratic Party is becoming an accomplice in the annihilation of the people. I want to tell you journalists to be clear and objective in your reporting of what is going on in El Salvador. I have often heard it said by persons who live abroad and do not understand what is going on here, "The Christian Democrats are there; they are carrying out reforms; what more do you want? Why do you complain?" So it should be made clear that yes, there is the Christian Democratic Party, and yes, there are reforms. But the only thing the people know is terrible repression [interview, *El Diario de Caracas*, March 19, 1980].

It is in this context that one has to understand his letter to President Carter. The United States has no right to intervene in El Salvador, no right to lend support to a policy that is said to be opposed to the oligarchy but in reality is opposed to the interests of the people, no right to provide military support just as repression grows in intensity (cf. his sermon of Feb. 17, 1980).

Romero certainly had no objections to a reform policy in itself, provided it really opened the way to reforms, and to the integration of the people and their organizations in the political process. But he did not regard the superficial reform policy of the junta as one that was viable for Christians. Nor did he believe that the people would support it in the long term.

Over his three-year period as archbishop, Romero's judgment on the people's self-liberation evolved to the point where, in the last three months of his life, he came to think of it as the historical force that offered most hope. He thought this for two reasons: the others would not work, and the popular organizations, which were the main protagonists of the people's interests, had gone through a long process to reach maturity.

It has already been pointed out that the reality of the poor and their being the "agents of their own destinies" had brought Romero face to face with the situation of the popular organizations. He gave over a large part of his third and fourth pastoral letters to this topic. Here I want to sum up briefly his attitude to the popular organizations, what he criticized in them, what the criticism meant, his support for them, and the hopes that they engendered in him. For though the general tendency of his attitude was clear, it was complex and nuanced.

Romero criticized everything he saw as wrong-headed or dangerous in the popular organizations, both from a Christian and from an ordinary human point of view. He criticized all that he regarded as dehumanizing in them, either in their effect on their members or in their effect on the country. He warned them severely against the danger of thinking that the point of view of their own organization was the only possible one, and against the danger of reductionism: seeing everything from a political angle and neglecting other areas of life. He accused them of being dogmatic and sectarian, of being divided among themselves, of being separated from other political groups and even from the people itself. He denounced some of their actions as being disproportionately violent. On occasion he even denounced their violence as little different from terrorism—though he did not think it so typical of the popular organizations as it was of the politico-military groups. He accused them of claiming to be more representative of the people than they actually were, of sometimes failing to take account of the religious feelings of the people and their most cherished expressions of those feelings. In some extreme cases, he said, they wanted to manipulate or even to destroy the people's Christian faith.

It is important to make clear what his criticism meant. His love for the truth moved him to denounce whatever he saw to be mistaken, though he perfectly well understood that so vast a social phenomenon as the popular organizations would be bound to make some mistakes. His criticism of them was different from that directed against the other two options for the liberation of the masses. He criticized the popular organizations because he had hopes for them. He wanted them to improve, to grow, and to serve the people better. He denounced the absolutization of politics because "one could, for all practical purposes, ignore all other real problems or mistake the basic ideological criteria" (fourth pastoral letter). He attacked sectarianism because "it changed what was a likely force for the people's good into an obstacle impeding radical social change" (ibid.). He attacked disparagement of the Christian faith because it showed no respect for the reality of the faith among the people, and because it "would be a mistake to place in opposition to each other the driving force within the organizations and the driving force within the church" (ibid.).

On the other hand, in the popular organizations Romero saw a range of humane, Christian values that were beneficial for the country as a whole and that the church would do well to learn. He admired the justice of their struggle, the moral weight of their cause, the generosity and strength of their commitment, and their readiness to devote their lives and their possessions to the people. These qualities were more in evidence among the popular organizations than they were in other political groups. And he admired their values although he knew that, alongside the Christians, there were also nonbelievers in the popular organizations. This was no reason for him not to give the organizations his admiration and support. He was convinced that "even outside the church's precincts, Christ's redemption has great power, and peoples struggling for freedom, even though they are not Christian, are inspired by the Spirit of Jesus" (third pastoral letter).

Toward the end of his life, though he kept up his criticism, he came to realize that the popular organizations had entered upon a stage that, taken all in all, he regarded positively. He had called for unity, and for the overcoming of sectarianism. With the creation of the CRM (*Coordinadora Revolucionaria de Masas,* Mass Revolutionary Coordinating Committee) and its opening up to other social and politically democratic forces, these ends seemed about to be attained. Romero did not live to hear of the formation of the FDR (*Frente Democrático Revolucionario,* Democratic Revolutionary Front) on April 2, 1980. But he knew of the first steps that were being taken, and was delighted by them. In fact, through the good offices of the archdiocesan Legal Aid Bureau he was, in a manner of speaking, to be found in the Halt to Repression document signed by several of the democratic groupings. The formation of a democratic front had been sought by several democratic groups. But it was made possible by the openness of the CRM and its desire to weld together other forces in society on behalf of the popular program.

He was also pleased when the CRM presented a unified platform, because that fact presupposed a wholly new form of unity. It was a response to his explicit request that the people know along which paths the CRM intended to lead the country. We cannot know what he would have thought about the content of the policy adopted by the CRM. The only thing we have is his reply, given in the interview already quoted, when he was asked about it: "I know of it, and I accept it as a basis for discussion among the people. There has to be a readiness to receive criticism and comment from every sector, so that it can be the people itself that forges the government it desires."

Finally, in the last stage of the CRM, he was anxious, and he insisted, that the new program should respect the people's human and religious values. The presence of many Christians in the popular organizations and the readiness of the organizations and the CRM to engage in dialogue with the church and other Christian institutions appeared to him to give some guarantees of such respect. He insisted on this partly because it was his clear duty as archbishop to do so, and partly from his awareness of what it means to be a Salvadoran. The popular program ought to find a place for Christianity because Christianity is an important part of the people's life.

Romero showed that he had great hopes for the popular program while it was being drawn up. He did not idealize it, however. He made suggestions for improving it, and kept demanding that it display greater maturity. From his homily of January 20, 1980, onward, he repeatedly referred to his hope in it. Not that he identified himself with it, or with any other current political program. Taking politics in the strict sense of the word, he could not do so, because of his position as archbishop. In any case he believed that it would be more fruitful for the development of the country if he kept a certain distance. But there is no doubt at all that he saw in the popular program the best, and the most workable, translation into political terms of the option for the poor that he so radically defended in pastoral terms.

Hence it would be a mistake to present Archbishop Romero as a man of the center, keeping himself equidistant from the left and the right. It would be a mistake because it would imply that he acted on the *negative* principle of avoiding extremes. In fact he acted out of *positive* principles, asking himself what would lead to deeper truth, greater justice, stronger possibilities for peace. The popular program, he found, had these in greater abundance and with greater potential. He wanted to avoid the trap that the very terminology "right," "left," and "center" offers, as if it were the job of an archbishop to choose the center *ex officio*. In the interview quoted above he was asked what the "left" meant for him. He replied, "I don't call them the forces of the left but the forces of the people. . . . What they call 'the left' is the people. It is the organization of the people . . . and their demands are the demands of the people." Romero did not choose not to choose—which, in effect, is what to be "of the center" means. He made a choice: he opted for the people.

THE CHURCH'S ROLE IN THE SALVADORAN CRISIS

Romero saw clearly that El Salvador was passing through a period of change, a period of agitation giving rise to conflict. In the conflict the protagonists of each of the three national options were trying to push their own program into the leading position. He also saw clearly that it was the church's duty to pass judgment not only on political programs, but also on the process of change itself. It ought to enter into it, so as to humanize it along Christian lines.

He took up a stance on the conflict inherent in the process and on violence. He had to decide whether or not violence was legitimate and how to humanize it wherever possible.

In making his fundamental ethical judgment on violence, Romero distinguished between the violence of provocation and the violence of response. He recalled the traditional doctrine of proportionate violence in legitimate self-defense, and expounded the degrees of violence as presented by Medellín.

Medellín clearly condemned the violence of provocation that springs from institutionalized injustice. It becomes institutionalized violence or, in the particular case of El Salvador, general repression. From this point of view he saw a violent response as legitimate and just. In the constitutions of the popular organizations he saw the first response to structural injustice. Their means were not essentially violent ones. They were rather those of social pressure. But when the popular organizations were attacked for making use of social pressure, then they had a right to defend themselves. This is how he put it in a carefully phrased paragraph in his fourth pastoral letter:

We are also aware that great numbers of *campesinos*, workers, slum dwellers, and others who have organized themselves to defend their rights and to promote legitimate changes in social structures are simply regarded as "terrorists" and "subversives." They are arrested, tortured, they disappear, they are killed without any concern for the law or for those legal institutions that are there to protect them. They have no chance to defend themselves or to prove their innocence. Confronted by this harmful and unjust situation they have frequently been forced to defend themselves, even to the point of having recourse to violence. And lately the response to this has been the arbitrary violence of the state.

Within the context of legitimate self-defense, Romero condemned what was out of proportion. He also condemned terrorist violence—more typical of paramilitary political groups than of the popular organizations. Though at times it may be difficult to distinguish between legitimate armed violence and out-and-out terrorism, he took great care to analyze situations and to condemn terrorism.

That is why he did not simply condemn violence "wheresoever it may come from." In a manner that is rarely to be found in the pronouncements of bishops he said, "The church cannot simply assert that it condemns all forms of violence" (fourth pastoral letter). He tried to analyze each case carefully and to judge in accordance with the de facto circumstances.

But Romero was not content simply to judge the legitimacy or illegitimacy of acts of violence. He also attempted to humanize courses of action that involved violence. Though there were cases when violence might be *just*, Romero tried to make it *good* as well. He put Salvadorans on their guard against those unfortunate by-products of violence that can occur even when violence is legitimate. He insisted on the need to overcome hate, to overcome the instinct for vengeance, the temptation to make violence the chief and the basic means of achieving one's ends. He energetically condemned what he called the mysticism of violence.

More positively, he promoted the use and effectiveness of peaceful means even when violence might be necessary to some extent. Romero was not a pacifist pure and simple. By nature he was a peaceful man. As archbishop he was a peacemaker. So as to humanize even the violence that was legitimate, he repeatedly drew attention to all the other elements that had to be employed in building up peace: justice, dialogue, truth, magnanimity.

Romero was also aware of the possibility of armed insurrection. He dwelt on the subject in his last pastoral letter, and he often alluded to it in his final homilies. Conscious of the influence he had in society at large, he tried by his actions to prevent the growth of a war mentality, though he had to recognize that there were already so many dead that the situation resembled an undeclared civil war. But he was always trying to avoid it, trying to find other means of bringing about radical changes. Recent events raised in him the hope that the popular cause might gather so much impetus, and bring together so many different sectors of society, that change might be the most peaceful, and the least violent, possible. Nonetheless he did not exclude the possibility of insurrection. He fought for reconciliation until the last, seeing it as one of his most important tasks. But when asked what would happen should reconciliation prove impossible, he replied laconically, "Well then, the church allows for insurrection when all other peaceful means have been exhausted" (interview, March 19, 1980).

Romero thought the popular program was the best one for the people of El Salvador, for it seemed that it was the policy best able to guarantee enduring structures of justice. But conscious of his role as a churchman, he insisted upon, and worked for, the ideal that it be achieved with what was best from among the people of El Salvador, and that it should incorporate the values of the people of El Salvador. Putting it theologically, he was concerned both for the kingdom of God, and for the men and women of that kingdom. With a rare and a deep understanding, he pleaded for a conversion of structures and a conversion of hearts.

It was evident that his interest was in persons and not simply in structures when he spoke as a Christian to Christians, and also when he spoke to the people of El Salvador as a whole. In the first instance he emphasized the explicit values of Christianity: faith in God, prayer, openness to Christ— realities that, for him, made men and women human. In the second case he promoted authentic Christian values, though they were not put forward as Christian, for the birth of a new people in El Salvador.

This new people ought already to be in the making, even in the present conflict, as we have seen. It ought to be looked on as the beginning of the future of a new society. Though we do not know what Romero thought of the manifesto of the CRM, I believe that he would have insisted upon analyzing the human, the cultural, the spiritual, and the Christian values of the people of El Salvador, and would have regarded this as the proper role for the church to play. He would have understood that a political manifesto is customarily more concerned with an analysis of a country's structural problems, but he would have remarked that, although new structures no doubt help, they cannot automatically resolve human problems. He recognized that structures do not change merely out of a people's goodness of heart, but neither will hearts change simply because of better structures. In this sense he stressed that the popular cause ought to acknowledge and enhance all that is best in the people of El Salvador, in their cultural inheritance and religious values.

Romero saw toward the end that to humanize this liberative process the church must be present within it. It ought not ignore it or judge it merely from the outside, despite all the conflict and ambiguity that are inherent in any such process. He himself was present within it. This is very clear both from his range of activities as archbishop and from all those innumerable particular occasions when he took it upon himself to dialogue with, to mediate on behalf of, and to stand alongside the people. It is also clear that he wanted all Christians, including the clergy, to be involved in the process and not try to avoid the most difficult aspect of it—that of associating themselves with politically committed Christians.

He believed that the church ought to be present in the process in a way specifically in accord with its nature. That is to say, the church ought to be an evangelical force that becomes a social force, directly, and a political force, indirectly. He believed this ought to happen for the good of the process and for the church's support to be more effective. Although, in the short term, it might seem that the church would be less effective if it stayed close to its own specific vocation in its involvement, Romero was convinced, and history has borne him out, that if it did so the church's influence would be greater and more humanizing in the long term.

He did not believe that it was the church's proper role to direct the process. The church should make its presence felt in the manner of leaven. De jure it was not the church's task to undertake political leadership, though he himself gave far-reaching social leadership. And de facto he knew that among the leaders in the process there were many Christians, as well as unbelievers. The church's presence ought not to come about by way of purely political means, but rather through the objective strength of its truth, its cogency, and its influence in society.

Romero regarded the church's presence in the process as being of the highest importance both for the process itself and for the future of the church. If it were not to be present then it would afterward be displaced by those—*ex hypothesi* outside the church—who had spent their blood and their lives for the popular cause. He did not share the common belief that the church has only an abstract right to speak to, and have an influence upon, society. A church that *ex hypothesi* has abandoned the people in its forward march cannot afterward try to put itself in the vanguard of the people.

Finally, Romero wanted the church to be present in the process for a simple and profoundly Christian reason: the incarnation. The first truth one says of Christ ought also be said of the church. But not infrequently, when the church is faced by new developments that involve conflict and ambiguity, it is tempted to stand to one side, to judge developments from the outside. The transcendence of the faith is commonly cited in defense of this attitude.

Romero believed profoundly in the transcendence of the faith. But he believed in it in a Christian manner. He believed that the church ought to "take flesh" in the world as it really is. It ought to maintain the transcendence of the faith not by alienating itself from, but by submerging itself in, particular situations, judging them, learning from them, always humanizing them, always trying to eliminate what is dehumanizing. The "more" that rises from the depths of humanity is that which directs the church toward the authentic transcendence of God.

It was, hence, because of the faith that Romero believed that the church ought always to make itself present, and to do so in a manner proper to the church. If the church fails to be present in current developments, then the church will simply stop being the Christian church, the church of Jesus, the church that believes in God.

Let us end where we began. If Archbishop Romero played a leading role in the church and in society, it was because of his profound faith in the God of Jesus. That is why he was such a spiritual, such a religious, man, such a close follower of Jesus. It was precisely because of these things that he knew how to renew the life of the church, and how to guide the nation along the road of liberation.

His martyrdom simply confirmed the truth of his life and his cause. His faith in God led him to foresee his martyrdom. He looked upon it as the final service he could render to the church and to his country. This is what he said in his last interview, one that he gave to *Excelsior* (Mexico City) just two weeks before his death:

> I have frequently been threatened with death. I must say that, as a Christian, I do not believe in death but in the resurrection. If they kill me, I will rise again in the people of El Salvador. I am not boasting; I say it with the greatest humility.
>
> As a pastor, I am bound by a divine command to give my life for those whom I love, and that includes all Salvadorans, even those who are going

to kill me. If they manage to carry out their threats, I shall be offering my blood for the redemption and resurrection of El Salvador.

Martyrdom is a grace from God that I do not believe I have earned. But if God accepts the sacrifice of my life, then may my blood be the seed of liberty, and a sign of the hope that will soon become a reality.

May my death, if it is accepted by God, be for the liberation of my people, and as a witness of hope in what is to come. You can tell them, if they succeed in killing me, that I pardon them, and I bless those who may carry out the killing.

But I wish that they could realize that they are wasting their time. A bishop will die, but the church of God—the people—will never die.

The Easter Church

First Pastoral Letter of Archbishop Romero,
Easter Sunday, April 10, 1977

To my beloved brothers and sisters, the auxiliary bishop, the priests, religious, and laity of the archdiocese of San Salvador; to you and to all men and women of good will, the Easter greeting of Jesus: peace be with you.

A TIME OF TRANSITION

On February 22, the feast of the Chair of St. Peter, the archdiocese of San Salvador lived through that mysterious moment of "apostolic succession," a characteristic of the human and historical side of Jesus' divine and eternal church. Salvadoran episcopal history began on September 28, 1842, when Pope Gregory XVI erected the diocese of San Salvador as a suffragan see of Guatemala. Four bishops followed each other in the new see until, on February 11, 1913, St. Pius X, the father of our ecclesiastical province, elevated it to the rank of metropolitan see. Since that date three important figures in the Salvadoran hierarchy have held the office of archbishop.

For the past thirty-eight years of turbulent history, Archbishop Luis Chávez y González successfully guided the ship of our local church. Now his distinguished but weary hands have turned over the finely balanced rudder to a new successor of the apostles. I have taken hold of it with all the respect and delicacy of one who feels that he has received an inheritance of inestimable value to help him continue to guide and sustain the church toward new and difficult horizons.

The work of my venerable predecessor will stand out when the ecclesiastical history of El Salvador comes to be written. During the thirty-eight years of his apostolate, God abundantly blessed the life of the church. The seminary, the number of vocations, the priests, the parish communities, the religious communities, the colleges, the schools, the work of catechesis, the organizations and initiatives taken for the betterment of men and women, the luminous teaching in his pastoral letters—all these will be chapter headings in the written record of his episcopacy. And it was backed up by the personal testimony of a holy life that faithfully traversed the road of his priestly vocation. Against this rock of authenticity and virtue have broken cowardly storms of calumny, but they have succeeded only in adorning his life, rather as rocks in the ocean are adorned by the furious foam of the waves.

A Paschal Moment

Were I to search for an appropriate adjective to describe this moment of apostolic succession in the archdiocese, I should have no hesitation in calling it paschal.

Yes. We are passing through a very beautiful Eastertide. It coincides with the Eastertide of our liturgical year. Only the spirit of a risen Christ who, down the years, lives in and builds up his church, can explain the rich heritage that my venerable predecessor Archbishop Chávez has handed on to me. Only the divine impulse of the Spirit of Easter can explain this unexpected beginning of my hierarchical service to the archdiocese. Never did I imagine so beautiful an entrance as pastor into this church of the divine Savior. In the special circumstances of this past Lent, the ecclesial mystery of Easter, which never fails to delight me as a Christian, has enriched my life, not only as a private individual but also as I have lived it from my position as a pastor in communion with the whole church: in a dialogue of common responsibility with my beloved clergy, in close involvement of concern and prayer with ecclesial communities and with the faithful. In communion with the church universal, I have shared in the fellow feeling and the solidarity of many of my brother bishops and of other dioceses. And, above all, I have had once again the support of the successor of St. Peter who, during my recent trip to Rome, entrusted to me Christ's charismatic commission: "strengthen your brothers" (Luke 22:32).

An Easter Greeting

All of this imposes upon my first pastoral letter addressed to the whole archdiocese a paschal theme and manner. It is my letter of introduction, my first greeting. In a spirit of optimism and of Christian hope it seeks to express:
• first of all, to my brothers and friends who are the priests of the archdiocese, my offer of, and hope for, a dialogue with each other, and of collaboration in the service of the People of God whom together we have to evangelize, sanctify, and rule;
• to the communities of religious, my pastoral affection and my gratitude for the way they enrich the life of prayer and contemplation, and for the many ways in which they bring into being, among our people, the divine mystery of the church;

• to generous lay people, all the vision and all the hope that the Second Vatican Council aroused in the hearts of pastors for the promotion of the lay vocation as a call to sanctity in the world, which they are to order according to the plans of God in committed collaboration with the church's apostolic mission;
• and to all men and women who await from the church an answer that will throw light on their doubts, their disquiet, and their problems, the certain promise that God is holding out his hand to them from the church, "to all who seek him with a sincere heart" (Eucharistic Prayer IV).

Especially is this Easter greeting directed to all my friends who, in different ways, expressed to me their loving welcome of, and adhesion to, the will of the Holy Father when he appointed me to this metropolitan see. It is also directed to those who, with much display of solidarity, shared the grief and the hope that were aroused by the murder of the never-to-be-forgotten Father Rutilio Grande—may he rest in peace—and by other attacks on the freedom of the church.

Toward Thoughtful Dialogue

And now, brothers, sisters, and friends, the greeting and the introduction become an invitation to thoughtful dialogue. I represent a church that wants always to converse with all men and women, so that it may pass on to them the truth and the grace with which God has entrusted it, in order that it may guide the world in conformity to his divine plan. Let us put the theme forward in the language of Easter, so as to retain the style of this letter's title: the church does not live for itself, but in order to bring to the world the truth and the grace of Easter. This is the essence of my letter. Its purpose is simply, in the daylight of this paschal hour, to present—with the sincere offer to enter into dialogue with everyone on—the church's identity and mission in these terms: (1) Easter: the origin and content of the church; (2) the church: sacrament and instrument of Easter; (3) the world: designated recipient of the truth and grace of Easter.

EASTER

What is Easter? What is the paschal mystery? It is simply the event of Christian salvation, through the death and the resurrection of our Lord Jesus Christ.

The Second Vatican Council made the paschal mystery the center of its reflections upon the church and its mission in the world. The council explains:

The wonderful works of God among the people of the Old Testament were but a prelude to the work of Christ the Lord in redeeming mankind and giving perfect glory to God. He achieved his task principally by the paschal mystery of his blessed passion, resurrection from the dead, and glorious ascension, whereby "dying, he destroyed our death and, rising, he restored our life."[1]

The Old Covenant Passover

The event of Christian salvation, then, which we call the paschal mystery, was being prepared for by "the wonders wrought by God among the people of the Old Testament." Hence, in order to understand the meaning and the manner of Christian redemption a little better, it is necessary to go back to the "wonders of the Old Testament." The historical and salvific manner of the redemption is mainly revealed to us in the Book of Exodus: God saves Israel, and thus will it be for every people, each within its own history. It is also revealed to us there what this redemption involves: a ransoming from death by means of the protection afforded by the blood of the lamb, while the avenging angel "passes over," taking only the lives of the firstborn of the Egyptians. It also involves a "passage" from slavery, through the sea and the desert, to a promised land, to freedom and repose.

The redeemed people celebrated that passover every year. But its celebration was more than simply a remembrance of things past. The whole process of redemption was made present in a profound liturgical and sacramental, prophetic and eschatological, sacrificial and communal sense. There were lived out again the "wonders" of the Lord. That is why it was said to those taking part, "On this day . . . you are leaving Egypt." The passover ritual was to be explained: "this is because of what Yahweh did for me when I came out of Egypt" (Exod. 13:4,8). The passover was always something in the here and now. God was the savior of Israel by way of its own history. The wonders were praised, and the sins against the covenant were denounced. The failures and the imperfections in their history did not dishearten them, because the passover was open to the eschatological future. In the strivings of the present there always shone out the hope of a more perfect passover, one beyond history, where there would be the happiness of the perfect paschal feast. The immolation of the lamb conveyed a sacrificial and communitarian meaning, as did the gathering of the family or group, which patriotism later extended to take in the entire national community.

Christ Our Paschal Victim Is Sacrificed

The whole of Israel's paschal mystery comes to its fulfillment in the final passover of Jesus. The preparatory symbol is transformed into the reality of the Christian passover. Upon the structure of that ancient passover Christ himself becomes its wondrous personification by means of his own "passage" from death to resurrection. "Christ our paschal victim is sacrificed" sings the church among the alleluias of the resurrection. The whole of his life and work are marked by that paschal sign: the passover was the hour appointed by the Father for the redemption of the world in Christ, and it was with a keen awareness that Christ approached his own "passover hour." His death upon the cross was the immolation of the true paschal lamb, and in a passover meal Jesus instituted a memorial, a eucharistic representation, which, in the midst of any human situation, will make present the wonder of the redemption.

Who can measure the redemptive power of this passage from death to resurrection? If in his death there were destroyed the empire of sin, of hell, and of death itself, in his resurrection there began now in history the reign of eternal life, holding out to us the opportunity for bold changes in history and in life.[2] In the resurrection God glorifies the Son (Acts 2:22 ff., Rom. 8:11), places the divine seal upon the act of redemption, which began at the incarnation and reached its consummation upon the cross. The resurrection made Jesus "Son of God in all his power" (Rom. 1:4), "Lord and Christ" (Acts 2:36), "leader and Savior" (Acts 5:31), "judge and Lord [of] everyone, alive or dead" (Acts 10:42), "the first to rise from the dead" (Acts 26:23; Rev. 1:5), and "Lord of glory" (1 Cor. 2:8). He is the first to have entered into the new world that is the ransomed universe. He has the power to offer to all who believe in him the gift of the Holy Spirit (Acts 2:38).

For Easter is also the coming of the Holy Spirit, the "power from on high," the spirit of truth and love, the advocate and consoler, the spirit of God through whom men and women can identify with Jesus in his victory over evil and in the renewal of their own lives. The "kingdom of heaven" is not something that comes only after death. That will be its perfect fulfillment. But it has already been inaugurated in history, among men and women, by the Risen One, by his passage from death to resurrection.

In Him Is Our Hope

When I described this moment in the life of our archdiocese as a "paschal hour," I was thinking of the superabundant power of faith, hope, and love that the risen Christ—living and working—has called forth in different sectors of our local church—even in sectors and persons who do not belong to, nor yet share in, our paschal faith. With the feelings of a pastor, I see that the spiritual riches of Easter, that greatest inheritance of the church, abound among us. I see that there is already being achieved among us here what was expressly desired by the bishops at Medellín, when they were speaking to young persons: "That the Church in Latin America should be manifested, in an increasingly clear manner, as truly poor, missionary and paschal, separate from all temporal power and courageously committed to the liberation of each and every man."[3]

THE CHURCH: SACRAMENT OF EASTER

Christ's church has to be an Easter church—that is to say, a church that is born of Easter and exists to be a sign and instrument of Easter in the world.

The Church Born of Easter

In the story of the lance (John 19:35) the fathers of the church found a mystical parallel between the birth of the church from the side of Christ sleeping upon the cross, and the formation of Eve from the side of Adam. There is also a beautiful paschal connection in St. Paul's linking the origin of the church with the sacrifice of Christ: "Christ loved the Church and sacrificed himself for her to make her holy. He made her clean by washing her in water with a form of words, so that when he took her to himself she would be glorious, with no speck or wrinkle or anything like that, but holy and faultless" (Eph. 5:25–27).

Jesus, who brought about our redemption beneath the paschal sign, longed to live on, in a paschal manner, in the life of the church. The church is the body of the risen Christ. Through baptism all those who belong to it live out that paschal tension, that "passage" from death to life, that "crossing over" that never ends and is called "conversion," the continual demand upon us to destroy whatever is sin and to bring into being ever more powerfully all that is life, renewal, holiness, justice. The Holy Spirit began to quicken this life of resurrection in the church from the very day of the resurrection itself when Jesus "breathed" the re-creating Spirit upon the Apostles (John 20:22). With Pentecost—fifty days after Easter—came the fulness of Easter. There then took place the great pouring out of charisms that were to make the church manifest to the world, and publicly to sanction the testimony of the Apostles. God thus forever anoints his church. He does so to identify it with Jesus in order that all the faithful may, in the same Spirit, have access with Jesus, to the Father.[4]

In other words, the Easter Christ continues, lives, in the Easter church. One cannot be part of this church without being faithful to his manner of "passing" from death to life, without a sincere movement of conversion and of fidelity to the Lord.

Sign and Instrument of Easter

"It was from the side of Christ as he slept the sleep of death upon the cross that there came forth the wondrous sacrament of the whole Church,"[5] "the universal sacrament of salvation," as Vatican II most beautifully describes it.[6] The council made the paschal mystery the central focus of its reflections on the church, for the whole purpose of the church's existence is to make obvious and operative, in the midst of humanity, the abundant energy of the death and resurrection of the Lord.

From this there arises the attractive characterization of a church that does not live for itself but so as to serve as Christ's instrument in the redemption of the whole of humanity. It is a great joy to me to emphasize this sense of service in a letter whose purpose is to introduce to you a pastor who wants to live out, and, as closely as possible, to share in, the feelings of the Good

Shepherd who "came not to be served but to serve, and to give his life" (Matt. 20:28).

The church, born at Easter to bring to all the grace of Easter, is described thus in one of the most profound Vatican II syntheses: "Christ, the one Mediator, established and continually sustains here on earth his holy Church, the community of faith, hope, and charity, as an entity with visible delineation, through which he communicates truth and grace to all."[7]

There are here the three elements that make the church to be the "universal sacrament of salvation": as the visible part of the sacrament, the hierarchical community; as the invisible sacramental content, the truth and grace of the Redeemer. To build the church will always mean to build upon these three foundational stones, so beloved of Christ himself: to gather a community in faith and love around the shepherd, and so makes Christ visible; to evangelize that community with Christ's unique truth, and from that community to evangelize the world; and to live out and pass on that Easter grace, which means to liberate oneself from sin, and to become a sharer in the divine sonship that Christ merited through his death and resurrection.

Or, to put it in the terms used by Pope Paul VI in his apostolic exhortation *Evangelii Nuntiandi*:

> Those whose life has been transformed enter a community which is itself a sign of transformation, a sign of newness of life: it is the Church, the visible sacrament of salvation. But entry into the ecclesial community will in its turn be expressed through many other signs which prolong and unfold the sign of the Church. In the dynamism of evangelization, a person who accepts the Church as the Word which saves normally translates it into the following sacramental acts: adherence to the Church, and acceptance of the Sacraments, which manifest and support this adherence through the grace which they confer.[8]

What Fidelity Demands

If the church's preaching is the "truth that saves" (Rom. 1:16), and if the Eucharist and the other sacraments it administers both signify and communicate the power to become children of God, this is because "grace . . . flows from the paschal mystery of the passion, death, and resurrection of Christ."[9]

Its paschal origins require of the church, as a demand of Christ, a careful fidelity to the risen Lord in order that it be true to its identity, and so it is obliged by the requirements of a world in need of salvation not to water down in any way its teaching and its ministry. This obligation arises from its service as sign and instrument of the truth and grace that, through the paschal mystery, redeem the world. The prophetic, priestly, and social functions that the church, in the name of the risen Christ, carries out among men and women ought to be in perfect harmony with the mind of Christ. This is more true today than ever before, when persons expect of the church an answer from the only Redeemer who can save them.

THE WORLD: THE BENEFICIARY OF EASTER

The church does not exist for itself. Its raison d'être is the same as that of Jesus: service to God to save the world. Vatican II said as much when treating of the mission of the church in the modern world:

> The council can provide no more eloquent proof of its solidarity with, as well as its respect and love for the entire human family with which it is bound up, than by engaging with it in conversation about these various problems. The council brings to mankind light kindled from the Gospel, and puts at its disposal those saving resources which the Church itself, under the guidance of the Holy Spirit, receives from its Founder.[10]

And when, in August and September 1968, the bishops of Latin America met together in Medellín under the authority of the pope to determine the form this noble service would take for our continent, they kept well in mind the fact that the Spirit of Easter urges the church to dialogue with, and to serve, our peoples. "We are," they said, "on the threshold of a new epoch in the history of our continent. It appears to be a time full of zeal for full emancipation, of liberation from every form of servitude, of personal maturity, and of collective integration."[11] The church cannot be indifferent, they proclaimed, when faced with "a muted cry [that] pours from the throats of millions of men, asking their pastors for a liberation that reaches them from nowhere else."[12]

A Religious and Human Mission

These legitimate aspirations of our people here and now are directed toward the church in the form of a challenge or, better, an evangelical appeal. That is one side of the coin. The other side is a growing awareness that the church has of its own mission not to shrink from this appeal but to have the wisdom and fortitude to speak the words, and to adopt the attitude, that Christ requires of it in this complicated situation. This is typical of the difficult times in which we live. "It is a time," Cardinal Pironio says, "of the cross and of hope, of possibilities and of risks, of responsibility and of commitment."[13] It is, above all, a time for prayer and contemplation so as to interpret, according to the heart of God, the signs of our times. They will help us to know how to offer the service that we, as church, owe to the just aspirations of our brothers and sisters.

The church cannot be defined simply in political or socio-economic terms. But neither can it be defined from a point of view which would make it indifferent to the temporal problems of the world. As Vatican II puts it: "the mission of the Church will show its religious, and by that very fact, its supremely human character."[14] And this is how Paul VI explains the blending of the church's two aspects, the religious and the human:

> Hence, when preaching liberation and associating herself with those who are working and suffering for it, the Church is certainly not willing to restrict her mission only to the religious field and dissociate herself from man's temporal problems. Nevertheless she reaffirms the primacy of her spiritual vocation and refuses to replace the proclamation of the Kingdom by the proclamation of forms of human liberation; she even states that her contribution to liberation is incomplete if she neglects to proclaim salvation in Jesus Christ.[15]

While taking account of the supremacy of the church's spiritual vocation and the predominant role of salvation in Jesus Christ, Pope Paul defends the linkage of true evangelization and human advancement, both because anthropology, theology, and the gospel demand it, and because to dissociate evangelization from human advancement "would be to forget the lesson which comes to us from the Gospel concerning love of our neighbor who is suffering and in need."[16] I very earnestly recommend that you study the whole of the third chapter of *Evangelii Nuntiandi*. It will help you to have a clearer idea of the liberation that the church promotes.

Service that Demands Conversion

The service offered by an Easter church to the needs of its people ought to begin, as the bishops at Medellín said, "in a spirit of eagerness for conversion and service. We have seen that our most urgent commitment must be to purify ourselves, all of the members and institutions of the Catholic Church, in the spirit of the Gospel."[17]

In a sincere analysis of this confession, Cardinal Pironio thinks along three basic lines:

> We Christians have not thoroughly assimilated ourselves to Jesus Christ (we may have known the gospel superficially, or have studied Christ technically, but we have not fully savored his mystery).
> We divorce faith from life (we content ourselves with preaching the faith or celebrating it liturgically, but we do not put love and justice into practice).
> By the same token, we have lost that Christian sensitivity to the anxieties of others, we no longer know how to brighten their hopes, and we have lost interest in the constructive molding of history.
> An Easter church, a Pentecost church, ought to be a church of conver-

sion, of a fundamental turning back to Christ—whose mirror we should be—and to the radical demands of the Sermon on the Mount.[18]

Sincere Cooperation

From the perspective of our identity as church, we also realize that our service to the people, precisely because it does not as such have a political or a socio-economic character, must seek sincere dialogue and cooperation with whomever holds political and socio-economic responsibility. The church does not do this because it has some technical competence or because it wants temporal privileges, but because the political community and other elements of society need to be reminded that they are at the service of the personal and social vocation of men and women. As Vatican II teaches:

> [The church] is at once a sign and a safeguard of the transcendent character of the human person. . . . [Therefore] it is only right . . . that at all times and in all places, the church should have true freedom to preach the faith, to teach its social doctrine, to exercise its role freely among men, and also to pass moral judgment on those matters which regard public order when the fundamental rights of a person or the salvation of souls require it. In this, it should make use of all the means . . . which accord with the Gospel and which correspond to the general good.[19]

Vatican II, while advocating this sincere cooperation, which in no way compromises the freedom and the autonomy of the church, is ready to renounce any kind of privilege when there is danger of tarnishing the purity of the church's testimony. The church in El Salvador, out of its concern for the welfare of its people, and because of its love for them, is always ready to enter into dialogue with civil authorities and with those Salvadorans who are economically or socially powerful. It has been grateful when it could count upon them, just as it suffers when relationships have deteriorated—to the detriment and confusion of the people—by misunderstandings or a lack of comprehension of its difficult responsibility to defend the rights of God and of humanity. The search for this understanding is one of the church's Easter hopes, the object of its prayers, and one of the aims of its apostolic work, so that it may be able to live out in its fulness the peace that the Risen One came to give us, and for which El Salvador has always dreamed.

CONCLUSION

Beloved brothers, sisters, friends. We have together lived through a Lent that was a way of the cross, and a Good Friday that has come to full flower in this bright and hopeful hour of the Easter of resurrection. Those of us— bishops, priests, religious, and laity—who are aware of what it means to be a church, the depository of all the energies working for the salvation of humanity in Christ, also understand the challenges and the risks of these difficult times. The major challenge arises from the hope placed in the church by the world. Let us be worthy of this hour. Let us know how to give reason for this hope by the witness of unity, of communion, of Christian authenticity, and of apostolic work. While carefully honoring the supremacy of the church's religious mission and of salvation in Jesus Christ, this apostolic work should also take into account the human dimension of the gospel message, and the demands that the religious and eternal spheres make upon history.

Our divine Savior will not cheat us of our hope. Let us appeal to the queen of peace, the heavenly patroness of our people, to intercede with him for us. May the mother of the Risen One defend our church, the sacrament of Easter. Like Mary, may the church live out this happy balance of the Easter of Jesus, which ought to characterize the true salvation of men and women in Christ—namely, to feel oneself already glorified in heaven as the image and first flowering of the future life, and at the same time to be, here on earth, the light for God's pilgrim people "as a sign of sure hope and solace until the day of the Lord come."[20]

I beg my beloved priests, religious, catechists, the Catholic colleges and schools and other agencies of our apostolate to study throughout the whole of Eastertide—that is, until Pentecost—the theme of this pastoral letter: Easter, the church, and the world.

NOTES

1. *Sacrosanctum Concilium*, §5.
2. See *Gaudium et Spes*, §§22, 38.
3. Medellín, "Youth," §15.
4. See *Lumen Gentium*, §4; cf. Eph. 2:18.
5. *Sacrosanctum Concilium*, §5.
6. *Lumen Gentium*, §48.
7. Ibid., §8.
8. *Evangelii Nuntiandi*, §23.
9. *Sacrosanctum Concilium*, §61.
10. *Gaudium et Spes*, §3.
11. Medellín, "Introduction," §4.
12. Medellín, "Poverty," §2.
13. *Escritos pastorales*, p. 206.
14. *Gaudium et Spes*, §11.
15. *Evangelii Nuntiandi*, §34.
16. Ibid., §31.
17. Medellín, "Message to the Peoples of Latin America."
18. *Escritos pastorales*, p. 211.
19. *Gaudium et Spes*, §76.
20. Ibid.

The Church, the Body of Christ in History

Second Pastoral Letter of Archbishop Romero,
Feast of the Transfiguration, August 6, 1977

To my beloved brothers and sisters, the auxiliary bishop, the priests, religious, and laity of the archdiocese of San Salvador; to you and to all Salvadorans of good will: the joy and hope of our divine Savior.

IN THE SPLENDOR OF THE TRANSFIGURATION

I wrote you my first pastoral letter for Easter, on April 10. That was four months ago. It was my "letter of introduction" and my "first greeting." The Lord wished to place my inception as pastor of this beloved archdiocese within the providential context of Lent, Passiontide, and Easter. That context inspired the theme of my first letter, and so I gave it the title "The Easter Church."

Today the world's divine Savior, who is the patron of our local church, illuminates, with the splendor of his transfiguration—as at a Salvadoran Easter—the path through history of our church and our nation. I believe it opportune to write again to you who, together with me, make up this portion of the people of God who "like a stranger in a foreign land, presses forward amid the persecutions of the world and the consolations of God."[1]

Because of what has happened in El Salvador both before and after that memorable Easter, and because of the intense life of the church at the time of those events in our archdiocese, an explanation of my actions is demanded. And no time seems more fitting to give it, none better to compare the road we have marched together as the people of God with the divine plans for our salvation, than now, in this new luminous and liturgical presence of the divine Savior.

Different Reactions

In good conscience, I believed my position to be that of the gospel. It has aroused a variety of reactions. Now it is necessary to give an explanation of

63

the church's stance as a basis for understanding, in the light of our faith, the different reactions aroused.

Some have been delighted. They feel that the church is drawing closer to their problems and anxieties, that it gives them hope, and shares their joys.

Others have been disgusted or saddened. They feel that the church's new attitude makes a clear demand upon them, too, to change and be converted. Conversion is difficult and painful because the changes required are not only in ways of thinking but also in ways of living.

Many Catholics of good will have been disconcerted, even to the point of hesitating to follow the church in the latest steps it has been taking. Instead they have preferred to seek refuge in the security of a tradition that spurns growth.

Others again, inspired more by selfish interests than by the church's purity and fidelity, have, pharisaically, been scandalized. They have even gone so far as to attack it in what is closest and most sensitive to the heart of the church of Christ: they are saying that it has been unfaithful to the gospel.

Thanks be to God, the faithful sons and daughters of the church are beyond number. Priests, religious, and laity, sincerely committed to the demands of the kingdom as proclaimed by Christ, have been bolstered in their faith, hope, and Christian commitment. With the church, they repeat with the apostle, "Let us go too, and die with him" (John 11:16).

A Word of Faith and of Hope

I have therefore come to regard it as a duty of my episcopal office to address myself to all the beloved sons and daughters of the church, as also to all other Christian brothers and sisters, and to all Salvadorans who look and hope for a temperate word that, from the standpoint of the faith and of our Christian hopes, would throw light on what is taking place.

Yes, it is a word of faith. I am not trying to replace the efforts of human reason necessary in the search for real, viable solutions to our grave problems. But with the light of faith I am secure in offering the contribution that is proper to the church, purifying and strengthening the power of reason, so as to free it from impure motives and to guarantee that it will have God's approval.

It is also a word of hope. The word of the church can be nothing else, because it is the word of the good news, of the gospel, of the liberation that Jesus goes on proclaiming to humankind by means of the church. But it is not an ingenuous hope that the church proclaims. It is accompanied by the blood of its priests and *campesinos*: blood and grief that denounce the obstacles and the evil intentions that stand in the way of the fulfillment of that hope. Their blood is also an expression of a readiness for martyrdom. It is therefore the best argument for, and a testimony to, the utterly certain hope that the church offers, as from Christ, to the world.

In the light, then, of our faith and hope in Christ, I am going to dwell on three major themes in this pastoral letter. (1) What are the changes in the present-day mission of the church? (2) These changes come about because the church is the Body of Christ in history, and because the church has to communicate the Lord's message and continue his eternal mission in keeping with the many changes that occur in history. (3) This is the ecclesiology that has come alive in our archdiocese. It comes alive in an archdiocese that, out of fidelity to the gospel, rejects as a calumny the charge that it is subversive, a fomentor of violence and hatred, Marxist, and political. It comes alive in an archdiocese that, out of the persecution it is undergoing, offers itself to God and to the people as a united church, one ready for sincere dialogue and cooperation, a bearer of the message of hope and of love.

THE CHURCH'S MISSION TODAY

What I am going to say here is nothing new. I think, however, that it is opportune to repeat it. It is something that has not been sufficiently assimilated. And there are a great number of Salvadoran speakers and writers who are telling others what the church is, and they are distorting its true nature and mission.

Church and World

Many things in the church have changed in recent years. One might instance changes in the liturgy, in the role of the laity, in religious life, in the training given in seminaries, and so on. But the fundamental change, the change that explains all the others, is the new relationship between the church and the world. The church looks upon the world with new eyes. It will raise questions about what is sinful in the world, and it will also allow itself to be questioned by the world as to what is sinful in the church.

This change is of the gospel, because it has helped the church recover its deepest Christian essence, rooted as it is in the New Testament.

This new relationship with the world has deepened the church's understanding in two directions: in the meaning of its presence in the world, and in the meaning of its service to the world.

In the World

Down the centuries the church has not always given full importance to what was really going on in the world. It is different now. From his first encyclical, *Ecclesiam Suam*, the present pope, Paul VI, asserted that "we ought not disregard the situation in which humanity finds itself today, in the midst of which we have to develop our mission."[2] The Second Vatican Council felt a profound sympathy for the problems of the modern world: "Today, the human race is involved in a new stage of history. Profound and rapid changes are spreading by degrees around the whole world."[3] And for our continent more particularly, the bishops of Latin America affirmed at Medellín that the peoples of these countries are "living a decisive moment of [their] historical process,"[4] and that there is in them an aspiration toward integral liberation that can be expressed in biblical language as "a foreshadowing of the new age."[5]

The changes taking place in the world are, for the church, a sign of the times that will help it to come to know itself better. It believes that, through these changes, God himself is speaking to it. It has to be aware of changes so as to respond to the word of God, and be able to gauge its actions in and for the world.

The modern church is conscious of being the "people of God in the world," or rather, of being a body of men and women who belong to God, but who live in the world. That is why Vatican II described the church as "the new Israel which while living in this present age goes in search of a future and abiding city.[6]

What is being asserted here is of capital importance. The element of transcendence that ought to raise the church toward God can be realized and lived out only if it is in the world of men and women, if it is on pilgrimage through the history of humankind. Therefore the council, as it opened its Pastoral Constitution on the Church in the Modern World, solemnly proclaimed:

> The joys and the hopes, the griefs and the anxieties of the men of this age, especially those who are poor or in any way afflicted, these are the joys and hopes, the griefs and anxieties of the followers of Christ. Indeed, nothing genuinely human fails to raise an echo in their hearts. For theirs is a community composed of men. United in Christ, they are led by the Holy Spirit in their journey to the Kingdom of their Father and they have welcomed the news of salvation which is meant for every man. That is why this community realizes that it is truly linked with mankind and its history by the deepest of bonds.[7]

At the Service of the World

The church is in the world for the benefit of humankind. This is the meaning of service. The council puts it in theological terms: the church is a "sign," a "sacrament." As sacrament and sign the church signifies and achieves something for human beings: it signifies and brings about "a very closely knit union with God and . . . the unity of the whole human race."[8]

The church is in the world so as to signify and bring into being the liberating love of God, manifested in Christ. It therefore understands Christ's preference for the poor, because the poor are, as Medellín explains, those who "place before the Latin American Church a challenge and a mission that it cannot sidestep and to which it must respond with a speed and boldness adequate to the urgency of the times."[9]

The Unity of History

So as better to grasp its relationship with the world, the church has also deepened its understanding of another concept: the relationship between the history of humankind and the history of salvation. For a very long time we were accustomed to think that human history, with all its joys and sorrows, achievements and failures, was something provisional, something ephemeral, something that, in comparison with the ultimate fulness that awaits Christians, was of little consequence. It seemed that the history of humankind and the history of salvation ran along parallel lines. The lines met only in eternity. In short it appeared that secular history was nothing more than a period of trial, leading to final salvation or condemnation.

The church has a different view of human history nowadays. It is not mere opportunism or a desire to adapt itself to the world that brings it to think differently. It is because it has genuinely recovered the insight, which runs throughout the pages of the Bible, into what God is doing in human history. This is why it has to take that history very seriously. Vatican II certainly recalled the traditional understanding of the church as being on pilgrimage toward that "future and abiding city,"[10] but added that the church at the same time reveals "in the world faithfully though darkly, the mystery of its Lord until, in the end, it will be manifested in full light."[11]

Medellín asserts the unity of history more clearly still:

Catechetical teaching must manifest the unity of God's plan. While avoiding confusion or simplistic identifications, it must always make clear the profound unity that exists between God's plan of salvation realized in Christ, and the aspirations of man; between the history of salvation and human history.[12]

Our continent's longing for liberation, even the partial achievement of that full liberation of body and soul, is a clear sign of the presence of God in history.[13]

With these affirmations Medellín put an end to the secular dualism we had subscribed to, the dichotomy between the temporal and the eternal, between the secular and the religious, between the world and God, between history and the church. "In the search for salvation we must avoid the dualism which separates temporal tasks from the work of sanctification."[14]

The Sin of the World

The relationship between the church, as the universal sacrament of salvation, and the world defines the church's firm attitude against the world's sin and lends strength to its urgent call to conversion. By the very fact that it is in the world and for the world, by the fact that it is in solidarity with the history of the world, the church encounters the world's dark side, the depths of its iniquity. It encounters that which brings about the moral downfall of human beings, that which degrades and dehumanizes them. The church takes very seriously the shadowy reality that surrounds us on all sides. It is sin that prevents the history of the world from being the history of salvation. It is sin that dissolves the profound unity between the two halves of history. Sin is slavery to the world. "Their senseless minds were darkened and they served the creature rather than the Creator."[15] That is what brings about the internal sundering of human history: the whole of human life, "whether individual or collective," is tragically affected by sin.[16]

The church's present thinking is as strict as ever with regard to the seriousness of individual sin. Sin is, above all, the act of one who, in the depths of his or her will, denies and offends God. But the church today, more than before, stresses the seriousness of sin in its social consequences. The evil of interior sin crystalizes in the evil of exterior, historical situations.

Medellín has underlined this tragic reality of sin, linking together its two dimensions: "the lack of solidarity which, on the individual and social levels, leads to the committing of serious sins, [is] evident in the unjust structures which characterize the Latin American situation."[17] And when Medellín attempts to sum up, in one phrase, what for our continent is the fundamental sin of the age, it has no hesitation in asserting that it is "that misery, [which] as a collective fact, expresses itself as injustice which cries to the heavens."[18]

It is, perhaps, in this understanding of sin that one finds one of the greatest changes, and the source of the greatest conflict, in the relationship between church and world. Down the centuries the church has, quite rightly, denounced sin. Certainly it has denounced personal sins, and it has also denounced the sin that perverts relationships between persons, especially at the family level. But it has begun to recall now something that, at the church's beginning, was fundamental: social sin—the crystalization, in other words, of individuals' sins into permanent structures that keep sin in being, and make its force to be felt by the majority of the people.

The Need for Conversion

In this new epoch of the church's history, what has always been true has become still more evident: there is need for conversion. As Medellín puts it, "for our authentic liberation, all of us need a profound conversion."[19] What it is important to stress, however, is that this sense of the need for conversion has been reinforced as the church looks upon the world. As all of us bishops of El Salavdor said in our Message from the Episcopal Conference on March 5, Christians "are aware of the radical *no* that God pronounces over our sins of omission."

The church is here speaking not only of the conversion that others ought to bring about in their lives, but is speaking in the first instance of its own conversion. This awareness of its own need for conversion is, historically, something very new, though it was said of the church in the past that it always had to be reformed (*semper reformanda*). The pressure for this conversion came not only when the church looked inward, at itself, with its defects and its sins, but also when it looked outward, at the sins of the world. The church has regained the basic attitude for conversion, which is to turn toward "those who are especially lowly, poor, and weak. Like Christ, we should have pity on the multitudes weighed down with hunger, misery, and ignorance. We want to fix a steady gaze on those who still lack the help they need to achieve a way of life worthy of human beings."[20]

It is in this encounter with the world of the poor that one finds the most pressing need for conversion. It is the love of Christ that urges us on (2 Cor. 5:14), that makes a clear demand upon us when we are faced with a brother or sister in need (1 John 3:17).

THE CHURCH, THE BODY OF CHRIST IN HISTORY

Why Are There Changes in the Church?

Clearly, then, the church has changed. It is obvious that the church, in recent years, has a new vision of the world and its relationship to it. Anyone who fails to understand, or to accept, this new perspective is incapable of understanding the church. To remain anchored in a nonevolving traditionalism, whether out of ignorance or selfishness, is to close one's eyes to what is meant by authentic Christian tradition. For the tradition that Christ entrusted to his church is not a museum of souvenirs to be protected. It is true that tradition comes out of the past, and that it ought to be loved and faithfully preserved. But it has always a view to the future. It is a tradition that makes the church new, up to date, effective in every historical epoch. It is a tradition that nourishes the church's hope and faith so that it may go on preaching, so that it may invite all men and women to the "new heaven and new earth" that God has promised (Rev. 21:1; Isa. 65:17).

What is it that bestows this energy, this perennial modernity, on the eternal tradition of the church? What is the reason for the current changes in the church as it confronts the world and the history of humankind? It is not opportunism, nor is it disloyalty to the gospel—two charges that have often been leveled at it in the recent past. The answer has to be sought in the very depths of our faith. Seen in the light of faith in the mystery of the church, the changes taking place are far from ruining it, or making it unfaithful to tradition. On the contrary, they make the church even more faithful and better identify it with Jesus Christ.

This is the theme of my letter: the church is the Body of Christ in history. By this expression we understand that Christ has wished to be himself the life of the church through the ages. The church's foundation is not to be thought of in a legal or juridical sense, as if Christ gathered some persons together, entrusted them with a teaching, gave them a kind of constitution, but then himself remained apart from them. It is not like that. The church's origin is something much more profound. Christ founded the church so that he himself could go on being present in the history of humanity precisely through the group of Christians who make up his church. The church is the flesh in which Christ makes present down the ages his own life and his personal mission.

That is how changes in the church are to be understood. They are needed if the church is to be faithful to its divine mission of being the Body of Christ in history. The church can be church only so long as it goes on being the Body of Christ. Its mission will be authentic only so long as it is the mission of Jesus in the new situations, the new circumstances, of history. The criterion that will guide the church will be neither the approval of, nor the fear of, men and women, no matter how powerful or threatening they may be. It is the church's duty in history to lend its voice to Christ so that he may speak, its feet so that he may walk today's world, its hands to build the kingdom, and to offer all its members "to make up all that has still to be undergone by Christ" (Col. 1:24).

Should the church forget this identification with Christ, Christ would himself demand it of the church, no matter how uncomfortable that might be, or how much loss of face it might entail.

Vatican II and Medellín represent for us Christians today the humble, honest attitude of the church in its concern to be the Body of Christ in this fascinating period of history.

The Person, the Teaching, and the Activity of Christ

To think of ourselves as the body of the world's divine Savior, in history, here in El Salvador, ought to be for our church, I believe, the principal message of this August feast day. For in the mystery of the transfiguration, our titular festival, the church contemplates, and year by year listens to, the message, the activity, and the person it has to embody on behalf of all Salvadorans of every generation.

The Person of Christ

It is the mysterious voice of the Father from out of the "bright cloud" that, on the "high mountain," presents Jesus to us as "my Son, the Beloved; he enjoys my favor. Listen to him" (Matt. 17:1–9). True God and true man. He is, as eternal Son, a mystery inaccessible to human reason. He can be accepted only in faith by believers. In saying that he is true God, faith asserts that in him is the ultimate truth, the ultimate answer to the mystery of the existence and of the history of humankind. Faith also asserts that this Christ, in his humanity, was brought back to life by the Father, and that he is now seated at the Father's right hand as the only Lord of the living and the dead. But the Christian faith makes another fundamental assertion as well, one that is still, as it has ever been, "to the Jews an obstacle that they cannot get over, to the pagans madness" (1 Cor. 1:23): the Father's eternal Son became man, became our brother, became like us in all things except sin (Heb. 4:15).

Only in the light of that Christ, of his actions and his teachings, can the church find the meaning of, and guidance for, its service in the world. The study and contemplation of Christ, therefore, should constitute the chief preoccupation of those of us who make up his church. I am now going to put before you a brief summary of Jesus' message. By comparing it with our church's stance we can see if, here and now, we are still the authentic Body of Christ in history.

Jesus Proclaims the Kingdom of God Especially to the Poor

"The time has come and the kingdom of God is close at hand. Repent, and believe the Good News" (Mark 1:15). This is the way Christ begins, and the way he sums up, his gospel message. His hearers understood what was meant: that they should live together in such a way that they feel themselves to be brothers and sisters, and hence also children of God. In the words of Jesus there were echoes of the ancient prophecies that proclaimed God's plan for the salvation of humankind. But in Jesus they come together to make a final impact: here and now upon this earth the kingdom of God has the mission of turning all men and women into children of the Father of Jesus Christ, whereby they become brothers and sisters. Or, to put it another way, in the effort to become brothers and sisters they also become children of God. Faith in God requires a certain moral conduct in this world, and in fulfilling this ethical requirement one is also building up faith in God.

In Jesus' proclamation of the kingdom, his preference for the poor is also evident. In his programatic discourse, he reads the prophecy of Isaiah that he himself fulfills: "The spirit of the Lord has been given to me, for he has anointed me. He has sent me to bring the good news to the poor, to proclaim liberty to captives and to the blind new sight, to set the downtrodden free, to proclaim the Lord's year of favor" (Luke 4:18-19). This preference of Jesus for the poor stands out throughout the gospel. It was for them that he worked his cures and exorcisms; he lived and ate with them; he united himself with, defended, and encouraged all those who, in his day, were on the margin of society, whether for social or for religious reasons: sinners, publicans, prostitutes, Samaritans, lepers. This closeness of Jesus to those who were marginalized is the sign that he gives to confirm the content of what he preaches: that the kingdom of God is at hand.

Jesus Calls to Conversion

That message of hope is, in Jesus, linked to a call to conversion. Jesus does not want to exclude anyone from God's kingdom; he calls everyone to a sincere conversion of heart, a conversion that manifests itself in objective deeds. Without that conversion there is no chance of entering the kingdom, for the entrance gate is narrow (Matt. 7:13) and the road difficult. One has to be ready to leave everything, even home and family. One has to be ready to lose an eye, an arm, or even life itself in order to enter the kingdom. In the gospels there are many examples of conversion, of every sort of person: the rich Zacchaeus, Nicodemus the lawyer, the Roman centurion, the woman who was a sinner, Levi the collector of taxes—sinners who became his faithful followers.

Jesus excluded no one, either from his message or from the invitation to enter the kingdom. He loved all his contemporaries. And because he loved them he sought their conversion, the change of heart that makes a person more human, and that is overshadowed by, or submerged under, riches, power, pride, security in the traditions of the law. What Jesus sought was that everyone should become a "new person," a member of the kingdom.

Jesus Denounces Sin

Jesus carried out his mission, his preaching, his service to men and women, in a particular world, a particular society. That is the profound meaning of what we Christians affirm when we speak of the incarnation of the Son of God: that he took flesh in the real history of his age. Like so many other eras of human history, that era was dominated by sin. To the positive proclamation of the kingdom of God, therefore, Jesus added the denunciation of the sin of his age. The kingdom of God is what Jesus proclaims; for him, then, sin is everything that gets in the way of the coming of the kingdom, makes it impossible or even destroys it. With the courage of a free man, therefore, he denounced the distorted image of God created by the manipulation of human traditions that destroy the authentic will of God (Mark 7:8-13). He denounced the distortion of the temple: from being a house of God, it had been turned into a den of thieves (Mark 11:15-17). He denounced a religion that was devoid of works of justice—as in the well-known parable of the Good Samaritan (Luke 10:29-37). He also denounced all those who made of their power a means to keep the weak and powerless in a state of oppression, rather than using it to serve them. He accused the wealthy of not sharing their wealth, the priests of imposing intolerable burdens (Luke 11:46), the wise of carrying off the key of knowledge and leaving the others without learning, the rulers of looking only to their own advantage and not to the service of their people (Matt. 20:25 ff.).

From the beginning of Jesus' public life, these denunciations brought in their train frequent attacks upon him (Matt. 2:1-2). They brought personal risk and even persecution. The persecution was to go on through the whole of his life until, at the end, he was accused of blasphemy (Mark 14:64) and of being an agitator among the masses. For these reasons he was condemned and executed.

The Church Continues the Work of Jesus

This is the message and the mission of Jesus that he, after he had risen, intended to go on preaching and living in the history of the world by means of his church. The church is the community of those who profess faith in Jesus Christ as the only Lord of history. It is a community of faith whose primary obligation, whose raison d'être, is to continue the life and work of Jesus. To be church is to preserve in history, in and through the lives of men and women, the image of its Founder. The church principally exists for the evangelization of the human race. Yes, it is an institution; it is made up of persons, and it has forms and structures. But all that is for a much more basic reality: the exercise of its task of evangelization.

The church has always borne it in mind that in this task it has to go on proclaiming its faith in Jesus Christ, and that it has to continue, in the course of history, the work that Jesus carried out. When doing this it is the Body of Christ in history.

The Sphere of Its Rights and Duties

This well-defined purpose of the church also defines its duties and its rights—above all, the right and duty of following and loving in freedom its only Lord, Jesus Christ, known in faith. Then comes the right and duty of proclaiming the gospel without hindrance and of cooperating, in accord with its proper autonomy, in building up the kingdom of God among men and women in the way Christ wants it to be done today. For that purpose it will use the means with which Christ himself has endowed it: preaching the word, administering the sacraments, above all celebrating the Eucharist—which will remind it, in an active, vital way, that it continues to be the Body of Christ. And it will also use those particular means that throw light on the question of what path is to be followed if the kingdom of God is to be realized. In other words: the church has to clarify faith in Jesus Christ and procedures for building up the kingdom of God in this world.

This is what the first Christians understood and lived out, those who "remained faithful to the teaching of the apostles, to the brotherhood, to the breaking of bread and to the prayers. . . . The faithful all lived together and owned everything in common; they sold their goods and possessions and shared out the proceeds among themselves according to what each one needed" (Acts 2:42, 44).

Down through its history the church has carried out, with greater or lesser fidelity, that ideal of those first Christians in its following of Jesus. There have been times when the Church has more clearly been the Body of Christ. There have been times when it was not so clear—indeed, when it has been disfigured because it has accommodated itself to the world, seeking rather to be served by the world than itself to serve the world. But at other times its sincere wish has been to serve the world. On those occasions it has experienced rejection by the sinful world, just as its Founder did, even to the extent of persecution. That was the fate of the first Christians, of Peter and John before the courts, of Stephen the deacon, of Paul.

Like Jesus, the Church Proclaims the Kingdom of God

In Latin America, in El Salvador, the church, like Jesus, has to go on proclaiming the good news that the kingdom of God is at hand, especially for the great majority who, in worldly terms, have been estranged from it—the poor, the low-income classes, the marginalized. This does not mean that the church should neglect the other classes in society. It wants to serve them also, to enlighten them. It also needs their help in building up the kingdom. But the church should share Jesus' preference for those who have been used for others' interests and have not been in control of their own destinies.

The Church Denounces Sin and Calls to Conversion

The church, like Jesus, has to go on denouncing sin in our own day. It has to denounce the selfishness that is hidden in everyone's heart, the sin that dehumanizes persons, destroys families, and turns money, possessions, profit, and power into the ultimate ends for which persons strive. And, like anyone who has the smallest degree of foresight, the slightest capacity for analysis, the church has also to denounce what has rightly been called "structural sin": those social, economic, cultural, and political structures that effectively drive the majority of our people onto the margins of society. When the church hears the cry of the oppressed it cannot but denounce the social structures that give rise to and perpetuate the misery from which the cry arises.

But also like Christ, this denunciation by the church is not inspired by hatred or resentment. It looks to the conversion of heart of all men and women and to their salvation.

The Church Throws Light on the Kingdom of God

Jesus fulfilled his mission in a particular kind of world, in a particular sort of society. Like him, the church does not simply proclaim the kingdom of God in the abstract. It also has to promote the solutions that seem most likely to bring the kingdom into being, those that are most just. The church is well aware that to solve today's problems is a supremely difficult and complex task. It knows, furthermore, that in the last analysis it is not for it to put forward concrete solutions. And it knows that, in this world, it will never be possible fully to achieve the kingdom of God. But none of that exempts it from the pressing duty of publicizing and promoting the means that seem best able to help toward the partial realization of the kingdom.

In recent years everyone has come to know that the church has an interest in speaking out on matters concerning the ordered, rational, living together of human beings. A great number of documents have been issued by the church, from Leo XIII's encyclical *Rerum Novarum* (1891) to the recent exhortation *Evangelii Nuntiandi* by Paul VI (1976), which attempt to give guidance on what, at particular moments, have been the crucial problems facing society. The church has done so in order that, in denouncing sin and drawing attention to the paths to solutions, it may bring to the world the kingdom of God.

On March 5 of this year we Salvadoran bishops wrote, in fulfillment of this duty incumbent on the church, "Just as injustice takes concrete forms, so the promotion of justice must take concrete forms. It should come as a surprise to no one that the church encourages particular methods of achieving justice. Among those particular methods there will be some that are matters of opinion, and the church, too, will have to continue to learn which methods best bring about the ideal of the kingdom of God." And we added in our collective message of May 17, "The church believes that the world is called to be subject to Jesus Christ by way of a slow but sure establishment of the kingdom of God. . . . It believes in the kingdom of God as a progressive change from the world of sin to a world of love and justice, one that begins in this world but has its fulfillment in eternity."

Duty Arises from Loyalty to Christ

Only by fulfilling its mission in this way can the church be faithful to its own mystery, which is to be the Body of Christ in history. Only by living out its mission in this way, with the same spirit in which Jesus would have lived it out at this time and place, can it preserve its faith and give transcendent meaning to its message so that that message not be reduced to mere ideology or be manipulated by human selfishness or false traditionalism. It will move toward that final perfection of the kingdom of God in the world to come only if it strives to achieve, in the history of human society here on earth, the kingdom of truth and peace, of justice and love.

THE ARCHDIOCESE OF THE DIVINE SAVIOR

On its titular feast this year, the archdiocese presents to its divine patron, as its most precious offering, itself—marked with the sad yet glorious signs of martyrdom and persecution. The marks are there precisely because it is being faithful to its vocation to be the Body of Christ in our history.

In effect, the whole of the ecclesiology sketched in the doctrinal part of this letter has been lived out by our archdiocese in the intensive work for the social apostolate carried on by my venerable predecessors, especially by Archbishop Luis Chávez y González. Our church's actions are not the result of some sudden or imprudent change. They follow the well thought out approach urged on the whole church by Vatican II, and on our own continent by the Second Latin American Episcopal Conference at Medellín. It was this that Archbishop Chávez y González tried to implement in our archdiocese.

There is need for a calm reflection on our archdiocese and upon its stance, both in order to strengthen sincere Christians in their faith and to clear up the confusion that the media have recently created in public opinion. The media have been vehicles of calumny against the church, and of attacks on its nature and its mission. Would that such reflection might also bring about a conversion deep in the hearts of those who, because of their own particular interests, go on attacking the church, or have doubts about it. Here, then, I shall try to show that the archdiocese has been faithful to the gospel, and for that very reason it has been persecuted. Yet out of this persecution arises a stronger unity that helps it to offer the people more effectively its message of hope and love.

Faithful to the Gospel

Precisely when the archdiocese is making a great effort to be faithful to the gospel one hears voices raised with the accusation that causes it the greatest distress: the charge of having betrayed the gospel. They are many and varied, these accusations, but they can be reduced to three headings: (1) the church preaches hatred and subversion; (2) the church has become Marxist; (3) the church has overstepped the limits of its mission and is meddling in politics.

These are serious accusations. They deserve serious treatment. But the following brief reply should be enough to convince those of sincere heart.

Neither Hatred nor Subversion

The church has never incited to hatred or revenge, not even at those saddest of moments when priests have been murdered and faithful Christians have been killed or have disappeared. The church has continued to preach Jesus' command "love one another" (John 15:12). This is a command that the church cannot renounce, nor has it renounced it, not even in recent months. On the contrary, it has recalled that other command, "pray for those who persecute you" (Matt. 5:44).

The church has also recalled that the love that it preaches has Jesus' love for its model, "love others . . . as I have loved you." There is no reducing this to a sentimental, or to an abstract, sort of love. It was a love freely given and it was an effective love, for he came to bring life even to his enemies. He sought their conversion so that he might free them from sin and bring them out of darkness. That is why the church, like Jesus, has no alternative but to extend its love to the rich and to the poor. It ought to sit down at table with all—but in the spirit of Jesus. Jesus entered the house of the rich man Zacchaeus in search of the conversion of that household (Luke 19:9). Zacchaeus repaid fourfold the goods he had defrauded others of, and he gave away half of his possessions to the poor. Jesus sat down at the table of the poor and of sinners to defend their rights, calling them, too, to conversion. Jesus' love was directed toward all men and women, but in different ways. To those who had become dehumanized because of their desire for profits, he clearly demonstrated, through his love, how to recover their lost human dignity; with the poor, dehumanized because pushed to the margins of society, he sat at table, also out of love, to bring hope back to them.

In what the church has done, there has never been any sign of hatred or revenge, only a remembrance of that great truth of Jesus: that love wants to make all men and women truly human. For that purpose it has to seek out the best way to restore human integrity to those who have lost it.

If one understands the words of love that the church preaches in this way, one can also understand what is meant by accusations of "sermons of subversion" or "violence." The church has not called upon the people to rise up against their brothers and sisters. But it has recalled two fundamental things. The first is what Medellín has to say about "institutionalized violence."[21] When there really is present a situation of permanent, structured injustice, then the situation itself is violent. Secondly, the church is aware that anything said in that situation, even something undoubtedly prompted by love, will sound violent. But the church cannot refrain from speaking out. It can in no way reject what Jesus said: "The kingdom of heaven has been subjected to violence and the violent are taking it by storm" (Matt. 11:12). For there is the violence of the struggle against one's own selfishness, against the inertia of one's own existence—more inclined, as it is, to dominate than to serve. And there is the violence with which one denounces what is wrong in a violent situation.

Nor Marxism

Another way of accusing the church of infidelity is to call it Marxist. Marxism is a complex phenomenon. It has to be studied from various points of view: economic, scientific, political, philosophical, and religious. One has, moreover, to study Marxism in terms of its own history. What the church asserts, and what, in its joint message of May 1, the episcopal conference has recalled, is that insofar as Marxism is an atheistic ideology it is incompatible with the Christian faith. That conviction has never changed in the church's history. In that sense, the church cannot be Marxist.

The real problem, however, arises from the fact that alongside the traditional condemnation of Marxism the church now lays down a condemnation of the capitalist system as well. It is denounced as one version of practical materialism.[22]

The church is very well aware that it coexists with a variety of ideologies and social practices. It has analyzed and reflected upon what there is for good or ill, what there is of attraction or temptation, in socialist thought and liberal ideology.[23] When listening to, and rendering its judgment upon, the various ideologies it is influenced in the first place by the moral concerns proper to the faith. It is not so much moved to give technical judgments about the concrete proposals that spring from different ideologies. With regard to this moral concern, the church's attitude has been constant from Leo XIII to Paul VI. Although there have been different ways of stating the church's concern, it has always been to defend the rights of the individual in the use of material goods so that human beings may live with dignity. When Pius XII, for example, spoke about private property he pointed very clearly to moral problems: "We wish to refrain from approving the conduct of some of the advocates of the right to private property, because, in their way of interpreting the use of, and respect for this right, they manage only, even more successfully than their opponents, to put it in danger."[24]

The church is not dedicated to any particular ideology as such. It must be prepared to speak out against turning any ideology into an absolute. As several of the Latin American hierarchies have said time and again in recent years, worldly interests try to make the church's position seem Marxist when it is in fact insisting on fundamental human rights and when it is placing the whole weight of its institutional and prophetic authority at the service of the dispossessed and weak. As the Episcopal Conference of Chile has said, and as our own has repeated, "it is also a help to Marxism—though indeed without wishing it—to regard as Marxist or to suspect of Marxism every effort for human dignity, for justice, and for equality, everything that seeks participation and opposes domination."[25]

Nor Meddling in Politics

Lastly, the correct relationship between the church and politics has to be recalled. It is understandable that the church's message and its activity, because it is Christ's message and activity, should have very lively repercussions, including repercussions on matters that may be called political, in the society within which it is active. But the church's activity does not take in— as an appropriate method of pursuing its goals—political parties or equivalent groups. It has to be repeated emphatically: the church does not engage in party politics.

The correct relationship between the church and the political community was defined by Vatican II. In the first place, both groups work for the same constituency: "both, under different titles, are devoted to the personal and social vocation of the same human beings."[26] Therefore the church holds out as the ideal that there should be a sincere cooperation between itself and the political community so that the people may be served more effectively— both parties, however, safeguarding their own autonomy. But in addition to such desirable collaboration the church has a right and an obligation to speak about the political sphere:

> It is only right . . . that at all times and in all places, the Church should have true freedom to preach the faith, to teach its social doctrine, to exercise its role freely among men, and also to pass moral judgment on those matters which regard public order when the fundamental rights of a person or the salvation of souls require it. In this, it should make use of

all the means—but only those—which accord with the Gospel and which correspond to the general good according to the diversity of times and circumstances.[27]

It is for those reasons that, over recent months and years, the Salvadoran church has been speaking out. Far from betraying the gospel, it has done no more than fulfill its mission. It has spoken out about events in this country precisely because it is interested in the good of each and every individual. This has been required of it for the defense of human rights and for the salvation of souls.

The Testimony of a Persecuted Church

To the calumnious accusations that the church has been adulterating the Christian message has been added a series of events that amount to persecution of the church. An archdiocesan communiqué dated July 11 sums up the principal abuses to which the church has been subjected: priests expelled from, or prevented from entering, the country; calumnies; threats and assassinations; entire parishes deprived of their clergy; lay ministers of the word and catechists prevented from carrying out their duties; the Blessed Sacrament profaned in Aguilares. And all are aware of the lengthy, anonymous, and calumnious campaign being waged in the press against church-related persons and even against the church itself and its mission, as the church and its mission have been understood ever since Medellín.

But rather than simply detail such sad memories again, it seems to me more important to engage in a Christian reflection upon all these abuses now that some persons have been denying—despite all these outrages—that there is any persecution. They are saying that what has happened is in fact the church's fault, and blame it for the violent situation that exists in our country.

In the first place, no one should be surprised that the church is being persecuted precisely when it is being faithful to its mission. The Lord foretold it: "A servant is not greater than his master. If they persecuted me, they will persecute you too" (John 15:20). Christians have been subjected to persecution from the very beginning.

Why is the church persecuted? As I said earlier, the church is not an end in itself; it has a mission to pursue. Persecuting the church, therefore, does not consist only in attacking it directly, depriving it of privileges, or ignoring it juridically. The most serious persecution of the church is that which makes it impossible for it to carry out its mission, and which attacks those to whom its word of salvation is directed.

Even though the church is juridically recognized in our country, in recent months its mission has been attacked, and so have its priests and catechists who were trying to proclaim, and helping to bring into being, the kingdom of God. The Salvadoran people has been subjected to attack. Its human rights have been trodden underfoot—and protection of these rights falls under the church's responsibility. It is the church's belief that this persecution affects Christ himself: what touches any Christian touches Christ, because he is in personal union with all Christians—especially in anything that involves the poorest of society. "Saul, Saul, why are you persecuting me?" asks Christ of everyone who is persecuting his members. And at the last judgment Christ will reveal that "in so far as you did this to one of the least of these brothers of mine, you did it to me" (Matt. 25:40).

It is in this profound sense that the church can speak of persecution and can plead that this persecution cease. The church is persecuted when it is not allowed to proclaim the kingdom of God and all it entails in terms of justice, peace, love, and truth; when it is not allowed to denounce the sin of our land that engulfs people in wretchedness; when the rights of the people of El Salvador are not respected; when the number mounts steadily of those who have disappeared, been killed, or been calumniated.

It is also important to keep in mind that the church is persecuted because it wills to be in truth the church of Christ. The church is respected, praised, even granted privileges, so long as it preaches eternal salvation and does not involve itself in the real problems of our world. But if the church is faithful to its mission of denouncing the sin that brings misery to many, and if it proclaims its hope for a more just, humane world, then it is persecuted and calumniated, it is branded as subversive and communist.

During this time of persecution the church of the archdiocese has never returned evil for evil, it has never called for revenge or hatred. On the contrary, it has called for the conversion of those who persecute it, and, in our country's difficult problems, it has tried always to promote justice and avert worse evils.

The church hopes, with the help of God, to continue to witness with Christian courage in the midst of all difficulties. It knows that only by so doing will it win credibility for what it is proclaiming: that it is a church that has taken its place alongside those who suffer. It will not be frightened by the persecution that it undergoes, because persecution is a reaction to the church's fidelity to its divine Founder and to its solidarity with those most in need.

The Unity of the Church

Service of the gospel and the persecution of the church have brought forth, as a precious fruit, a unity in the archdiocese to a degree hitherto unknown. It is a great joy for me to be able to say that so many barriers have been removed. Never has there been such a degree of unity among clergy, religious, and laity. Letters of solidarity and of encouragement to go on living out this testimony have been innumerable. They have come from cardinals, bishops, episcopal conferences, from clerical, religious, and lay societies. Support has also come from many of our separated brothers and sisters, both inside and outside the country. I wish publicly to thank them for their fraternal, Christian solidarity. I also remember—and with great happiness, because they have been expressions of unity—the many and various liturgical gatherings, the processions, the countless meetings and private contacts with communities, and with all kinds of persons. This unity, this solidarity, are to me a clear sign that we have chosen the right course.

But, yet again, the events of recent months remind us that Christian unity comes not only from a verbal confession of the same faith, but also from putting that faith into practice. It arises out of a common effort, a shared mission. It comes from fidelity to the word and to the demands of Jesus Christ, and it is cemented in common suffering. Unity in the church is not achieved by ignoring the reality of the world in which we live. So, even though the demonstrations of unity have been impressive, they have not been complete. Some among those who are called Christians have not contributed to the unity of the archdiocese, either out of ignorance, or in order to defend their own interests. Anchored in a false traditionalism, they have misunderstood the actions and the teachings of the contemporary church. They have pretended not to hear the voice of Vatican II and of Medellín. They have been scandalized at the church's new face.

Therefore I once again appeal for the unity of all Catholics. It is something for which I have a keen desire. But we cannot, as the price of this unity, abandon our mission. Let us remember that what divides us is not the church's actions but the world's sin—and the sin of our society. What has happened in our archdiocese is what always happens in the church when it is faithful to its mission. When the church enters into the world of sin to liberate and save it, the sin of the world enters into the church and divides it: it separates those who are authentically Christian and persons of good will from those who are Christian only in name and appearance.

The archdiocese needs unity now more than ever before, to make it credible and to make it more effective. The church becomes credible when it unifies all its efforts not for its own benefit but in the service of the gospel of Christ. And the church needs unity to be effective. The church has lost many priests and catechists in recent months. On the other hand, happily, its pastoral work is increasing through the increasing awareness of many Catholics. The church sees that it must take on new tasks in social communication, such as by our weekly publication *Orientación* and our radio station YSAX, new tasks in the Catholic schools, to move forward in an authentically Christian and social apostolate, new tasks in the parishes where the laity really want to put their voice and their effort to the service of the church's mission of evangelization.

In our particular circumstances, and at this especially privileged time for our archdiocese, unity ought to be brought about around the gospel, through the authoritative word of the divine Pastor. I earnestly want all priests, diocesan and religious, and all other members of religious orders, to unite their efforts around the directives that come from the archdiocese, even if that means giving up long-established points of view and perspectives. I above all want the laity also to be effective collaborators with the bishop, especially so today when the number of clergy has noticeably declined.

There is no doubt that courses of action taken by the archdiocese in recent months have borne fruit in the interest shown by many young persons for the priestly and the religious life. But there is also no doubt that through the persecution of the clergy the Lord is clearly calling upon the laity to shoulder its responsibilities within the church. This is a time when all of us Catholics should feel ourselves truly a church, when we should give to all the testimony of our faith, when we should all collaborate in evangelization, both by spreading faith in Christ and by extending his kingdom, translating it into structures of justice and peace.

The Hope of the Church

It may seem paradoxical, but in our archdiocese there has never been as much hope as there is now, at one of the most difficult times in its history. Persecution has not produced discouragement, retreat, or confusion. It has rejuvenated Christian hope. This has been demonstrated by the bravery with which many Christians, clerical and lay, rural and urban, have acted in recent months. It has been shown, too, in a tide of conversions. And, according to what has been said in hundreds of letters and telegrams, it has been demonstrated by the solidarity of many Christians with our actions.

Christians have hope. "Nothing can come between us and the love of Christ," said St. Paul (Rom. 8:35). And taking this idea further, we may say that not even all the deaths, the expulsions, the sufferings are able to part us from the love of Christ, and from following his way. Here, in the love of Christ, is the foundation of our hope.

But this hope takes shape only when persons work together as brothers and sisters. That is why our hope in Christ makes us wish for a more just world, a more comradely world. That is why the church of our archdiocese takes interest in, and hopes for, a new and better image for El Salvador, at home and abroad. Precisely for that reason our church says again that the object of its hope is linked inseparably with social justice, with a real improvement in the lot of the people of El Salvador, and especially an improvement in the lot of the impoverished, landless masses, with defense of their human rights, such as the right of life, to education, to housing, to medicine, and to organize, particularly in the case of those who more easily fall victim to the oppression that strips them of that right.

Finally I want to repeat my hope, which is the hope of all in the archdiocese, that the government may understand how right and humanitarian has been the church's course of action, and that the church cannot cease to act in this way, for it is part of its mission of integral evangelization. The church has no desire that its relationship with the government should continue to be tense. On the contrary, the ideal put forward by Vatican II was that of arriving at sincere cooperation. But for that to be the case, there has to exist a solid basis of sincere service to all Salvadorans. To the president's offer of dialogue, therefore, the church repeats its readiness, so long as dialogue uses a common language, and not a vocabulary that runs down and defames the church, and provided that events restore to the church the confidence it has lost in the government. Examples of acts of justice and reconciliation would include: an explanation of what has happened to the many citizens who have disappeared; an end to arbitrary arrests and torture; permission to return home, under a guarantee of liberty, to all who have fled as victims of terror; the return to El Salvador of those of the clergy who have been banned without just reason; a review of expulsion orders served on clergymen, giving them a hearing in court.

Church-state conversations, in a climate of justice and confidence, of love for the common good of the people, would in no way be a matter of seeking privileges. They would not be based upon any competence of a political kind. They would be intended to bring about sincere cooperation between government and church so as to create a just social order, one that would gradually eliminate unjust structures and would encourage the new society that the country needs in order to maintain and live within new structures of justice, peace, and love.

CONCLUSION

Each year this Body of Christ in history, this church of the archdiocese, understands better that the August 6 feast day is something more than just a titular feast. It is rather the celebration of a covenant that binds all Salvadorans to each other, all Salvadorans baptized with the baptism of the world's divine Savior, even to the extent of an identification in thinking and in destiny. All of us who have been baptized form the church, and the church makes Christ present in the history of our country.

In constructing the history of El Salvador our Christian commitment leaves us no room for any inspiration, or for any objective, distinct from the message and the inspiration of Christ. If we are not faithful to this commitment, if we do not construct a better homeland that reflects, within our history, the final kingdom of heaven, then we would be betraying our faith, and even betraying our homeland. Our fidelity to Christ, the Lord of our history, will bring us the deep satisfaction of having been, with him, the builders of his kingdom here in El Salvador, for the happiness of all Salvadorans.

The queen of peace is also one of our country's principal patrons. She is the mother of the first body of Christ and so mother also of the Body of Christ that continues through history. May she look after our church and our homeland with a mother's powerful protection. Beneath the sign of her peace may there come to be, here among the people of El Salvador, the kingdom of God that through his church, Christ continues to preach, a kingdom that "does not interfere with your prerogatives but heals everything human of its fatal weakness, transfigures it, and fills it with hope, truth, and beauty."[28]

NOTES

1. *Lumen Gentium*, §8.
2. *Ecclesiam Suam*, §5.
3. *Gaudium et Spes*, §4.
4. "Introduction," §1.
5. "Justice," §5.
6. *Lumen Gentium*, §9.
7. *Gaudium et Spes*, §1.
8. *Lumen Gentium*, §1.
9. "Poverty," §7.
10. *Lumen Gentium*, §9.
11. Ibid., §8.
12. "Catechesis," §4.
13. See "Introduction," §5.
14. "Justice," §5.
15. *Gaudium et Spes*, §13.
16. Ibid.
17. "Justice," §2.
18. Ibid., §1.
19. Ibid., §3.
20. Vatican II, Message to the World, Oct. 21, 1962, §9.
21. "Justice," §16.
22. See the joint message of the episcopal conference, May 1, 1977.
23. Paul VI, *Octogesima Adveniens*, §§30–37.
24. March 7, 1948.
25. §4.
26. *Gaudium et Spes*, §76.
27. Ibid.
28. Vatican II, Message to Governments.

The Church and
Popular Political Organizations

*Third Pastoral Letter of Archbishop Romero, Coauthored by
Bishop Arturo Rivera y Damas, Bishop of Santiago de María,
Feast of the Transfiguration, August 6, 1978*

To our beloved brothers and sisters, the auxiliary bishop of San Salvador,
the priests, religious, and laity of the archdiocese of San Salvador and the
diocese of Santiago de María; to you and to all men and women of good
will: the peace of Jesus Christ, our divine Savior.

IN THE LIGHT OF THE TRANSFIGURATION,
AND OF THE MEMORY OF PAUL VI

We, the archbishop of San Salvador and the bishop of Santiago de
María, had already been thinking of sending this pastoral letter to our
dioceses to mark our return from our *ad limina* visit to Rome and as an act
of homage to our divine Savior on our patronal feast of the transfiguration.

Never did we imagine, however, that the sudden death of his Holiness
Paul VI, now of happy memory, would give both these events a new significance.

Who could have imagined the eloquent coincidence of Paul VI's death
and our own titular feast of the transfiguration! The final message of his
lucid teaching—the short address he had written to be read at the angelus of
August 6—now becomes for us a cherished family heirloom because it was
inspired by the divine Patron of El Salvador: "That body transfigured before the astonished gaze of his disciples," his Holiness said, "is the body of
Christ our Brother, but it is also our body summoned to glory. The light
that floods over it is, and will be, our share in that inheritance of splendor.
We are called to share this glory because we are sharers in the divine nature." From this vision of transcendence that illuminated the last day of his
mortal life, the pontiff turned his gaze back to earth in anxious concern for
the poor. And he made an appeal to the world for social justice as he re-

flected that economic and social circumstances would prevent many from enjoying a well-earned rest during the traditional summer holidays.

Our audience with the supreme pontiff of the church, together with his wise pastoral advice, gained, through his death, the solemn character of a last testament. The same pattern of turning toward the absolute and eternal, together with a concern for the ordinary needs of our people, "confirmed" our episcopal service when, on that unforgettable June 21, he spoke to us with the tenderness of a father. He was already aware of the approach of death, but he spoke with the firmness and clarity of a prophet who had long known, and known well, the historical situation of El Salvador. He exhorted its pastors to guide and strengthen its people along the paths of justice and love for the gospel.

We feel, then, that the light with which our letter seeks to illuminate the pathway for our dioceses is the true light of the gospel and of the church's magisterium. We feel that the transfiguration of Christ, which, in a great pope's last hour, illuminated the divine vocation of men and women and exposed the unjust inequalities of this world, has the strength and brightness to offer us—through an analysis of the events that are threatening to drown us in a sea of bitterness and confusion—an effective answer to the questioners who look to us for a way out of the difficult situation through which the country is currently passing.

In Accord with the Universal Magisterium

The Father offers us the divine Transfigured One as the Son in whom he is well pleased and tells us to listen to him as Savior and Teacher of the world.

The church, which is the extension of the teaching and salvation of Christ, would be wrong to remain silent when faced with concrete problems. The testimony of the Second Vatican Council, always the point of reference for the teaching of Pope Paul VI; its application to Latin America through the documents of Medellín; the recent popes, many Latin American episcopates, and our own tradition in the church of El Salvador, show us that the church has always made its presence felt when society clearly seemed in a "sinful situation,"[1] in need of the light of the word of God and the word of the church in history. This prophetic mission of the church in defense of the poor, who have always had a special place in the heart of the Lord,[2] numbers among its apostles in Latin America such men as Fray Antonio de Montesinos, Fray Bartolomé de Las Casas, Bishop Juan del Valle, and Bishop Antonio Valdivieso who was assassinated in Nicaragua because of his opposition to the landowner and governor, Contreras.

To these eloquent testimonies of the church, both universal and local, we join today our own humble voice. In obedience to the exhortation of his Holiness, we hope that it will serve to guide and encourage the beloved people we serve as pastors.

Our True Intention

We realize that we risk being misunderstood or condemned, through malice or naivety, as inopportune or ignorant. It is, however, our honest intention to dispel the inertia of the many Salvadorans who are indifferent to the suffering in our land, especially in rural areas. It is true that there is some awareness in society of the plight of urban workers and of independent merchants harassed by acts of arson, and even of the crowded slums and shantytowns. Nevertheless we are concerned about the indifference shown by many urban groups to rural hardship. It seems to be accepted as inevitable that the majority of our people be weighed down by hunger and unemployment. Their sufferings, injuries, and deaths seem to have become routine. They no longer make us ask "Why is this happening? What should we do to avoid it?" How can we answer the question the Lord put to Cain, "What have you done? Listen to the sound of your brother's blood, crying out to me from the ground" (Gen. 4:10).

The Duty and Danger of Speaking Out

It is also our intention to clarify yet again the attitude of the church to human situations that, by their very nature, involve economic, social, and political problems. "The church is meddling in politics," we keep hearing, as if that were proof that it had abandoned its mission. And the church is also misrepresented and slandered in order to discredit and silence it because the interests of a few are not compatible with the logical consequences that follow from the church's religious and evangelical mission in the human, economic, social, and political spheres.

The church's prophetic mission in the world is also mentioned on our patronal feast day when Peter, who was a witness of the transfiguration, compares it to "a lamp for lighting a way through the dark" (2 Pet. 1:19), something to which Christians ought to pay attention if they are not to be seduced by "cleverly invented myths" and the opinions of this world (2 Pet. 1:16).

We are well aware that what we have to say, as with every attempt to sow the seed of the gospel, will run the risk of the seed in the parable of the sower: there will be those, even those of good will, who will not understand, because the misery of the poor and, above all, of the *campesinos* is remote from them and tragically forms a part of the history of their country to which they have become accustomed. There will also be those who will "look without seeing and listen without hearing or understanding" (Matt. 13:14). There will be those, too, who prefer the darkness to the light because their actions are evil (John 3:19). However, thank God, we are sure we can also count on some honest and brave souls who will be ready to draw near to the light, who will not conform themselves to this world (Rom. 12:2), and who will cooperate in "the birth pains" of a new creation (Rom. 8:22).

Two Themes: Popular Organizations and Violence

The situation in our country and the questions of our Christians, especially of rural worker families, make it our duty to clarify as far as possible these two problems: the problem of what are called "popular organizations," which should perhaps be given a name that more accurately reflects their nature and aims, and the problem of violence, which is daily in greater need of the distinctions and classifications of sound Christian moral teaching.

We shall, therefore, divide our pastoral letter into three parts: (1) the situation of popular organizations in El Salvador; (2) the relationship between the church and popular organizations; (3) the church's teaching on violence.

Our Limitations Necessitate Dialogue

Because these problems have assumed a new form, we understand the disquiet that causes many, particularly *campesinos,* to ask: "What are we to make of these 'popular organizations,' which are independent of the government, especially when, alongside and bitterly antagonistic toward them, government organizations are growing up? Does being a Christian mean one has to join some popular organization seeking radical changes in our country? How can one be a Christian and accept the demands of the gospel and yet join some organization that neither believes in nor has sympathy with the gospel? How ought a Christian to resolve the conflict between loyalty to the gospel and the demands of an organization when it may not be in accordance with the gospel? What is the relationship between the church and these organizations?"

On the question of violence, Salvadorans are asking where, in the situation of our country, the line should be drawn between what is and is not permissible in the light of the law of Christ. As pastors, we have a duty to give a Christian answer, an answer of the church, to these problems that trouble so many consciences. We are, however, also aware of our limitations. Vatican II recognized them when it warned the laity not to think that "pastors are always such experts, that to every problem which arises, however complicated, they can readily give a concrete solution."[3]

Although the problems we shall address are old ones, they have often taken quite new forms in the recent history of our country. Therefore, because of the novelty of the subject and the natural limitations of its authors, our pastoral letter quite deliberately offers no more than the Christian principles on which a solution must be based. It is a call to the whole people of God to reflect on these matters in local churches, in communion with their pastors and with the universal church, in the light of the gospel, and in fidelity to the true identity of the church.

This is not an attempt to evade the seriousness of the problem. We are following the spirit of the church's magisterium, which Paul VI in his letter *Octogesima Adveniens,* defined as follows:

It is up to the Christian communities to analyze with objectivity the situation proper to their own country, to shed on it the light of the Gospel's unalterable words, and to draw principles of reflection, norms of judgment, and directives for action from the social teaching of the Church. . . . It is up to these Christian communities, with the help of the Holy Spirit, in communion with the bishops who hold responsibility and in dialogue with other Christians and all men and women of good will, to discern the options and commitments that are called for in order to bring about the social, political, and economic changes seen in many cases to be urgently needed.[4]

In order to make community reflection easier, we are offering, in a separate pamphlet, three clarificatory notes. They are not integral parts of the text of this letter, but simply additional notes intended to arouse thought and to stimulate study. They deal with (1) the national context in which the church fulfills its mission; (2) the word of God on human misery; (3) the most recent teaching of the church. One can find fault with these notes; nonetheless we think the study of them very useful if the problems touched on in this letter are to be better understood in relation to the situation in this country, and from a biblical and ecclesial perspective. For it is only by listening, starting from the facts and their analysis, to the cries of the poor, and by hearing the word of Jesus and of his church, that we can find a solution, and a pastoral response, to the problems we are going to discuss.

For this reflection we also recommend that you keep in mind the first two pastoral letters of the archbishop of San Salvador, "The Easter Church" and "The Church, the Body of Christ in History." These focus explicitly on the nature and mission of the church, to both of which we shall make reference only when it is essential to our central theme.

PART ONE
THE SITUATION OF POPULAR ORGANIZATIONS IN EL SALVADOR

Within the context of our national situation, the proliferation of popular organizations is one of those phenomena of which Vatican II makes mention when, calling upon Christians to reflect and discern, it says, "The People of God . . . motivated by this faith, labors to decipher authentic signs of God's presence and purpose in the happenings, needs, and desires in which this People has a part along with other men of our age."[5]

In this pastoral letter we have no intention of studying the origins, history, and objectives of these organizations. We want simply, in this section, to restate the right to organize and to denounce the violation of that right in our country. In the next section we shall deal with the relationship between the church and the popular organizations.

The Right to Organize

The United Nations' Universal Declaration of Human Rights, to which this country is a signatory, and article 160 of our Constitution, proclaim the right of all citizens to assemble and to form associations.

This right, whose proclamation is one of the achievements of our civilization, has been repeatedly affirmed by the church: "From the fact that human beings are by nature social," said Pope John XXIII in the encyclical *Pacem in Terris*, "there arises the right of assembly and association."[6] The Second Vatican Council reminded us once again that "among the basic rights of the human person is to be numbered the right of freely founding labor unions. . . . These should be able truly to represent [workers]."[7] For our own continent Medellín recalled that "in the intermediary professional structure the peasants' and the workers' unions, to which the workers have a right, should acquire sufficient strength and power."[8]

The Violation of This Right in El Salvador

Unfortunately there is an enormous difference between legal declarations and reality in our country. Various political, trade union, worker, rural, cultural, and other associations do exist here. Some of them enjoy legal recognition, others do not. Some of them—with or without legal recognition—are able to function freely, others are not. However, we do not now want to concentrate on the legal aspect of formal recognition. We are more interested in examining the practical freedom of any human group to exercise its natural right of association and the support and cooperation it can expect from an authority genuinely concerned with the common good "whereby men, families, and associations more adequately and readily may attain their own perfection."[9]

It is here, faced with the absence of this real freedom, that we have to denounce the violation of this human right of association proclaimed by our Constitution and by an international declaration of human rights accepted by our country.

We note, specifically, under this heading, the following three abuses:

Discrimination among Citizens

The first conclusion of any impartial analysis of the right of association must be that groups in agreement with the government or protected by it have complete freedom. Organizations, on the other hand, that voice dissent from the government—political parties, trade unions, rural organizations—find themselves hindered or even prevented from exercising their right to organize legally and work for their aims, just though these may be.

It is, then, a situation in which the fundamental right mentioned above is violated.

Harm Done to the Majority

This discrimination results in yet another violation of our democratic rights—for let us not forget that the meaning of the Greek word *demos* is the totality of the citizens. It is a fact, and one for which there is daily fresh evidence, that economically powerful minorities can organize in defense of their interests and very often to the detriment of the great majority of the people.

They can mount publicity campaigns, even in opposition to the government; they can influence important items of legislation, as in the case of agrarian reform and the Law for the Defense and Guarantee of Public Order. By contrast, other groups among the mass of the people meet only difficulties and repression when they try, in an organized way, to defend the interests of the majority.

This situation inflicts at least two serious injuries on our people; it infringes upon their dignity, their freedom, and their equal right to participate in politics, and it leaves without protection those who need it most. "The aspiration to equality and the aspiration to participation [are] two forms of human dignity and liberty," said Pope Paul VI in *Octogesima Adveniens.*[10] There is indeed, in this state of affairs, a blatant inequality between citizens as regards participation in politics depending on whether they belong to the powerful minority or to the poor majority, and whether or not they enjoy official approval.

With regard to the lack of protection for those who need it most, let us recall that, as we said in our message of January 1, historically, genuine laws were made to protect the weakest, those who, without the law, are prey to the powerful. The protection of the weakest was also the historical origin of the different groupings among the majority, the modern unions of urban and rural workers. What forced them to unite in the first place was not just their civil right to participate in the political and economic management of their country, but the simple basic need to survive, to exercise their right to make their conditions of life at least tolerable. It is here, in this basic exigency, that the need for legislation and the need for organization coincide. The absurd response to this basic need is—without any attempt to distinguish between true and false—indiscriminate repression. "Clandestine forces of subversion" is the term used to describe those who are trying to improve society and its laws, so that its benefits and ideals do not exclude those who also contribute to producing the wealth—great or little—of the country.

Conflict among Campesino Groups

Though we do not want to go into great detail, we cannot at this point ignore the tragedy in this country of organizations, composed mainly of *campesinos*, at odds with one another. Recently they have even engaged in violent conflict.

It is not—solely or ultimately—ideologies that have divided them and brought them into conflict. The members of these organizations do not, for the most part, think differently about peace, work, or the family. The most serious aspect of the situation is that rural Salvadorans are being divided by the very thing that most deeply unites them: the same poverty, the same need to survive, to give something to their children, to provide bread, education, and health care for their families.

What is happening is that, in order to escape from their common poverty, some are corrupted by the benefits offered by progovernment organizations. In return they are employed in various repressive activities that regularly include informing on, threatening, kidnapping, torturing, and even, in some cases, killing their fellow *campesinos*. Others, active in organizations independent of the government or opposed to it, strive to find more satisfactory ways of escaping their precarious situation. Finally special attention should be paid to those groups of Christian communities that have so often been the target of misrepresentation and manipulation. These groups meet to reflect on the word of God, which, if it is a word incarnate in real situations, always awakens the Christian conscience to its duty to work for a more just society through the various political choices suggested by that faith and conscience.

Why the Right to Organize and Why Especially for the Rural Poor?

It is very sad to have to present to the divine Patron of our nation on this titular feast a rural population that, paradoxically, is organized to divide and destroy itself. So, thinking for the moment chiefly of the *campesinos*, and recalling the fundamental right of all men and women to organize, we invite you to lift your minds and hearts to our divine Savior. He is the ultimate basis of all the rights and all the duties that regulate human relationships.

He is not a God of death or of fratricidal confrontation. He did not give us a social nature so that we should destroy ourselves in mutually hostile organizations, but so that we could complement our individual limitations with the strength of all, united in love. Under the law of his justice and his commandment of love, human rights ought to be exercised in such a way that they do not become the cause of fractricidal strife. The right to organize is not absolute: it does not make unjust ends or methods legitimate. It is a right to join forces in order to achieve, by just means, ends that are also just and conducive to the common good.

The right to organize must be exercised on the basis of the dignity of the individual. The criterion for organizing, whether at the political, cultural, or trade union level, is the defense of legitimate interests, whether or not they are contained in a specific piece of legislation or an interpretation of it.

Again, in regard to the right to organize, we uphold the national Constitution when it recalls the limits imposed by morality and rejects anarchical theories of the use of rights. Our intention, in demanding that the right of association be enjoyed by all Salvadorans, with particular emphasis on the rural population, is certainly not to defend terrorist groups or support anarchist movements and irrational, subversive ideologies. We have in the past often denounced the fanaticism of violence or class hatred, and we have reiterated the principle of the Christian moral teaching that the end does not justify criminal means and that there is no freedom to do evil. We therefore defend the right to make just demands and denounce the dangerous and evil-minded oversimplification that seeks to misrepresent them and condemn them as terrorism or unlawful subversion.

No one dare take away, least of all from the poor, the right to organize, because the protection of the weak is the principal purpose of laws and of social organizations.

That is why we have said that we want, in this letter, to stress the right of *campesinos* to form organizations. They are the ones who, today, encounter the greatest difficulty in exercising this right.

Historically, poor landworkers are the class with which society has least concerned itself. Pope John XXIII, who was never ashamed of his poor, rural origin, advocated the changes necessary so that poor landworkers "no longer regard themselves as inferior to others."[11] And he warned that "farmers should join together in fellowships. . . . For today it is unquestionably true that the solitary voice speaks, as they say, to the winds."[12]

The Second Vatican Council reminded us that poor landworkers do not simply want better living conditions but also "to take part in regulating economic, social, political, and cultural life."[13] During his journey to Colombia, Pope Paul VI solemnly affirmed to the *campesinos* of Mosquera, "You are aware of your needs and your sufferings, and, like many others in the world, you are not going to accept that these conditions continue forever without being able to bring about the needed remedies." He reminded them that they belong to the human family without discrimination, to the fellowship of humankind.[14]

Medellín reemphasized this right[15] and it has been reiterated since then by several Latin American hierarchies: Colombia, July 1969; Honduras, January 1970; Peru, December 1975; and others. Our own episcopal conference has also spoken out clearly in defense of the *campesino* right of association. In line with the position taken up by our own hierarchy, we have no hesitation in reaffirming the right of men and women living in the countryside to form associations, and, indeed, encouraging the formation of such associations. In so doing we do not speak, as pastors, with a particular political view but with the Christian view that the poor should have sufficient strength not to be the victims of the interests of a minority, as they have been in the past.

Medellín made it quite clear that, in the particular situation of Latin

America, it is an "eminently Christian task" and, therefore, part of the "pastoral policy" of the Latin American hierarchy "to encourage and favor the efforts of the people to create and develop their own grassroots organizations for the redress and consolidation of their rights and the search for true justice."[16]

PART TWO
THE CHURCH AND THE POPULAR ORGANIZATIONS

A New Problem

Our subject here is not the attitude of the church to the different political parties: that has already been examined and is well known. The issue is how the church should see and perform its particular mission within the process of organization that is now taking place at such speed among the people, primarily among the rural poor. It might well be thought that this proliferation of "popular organizations" is for us one of the "signs of the times" that challenge the church to exercise its power and duty of discernment and guidance in the light of the word of God that has been given to it to be applied to the problems of history.

We have already said that there is a new challenge here, not only for the church, but also for the organizations themselves and society in general. Therefore common reflection, with the help of the Holy Spirit and in communion with the bishops responsible, as recommended in the passage quoted above from Paul VI's *Octogesima Adveniens*, will be a sure path to understanding and to keeping an evangelical balance between the identity and duty of the church and the social and political concerns of the people. We shall first make three statements of principle and then apply them to our situation.

Three Statements of Principle

We can consider the relationship of the church to the popular organizations at two different levels, practical and theoretical.

At the practical level, much depends on the de facto historical situation. That is to say, when the church has to make judgments or advise people looking for guidance based on the gospel about immediate political commitments, the church must study each situation from a pastoral point of view, show respect for the rightful plurality of solutions, and not identify itself with any one of them, because the church has to respect the freedom to make specific political choices.

At the theoretical level, in regard to the relationship between the church and any organization that has as its objectives social and political justice, we want to lay down three principles.

The Church's Own Nature

The first principle we take as it stands from the Second Vatican Council:

> Christ, to be sure, gave his Church no proper mission in the political, economic, or social order. The purpose which he set before it is a religious one. But out of this religious mission itself come a function, a light, and an energy which can serve to structure and consolidate the human community according to the divine law.[17]

These more religious aspects of the mystery of the church can be studied in the archbishop of San Salvador's first two pastoral letters. They are not the main subject of this one, although we have them very much in mind in order to maintain the true nature and mission of the church in its relationship with other human organizations.

In his exhortation *Evangelii Nuntiandi*, Paul VI describes the two chief religious bonds that give cohesion and its own particular style to the community that is the church:

> Those who sincerely accept the Good News, through the power of this acceptance and of shared faith, therefore gather together in Jesus' name in order to seek together the Kingdom, build it up and live it. They make up a community which is in its turn evangelizing. . . . Such an adherence, which cannot remain abstract and unincarnated, reveals itself concretely by a visible entry into a community of believers. Thus those whose life has been transformed enter a community which is itself a sign of transformation, a sign of newness of life: it is the Church, the visible sacrament of salvation. But entry into the ecclesial community will in its turn be expressed through many other signs which prolong and unfold the sign of the Church. In the dynamism of evangelization, a person who accepts the Gospel as the Word which saves normally translates it into the following sacramental acts: adherence to the Church, and acceptance of the Sacraments, which manifest and support this adherence through the grace which they confer.[18]

Thus, one must not lose sight of this specific task of the church: evangelization. The word of God creates a church community united in itself and with God by means of sacramental signs, chief of which is the Eucharist. This is why the council said that "the Church is in Christ like a sacrament or as a sign and instrument both of a very closely knit union with God and of the unity of the whole human race."[19]

However, on accepting this word of God, Christians find that it is a living word that brings with it awareness and demands. That is to say, it makes them aware of what sin and grace are, and of what must be resisted and what must be built up on earth. It is a word that demands of our consciences and of our lives not only that we judge the world by the criteria of the kingdom of God, but that we act accordingly. It is a word of God that we must not only hear but put into practice.

This is what the church has been doing in its pastoral work: gathering men and women around the word of God and the Eucharist. We cannot give up the right to do this. It is a duty demanded of us by the very nature of the church. To this level of pastoral work belong our attempts to set up and encourage basic ecclesial communities. These are the organized communities that arise around the word of God, a word that brings persons together, makes them aware, and makes demands upon them, and around the Eucharist and the other sacramental signs, to celebrate the life, death, and resurrection of Jesus, celebrating at the same time our human effort to open ourselves to the gift of a greater humanity. Of these basic ecclesial communities Paul VI said:

> They spring from the need to live the Church's life more intensely, or from the desire and quest for a more human dimension such as larger ecclesial communities can only offer with difficulty. . . . These communities will be a place of evangelization, for the benefit of the bigger communities, especially the individual Churches. And . . . they will be a hope for the universal Church.[20]

These communities have to be maintained and strengthened because they are the vital cells of the church. They embody the whole concept of the church and its unique mission. Pastors and lay ministers must take care that this identity and mission be maintained in all its purity and autonomy so that these communities are not confused with other organizations and, above all, are not manipulated by them.

It is very important that pastors and others engaged in pastoral work should keep in mind the comments of Paul VI and the other bishops at the 1974 Synod of Bishops when they pointed out dangers that were likely to turn these communities aside from their ecclesial pursuits and evangelical objectives. We want to draw particular attention, in line with our theme, to the warning "not [to] allow themselves to be ensnared by political polarization or fashionable ideologies, which are ready to exploit their immense human potential."[21]

The church is also fully aware, through its own experience, that the typical ecclesial community can also arouse in Christians an explicitly political vocation. We have said that the word of God, which nourishes the ecclesial community, is a word that makes persons aware and makes demands upon them, and that this word must not only be heard but also put into practice. This demand and action in response to it can awaken political commitment in a Christian. Moreover, Vatican II states:

> Great care must be taken about civic and political formation, which is of the utmost necessity today for the population as a whole, and especially

for youth, so that all citizens can play their part in the life of the political community. Those who are suited or can become suited should prepare themselves for the difficult, but at the same time, the very noble art of politics, and should seek to practice this art without regard for their own interests or for material advantages.[22]

However, when political vocations appear in the ecclesial community, the church has no special role in determining the specific means to be chosen to achieve a more just society. While respecting the autonomy of politics, it will continue to maintain its own properly ecclesial character as outlined above.

The Church at the Service of the People

The second principle that we must lay down is that the church has a mission of service to the people. Precisely from its specifically religious character and mission "come a function, a light, and an energy which can serve to structure and consolidate the human community according to the divine law."[23]

It is the role of the church to gather into itself all that is human in the people's cause and struggle, above all in the cause of the poor. The church identifies with the poor when they demand their legitimate rights. In our country the right they are demanding is hardly more than the right to survive, to escape from misery.

This solidarity with just aims is not restricted to particular organizations. Whether they call themselves Christian or not, whether they are protected by the government, legally or in practice, or whether they are independent of it and opposed to it, the church is interested only in one thing: if the aim of the struggle is just, the church will support it with all the power of the gospel. In the same way it will denounce, with bold impartiality, all injustice in any organization, wherever it is found. By virtue of this service that it is the church's duty to render, through its faith, to the thirst for justice, it was stated at Medellín that the direction to be taken by pastoral policy in Latin America was "to encourage and favor the efforts of the people to create and develop their own grassroots organizations for the redress and consolidation of their rights and the search for true justice."[24]

The church is well aware of the complexity of political activity. However, and we repeat it, it is not, nor ought it to be, an expert in this sort of activity. Nevertheless it can and must pass judgment on the general intention and the particular methods of political parties and organizations, precisely because of its interest in a more just society. The economic, social, political, and cultural hopes of men and women are not alien to the definitive liberation achieved in Jesus Christ, which is the transcendent hope of the church.[25]

No less can the church shirk the task of defending the weak and those in real need, whatever the nature of the groups or individuals who support their just causes. As Paul VI remarked:

It is well known in what terms numerous bishops from all the continents spoke of this at the [1974] synod, especially the bishops from the Third World, with a pastoral accent resonant with the voice of the millions of sons and daughters of the Church who make up those peoples. Peoples, as we know, engaged with all their energy in the effort and struggle to overcome everything which condemns them to remain on the margin of life: famine, chronic disease, illiteracy, poverty, injustices in international relations and especially in commercial exchanges, situations of economic and cultural neo-colonialism sometimes as cruel as the old political colonialism. The Church, as the bishops repeated, has the duty to proclaim the liberation of millions of human beings, many of whom are its own children—the duty of assisting the birth of this liberation, of giving witness to it, of ensuring that it is complete. This is not foreign to evangelization.[26]

In this service of solidarity with the just causes of the poor, we have not forgotten the duties of the poor themselves and the demands on them to show respect for others. When we have mediated in conflicts, when we have denounced attacks on dignity, life, or liberty, and on other occasions when we have shown this solidarity, we have always tried to be just and objective, and we have never been moved by, nor have we ever preached, hatred or resentment. On the contrary, we have called for conversion. We have pointed to justice as the indispensable basis of the peace that is the true objective of Christians. Among its services to the people the church has performed countless works of charity for the welfare and Christian education of the poor, works that give the lie to those who accuse it of only agitating and never acting.

The Role of the Struggle for Liberation in Christian Salvation

This is the third principle that, at the theoretical level, guides our reflection on relations between the church and popular organizations. These organizations are forces for the achievement of social, economic, and political justice among the people, especially among the rural poor. The church, as we have said, fosters and encourages just attempts at organization and supports whatever is just in their demands. The church's service to these legitimate efforts for liberation would not, however, be complete if it did not bring to bear on them the light of its faith and its hope, and point out their place in the overall plan of the salvation brought by our Redeemer, Jesus Christ.

The overall plan of the liberation proclaimed by the church:

1) involves the whole person, in all dimensions, including openness to the absolute that is God, and to that extent it is linked to a certain understanding of human nature—an understanding that cannot be sacrificed to the demands of any particular strategy, tactic, or short-term expedient;

2) is centered on the kingdom of God and, although its mission is not limited to religion, it nevertheless reaffirms the primacy of humanity's spiritual vocation and proclaims salvation in Jesus Christ;

3) proceeds from a scriptural vision of human nature, is based on a deep desire for justice in love, implies a truly spiritual dimension that has as its final aim salvation and happiness with God;

4) demands a conversion of heart and mind, and is not satisfied with merely structural changes;

5) and excludes violence, considering it "unchristian and unscriptural," ineffective and out of keeping with the dignity of the people.[27]

If the church, in its support for any group in its efforts to achieve liberation in this world, were to lose the overall perspective of Christian salvation, "it would lose its fundamental meaning. Its message of liberation would no longer have any originality and would easily be open to monopolization and manipulation. . . . It would have no more authority to proclaim freedom as in the name of God."[28]

On the other hand, by cultivating faith and hope in this overall plan of Christ's salvation, the church preaches the real reasons for living, and it puts forward the most solid grounds possible to help persons become aware of themselves as truly free and ready to work with serene confidence for the liberation of the world. Acting in this way the church "is trying more and more to encourage large numbers of Christians to devote themselves to the liberation of men. It is providing these Christian 'liberators' with the inspiration of faith, the motivation of fraternal love, a social teaching which the true Christian cannot ignore and which he must make the foundation of his wisdom and of his experience in order to translate it concretely into forms of action, participation, and commitment."[29]

The Charism of Paul VI

To end this statement of principles, which should help us to understand more readily the relationship that should exist between the church and organizations working for social justice, our thoughts turn once more in grateful reverence to the memory of Pope Paul VI. We give thanks for the charismatic clarity of his teaching and for the pastor's love he showed for us, the people of El Salvador.

His teaching, endowed with a remarkable ability to explain the theology of the church's relationship with the world, has clarified our own reflections. It has led us forward, guiding us by means of many documents on social and ecclesiological questions. We invite the whole community of our dioceses to join us in our reflections so that our teaching, commitment, and action in this delicate area may be more precise.

The pastoral love that the pope enjoined on us as his last wish for El Salvador quickens our pastoral instincts in our desire to reach a balanced understanding of and support for the justice that our people is seeking with eagerness and hope.

Application of the Principles

Using the three ecclesiological criteria explained above, we are in a position to judge the relationship of the church to the social groups that organize to struggle for justice in the political sphere. From these principles we should be able to work out what these organizations can hope for, or even demand, from the church in accordance with its mission and what cannot be expected because it is outside the church's competence.

Let us therefore continue our dialogue by applying the principles to various problems presented by the church's relationships with the popular organizations.

A Relationship of Origination

Some popular organizations are known to be of Christian inspiration and even have names that reflect it. Their historical origin is closely linked with the life and activity of some Christian community. This fact, which is not exclusive to our period or our country, has been maliciously distorted here to the point of identifying the church with certain popular organizations. The church has been held responsible for the particular means chosen by these organizations with full autonomy and on their own responsibility to achieve their aims.

We have already explained that this relationship of origination is possible and natural when we talked about the power of the word of God, which nourishes the Christian faith of the ecclesial community, to awaken consciousness and make demands. In many *campesinos* this word has encouraged the parallel growth of an active awareness of both faith and the justice that faith demands, and this may also lead to a political calling.

Faith and Politics: United but not Identified

This is where the problem arises: faith and politics ought to be united in a Christian who has a political vocation, but they are not to be identified. The church wants both dimensions to be present in the total life of a Christian and has emphasized that faith lived out in isolation from life is not true faith. However, one also has to be aware that the task of the faith and a particular political task cannot be identified. Christians with a political vocation should strive to achieve a synthesis between their Christian faith and their political activity, but without identifying them. Faith ought to inspire political action but not be mistaken for it.

It is important to be very clear about this when the same persons who belong to ecclesial communities also belong to popular political organizations. If they do not bear in mind this distinction between the Christian faith and their political activity, they can fall into two errors: they can substitute for the demands of the faith and Christian justice the demands of a particular political organization, or they can assert that only within a particular organization can one develop the requirements of Christian justice that spring from the faith.

What Can and What Cannot be Demanded of the Church?

Thus, when Christians organize themselves into any sort of association, be it a political party, trade union, or popular organization, they ought to be well aware of precisely what belongs to the realm of the faith and what to the realm of politics, and respect the autonomy of each. A political organization ought to have a clear notion of what can be asked, or even demanded of the church, and of what cannot be demanded, because it would be asking for something the church cannot give and would be seriously compromising the legitimate autonomy of politics.

What we have said to clarify the nature and mission of the church also makes clear what any organization, Christian in inspiration or not, can ask of the church. It can expect the church to advocate civil rights, such as the right of association, the right to strike, the right to demonstrate, and the right to free speech. No organization, even if Christian in inspiration or name, can, however, require that the church as such or any feature or activity clearly recognizable as ecclesiastical (such as religious ceremonies, preaching, processions, etc.), be turned into direct means of propaganda for political ends. We have already said that the church, for its part, is always ready to make use of the only power it possesses—the power of the gospel—to throw light on any kind of activity that will better establish justice.

Loyalty to the Christian Faith

This brings us to another problem that we want to delineate as clearly as possible. To struggle for justice in a popular organization it is not necessary either to be a Christian or explicitly to accept faith in Christ. One can be a good politician or work hard to bring about a more just society without being a Christian, provided that one respects, and takes account of, the human and social value of the individual.

Those, however, who claim to be Christians, and who organize as such, have the duty of confessing their faith in Christ and, in their social and political activity, of using methods that are consonant with their faith.

We well understand that at times it is difficult to distinguish what is specifically Christian from what is not. And Christianity, being a historical religion, meets new situations that require new answers. Hence it is understandable that confusion arises in a new situation. One thing must, however, be quite clear: that what is final and absolute for a Christian, even for one involved in political activity, has to be faith in God and the need to achieve justice according to the norms of the kingdom of God.

We also understand that political activity tends to absorb, indeed to monopolize, a person's interest. This is a perfectly normal phenomenon of human enthusiasm. However, there arises at times a tension between two loyalties, loyalty to the faith and loyalty to the organization. At times it will not be easy to live out this tension. Here too, as with everything that is new, it will be necessary to learn by trial and error. It is, however, our pastoral duty, even taking into account the difficulties we have outlined, to remind you that, however great this tension between the two loyalties, the final and definitive loyalty of a Christian can never be to a human organization, no matter what advantages it may offer, but to God and to the poor, who are the "least of the brethren" of Jesus Christ.

Authenticity, not Manipulation

We therefore urge Christians who belong, formally or in practice, to any organization with just social, political, and economic aims to profess their faith openly so that it becomes their ultimate point of reference and they can grow in it. Yet, in their theoretical convictions and concrete applications, they must not fall into the temptation of pride and intransigence, as though the legitimate political choice to which their faith has led them were the only way of working wholeheartedly for justice.

We also remind them of the duty of expressing their faith in loyal solidarity with the church and openness to the transcendence of God through the sacramental signs of his grace, through prayer and meditation on the word of God. This is the only way to ensure that a commitment to justice and the Christian political vocation grow in tandem. This mutual interaction between an explicit faith and dedication to justice will be the guarantee that one's faith is not vain, but is accompanied by works, and at the same time that the justice one is seeking is indeed the justice of the kingdom of God.

However, if some Christians, having been moved in the first instance by their Christian faith to take up a stance in favor of the poor, sadly have come to lose that faith and now think it useless, we urge them to be sincere and not to exploit the faith, which they no longer share, in order to achieve political objectives, no matter how just.

Not Every Christian Has a Political Vocation

A Christian cannot be forced to join a specific political party or organization. It must be remembered, on the one hand, that every human activity has, and cannot avoid having, political repercussions in the broad sense and so constitutes an inescapable degree of political involvement, a certain capacity for deciding between different political courses and, above all, a strong critical sense. On the other hand, it must be remembered that not every Christian has a political vocation—that is to say, the qualities and the desire necessary to fight for justice by specifically political means.

There are other means of carrying on this struggle—for example, by education for liberation (Medellín), or by evangelization aware of human rights and the process of the liberation of peoples.[30]

Politics, as a vocation, as a legitimate human and Christian dimension of life, has no right to be considered the only possible way to perform the inescapable duty of every Salvadoran to work for the establishment of a more just order in our country.

We are not saying this to encourage inactivity or idleness, but so that all of you will think about your vocation to devote your life to the service of others.

Clergy and Laity in Collaboration with the Hierarchy

We now want to address ourselves to our beloved clergy and to those respected lay persons who, like the clergy, work closely with the hierarchy and therefore need a special commission or authorization that makes them, through this work, to some degree representatives of the teaching and ministry of the church among the people.

It is with great joy that we affirm that the work of our clergy and laity is daily becoming more involved with, and committed to, the cause of our divine Pastor, and of the world in which we live. Our pastoral activity is becoming continually more aware of the total liberation demanded of us by the gospel, and by the authoritative teaching of the bishops of the universal church and that of the Latin American bishops assembled at Medellín.

It is becoming increasingly clearer that the call to conversion addressed to all is more effective and authentic when it follows the gospel strategy of taking the good news of salvation first to the poor, while reminding them too of the demands of their conversion (Luke 4:18).

This is our pastoral approach. It received its most authoritative and direct support from Paul VI's *Evangelii Nuntiandi* and its practical application to our dioceses in the San Salvador pastoral week (Jan. 5–10, 1976). We cannot stray from this approach without being unfaithful to our consciences, to the hopes of the people, and, above all, to the word of the Lord.

For this reason we urge our beloved clergy and laity to guard the evangelical purity of this approach and, in guarding it, not to be afraid of the boldness it will often demand of us. We well understand the risks involved in this purity and boldness. It is normal, and indeed frequently happens, that priests and their closest lay collaborators, precisely because they want to preach a realistic and committed gospel, should have a keen awareness of political problems and, as citizens, should feel more drawn toward one political party or popular organization than to another. Likewise it is understandable that, when they are asked, they will work to guide, in a Christian perspective, the political activities of Christians striving for justice.

It is, however, our duty to remind them that, in whatever priestly or pastoral work they are asked to perform by individuals, political parties, or other organizations, they should make it their first concern to be animators and guides in faith and in the justice that faith demands, in accordance with the general Christian principles we have already dwelt on.

This is the priceless, necessary, and irreplaceable service we have to offer the world. In dealing with the detailed problems resulting from day-to-day political activity, politicians and experts are usually better qualified to make analyses and suggest solutions. In any case, the priest's task is to provide the stimulus that comes from the Spirit of the Lord. This must be related to actual situations but it must also be an authentic stimulus in faith. The priest's main task is to keep alive the gospel standards of thought and action, to remind the faithful, as Jesus did, of the love of the Father for all, and to urge them on to follow Jesus in implanting the kingdom of God on earth. The fulfillment of this task will always be partial and limited, but the inspiration and help that a priest can give toward it will be of immeasurable value for the faith of the whole church. It will bring together, without identifying the two or reducing one to the other, the dimension of faith and the need for justice. It will ensure—so we believe as Christians—that real advances in justice are in accordance with God's plan, without which no social progress can be genuine or lasting.

If, in an exceptional case, a priest were asked to work more closely in the political process—and the case would be exceptional because the priest would be acting in a supplementary role that has nothing to do with the normal vocation and ministry of a priest—it would be for the bishop, after a frank discussion with the priest in the light of faith, to make a Christian judgment on the apostolic value of the work in question.

Lay persons who have been taken into the service of the church by reason of a special hierarchial commission—catechists, celebrants of the word, and others—must not forget that this makes them conspicuous representatives of the hierarchy and of its ministry and teaching. Just as priests and bishops ought to be, so too are they a sign of the unity of all the church's children, in the local and in the universal church. This responsibility, which gives them a leading and unifying role within the people of God, ought to make them careful about sympathizing with, or joining, any popular organization. If playing an active role within an organization deprives them of the credibility and efficiency among the people of God that they need for pastoral work, then there is a stong pastoral reason why they ought, after serious reflection before the Lord, to choose between the two activities.

Non-Christian Organizations

Our reflections on the church and popular organizations have so far been concerned chiefly with organizations that are professedly Christian. We have not, however, forgotten that many of our Salvadoran brothers and sisters are active in organizations that do not profess to be Christian. Much of what has already been said about Christian organizations in their relationship with the church is equally true of non-Christian organizations. The fundamental criteria have already been stated: support for the human right of association, especially when the situation in the country leads one to think of such organizations as among the most important means for establishing justice; support also for the freedom that every individual has to make their own choices and not be forced to join this or that group; support for the just ends of any organization; support for the autonomy of the political and social activities of organizations, just as the church requires any person or organization to respect the autonomy of its own nature and its mission, and not to use it or subordinate it to the aims of some other organization. The church also has the right and duty to exercise, in relation to any organization, Christian or not, its prophetic function of encouraging what is in keeping with the revelation of God in the gospel and of denouncing all that is in contradiction to this revelation and constitutes the sin of the world.

There is, however, a further connection, more fundamental and based on faith, between the church and popular organizations even if they do not profess to be Christian. The church believes that the action of the Spirit who brings Christ to life in human beings is greater than itself. Far beyond the confines of the church, Christ's redemption is powerfully at work. The strivings of individuals and groups, even if they do not profess to be Christian, derive their impetus from the Spirit of Jesus. The church will try to see them in this way in order to purify them, encourage and incorporate them, together with the efforts of Christians, into the overall plan of Christian redemption.

We are well aware that, despite our intentions and all our efforts to provide adequate guidance to the political dimension of the faith of our brothers and sisters, especially of the rural population, there are still many questions waiting to be answered. Much thinking remains to be done. We must do it together, pastors and people of God, never separated from our union in Christ. We must do it in the light of our faith and of the social situation of our country.

PART THREE
THE JUDGMENT OF THE CHURCH ON VIOLENCE

In connection with the subject of popular organizations, the problem of violence arises spontaneously because, in the efforts of these groups to obtain their social, political, and economic objectives, violence is often regarded as a suitable means. That is why our pastoral mission now obliges us to offer principles from the church's moral teaching to guide the thinking of our communities.

We shall consider the following points: (1) different types of violence; (2) the church's moral judgment on violence; (3) its application to the situation in El Salvador.

The Reality and the Ideal

How painful it is to have to offer to our divine Savior, together with the hopeful prayers of his people gathered together in the light of his transfiguration, the horrifying spectacle of the situation in our country, stained as it is with so much blood, so many attacks on the dignity, the liberty, and even on the lives of our citizens. We live, nationally, in an explosive situation, heavy with the fruits of violence. We often see demonstrations end with the shedding of the blood of the demonstrators and sometimes of members of the security forces. In many places recently, especially in the countryside, there have been violent conflicts, sometimes on the scale of a military operation, extending over wide areas. There are many households that grieve for the victims of kidnapings, murder, torture, threats, arson, and so on.

In this situation, where consciences can lose all sensitivity, we have to go on repeating, even if we are a voice crying in the wilderness, "no to violence, yes to peace."

The church is quite clear about this ideal, no matter how much calumny and persecution may have tried to distort its message: "We forcefully reaffirm our faith in the productiveness of peace"—this was the voice of the Latin American episcopate at Medellín—"this is our Christian ideal . . . not hate and violence, but . . . the strong and peaceful energy of constructive works."[31]

Today, in this pastoral letter, we are also fulfilling the final charge laid upon us by Paul VI at the audience during our *ad limina* visit of June 21, 1978. He urged us to show pastoral solidarity with our fellow Salvadorans. He spoke of their efforts to obtain justice and charged us to guide them in the path of a just peace, and to help them resist the easy temptation of violence and hatred.

Different Types of Violence

However, although it is easy enough to put forward the ideal of peace, it is much less easy to deal with the reality of violence, which, historically, seems inevitable so long as its true causes are not eliminated. Normally speaking, and save in pathological cases, violence is not part of human nature. Persons do not find self-fulfillment in humiliating, harming, kidnaping, torturing, or killing others. Violence has other roots, which have to be exposed. To do that we must analyze the different types of violence along the lines suggested by the bishops of Latin America at Medellín.

Institutionalized Violence

The most acute form in which violence appears on our continent and in our own country is what the bishops of Medellín called "institutionalized violence."[32] It is the result of an unjust situation in which the majority of men, women, and children in our country find themselves deprived of the necessities of life.

This violence finds expression in the structure and daily functioning of a socio-economic and political system that takes it for granted that progress is impossible unless the majority of the people are used as a productive force under the control of a privileged minority. Historically we come across this sort of violence whenever the institutional structures of society operate to the benefit of a minority or systematically discriminate against groups or individuals who defend the true common good.

Those responsible for the institutionalization of violence, and for the international structures that cause it, are those who monopolize economic power instead of sharing it, those "who defend them through violence," and all "those who remain passive for fear of the sacrifice and personal risk implied by any courageous and effective action."[33] This institutionalized violence is firmly and dramatically a fact of life in our country.

The Repressive Violence of the State

Alongside institutionalized violence there frequently arises repressive violence—that is to say, the use of violence by the state security forces to contain the aspirations of the majority, violently crushing any signs of protest against the injustices we have mentioned.

This is a real form of violence. It is unjust because through it, the state, acting from above and with all its institutional power, defends the survival of the prevailing socio-economic and political system. It thus prevents the people from having any real chance of using its fundamental right to self-government—the people being the ultimate source of political power to find a new institutional road toward justice.

Seditious or Terrorist Violence

There is another dangerous kind of violence that some call "revolutionary," but which we prefer to describe as sedition or terrorism, for the word "revolutionary" does not always have the pejorative sense we intend here. We are talking of the violence that Paul VI referred to as "the explosive revolutions of despair."[34] This form of violence is usually organized and pursued in the form of guerrilla warfare or terrorism and is wrongly thought of as the final and only effective way to change a social situation. It is a violence that produces and provokes useless and unjustifiable bloodshed, abandons society to explosive tensions beyond the control of reason, and disparages in principle any form of dialogue as a possible means of solving social conflicts.

Spontaneous Violence

We call violence spontaneous when it is an immediate, not a calculated or organized, reaction by groups or individuals when they are violently attacked in the exercise of their own legitimate rights in protests, demonstrations, just strikes, and so on. In being spontaneous and not deliberately sought, this form of violence is marked by desperation and improvisation, and so cannot be an effective way of securing rights or bringing just solutions to conflicts.

Violence in Legitimate Self-Defense

Violence can also be used in legitimate self-defense, when a group or an individual repels by force the unjust aggression to which they have been subjected. This violence seeks to neutralize, or at least to bring under effective control—not necessarily to destroy—an imminent, serious, and unjust threat.

The Power of Nonviolence

To complete this classification of violence it is only right to include the power of nonviolence, which today clearly has its own eager students and followers. The gospel's advice to turn the other cheek to an unjust aggressor, far from being passivity and cowardice, is evidence of great moral strength that can leave an aggressor morally defeated and humiliated. "The Christian can fight, but prefers peace to war," was what Medellín said about this moral force of nonviolence.[35]

The Church's Moral Judgment on Violence

While we were making our *ad limina* visit, the *Osservatore Romano*, the semiofficial mouthpiece of the thinking of the Holy See, published a valuable article entitled "The Democratic State and Violence."[36] We believe it will be helpful to make use of its arguments to bring up to date the church's traditional teaching on violence, of which the bishops at Medellín also spoke.

"Recourse to violence," remarked the paper, "is a sad habit of humankind, and is one of the most obvious signs both of the imperfection that is part of human nature anywhere and under any system, and also of the constant need to start again from the beginning the work of personal perfection and of social improvement to contain and control the instincts that keep on reappearing in human life and lead to the struggle of person against person."

However, despite the fact that the church thinks of any sort of violence as a sign "of the imperfection that is part of human nature," and despite the fact that it continually emphasizes its preference and its love for the ideal of peace, the church makes a different judgment on different types of violence. That judgment can range from prohibition and condemnation to acceptance in certain conditions. We shall now recall some moral principles that should bind the conscience of any honorable person:

1) The church has always condemned violence pursued for its own sake, or wrongly used against any human right, or used as the first and only method to defend and advance a human right. Evil may not be done to promote good.

2) The church allows violence in legitimate defense, but under the following conditions: (a) that the defense does not exceed the degree of unjust aggression (for example, if one can adequately defend oneself with one's hands, then it is wrong to shoot at an aggressor); (b) that the recourse to proportionate violence takes place only after all peaceful means have been exhausted; and (c) that a violent defense should not bring about a greater evil than that of the aggression—namely, a greater violence, a greater injustice.

3) Because it is the root of greater evils, the church has condemned institutionalized violence, repressive violence by governments, terrorist violence, and any form of violence that is likely to provoke further violence in legitimate self-defense.

4) The Medellín document on peace, quoting a text from Paul VI's encyclical *Populorum Progressio,* mentions the legitimacy of "insurrection" in the very exceptional circumstances of an "evident and prolonged 'tyranny

that seriously works against fundamental human rights and seriously damages the common good of the country,' whether it proceeds from one person or from clearly unjust structures.'' It immediately goes on, however, to warn of the danger of occasioning, through insurrection, "new injustices . . . new imbalances . . . new disasters"—all of which would justify a condemnation of insurrection.[37]

5) For this reason too the church has taught—and the present situation gives tragic relevance to this teaching—that a government ought to use all its moral and coercive power to guarantee a truly democratic state, one based on a just economic order, in which justice, peace, and the exercise of every citizen's fundamental rights are defended. So the government ought to strive to make "increasingly hypothetical and unreal the situation in which recourse to force by some individuals or groups can be justified by the existence of a tyrannical regime in which the laws, the institutions, and the government, instead of recognizing and promoting fundamental liberties and other human rights, tread them underfoot, reducing their citizens to the condition of an oppressed people.''[38]

6) The church prefers the constructive dynamism of nonviolence: "The Christian is peaceful and not ashamed of it . . . not simply a pacifist, for he can fight, but prefers peace to war. [The Christian] knows that violent changes in structures would be fallacious, ineffectual in themselves, and not conforming to human dignity.''[39]

Application to the Situation in El Salvador

From this general teaching of the church on violence, we put forward the following applications and guidelines for the situation in our dioceses.

Believe in Peace

We proclaim the supremacy of our faith in peace and we appeal to everyone to make determined efforts to secure it. We cannot place all our trust in violent methods if we are true Christians or even simply honorable persons.

Work for Justice

The peace in which we believe is, however, the fruit of justice: *opus iustitiae pax.* As a simple analysis of our structures shows and as history confirms, violent conflicts will not disappear until their underlying causes disappear. To that extent, as long as the causes of our present distress persist, and as long as the powerful minority persists in its intransigence and refuses to accept even the smallest changes, there will be renewed outbreaks of violence. Further use of repressive violence will unhappily do nothing more than increase the conflict "and make less hypothetical and more real the situation in which recourse to force, in legitimate self-defense, can be justified." We therefore regard as a most urgent task the establishment of social justice.

Every individual has the potential for a healthy degree of aggression. It is an endowment by nature to enable persons to overcome the obstacles in their lives. Courage, boldness, and fearlessness in taking risks are notable virtues and values among our people. They have to be built into society, not to put an end to lives but so that law and justice may be achieved for all, and especially for those who today are most cut off from their benefits.

Reject the Fanaticism of Violence

The cult of violence, which becomes almost a mystique or religion for some individuals and groups, is doing immeasurable harm to our people. They preach violence as the only way to achieve justice and they propound and practice it as a method to bring justice to this country. This pathological mentality makes it impossible to check the spiral of violence and it contributes to the extreme polarization of different groups within our society.

Use Peaceful Means First

Even in legitimate cases, violence ought to be a last resort. All peaceful means must first be tried. We are living in explosive times and there is a great need for wisdom and serenity. We extend a fraternal invitation to all, but especially those organizations that are committed to the struggle for justice, to proceed courageously and honorably, always to maintain just objectives, and to make use of nonviolent means of persuasion rather than put all their trust in violence.

CONCLUSION

Christ's Aggressive Friends

We want to end our reflections by contemplating the splendid vision of peace offered by the transfigured Lord. It is striking that the five persons chosen to accompany the divine savior in that theophany on Mount Tabor were five men of aggressive temperaments and deeds. Moses, Elias, Peter, James, and John can be described in the terms used of Christians at Medellín, "they are not simply pacifists, because they are capable of fighting, but they prefer peace to war." Jesus channeled the aggression of their temperaments toward a rich work of construction, of building up justice and peace in the world.

Let us ask the divine Patron of El Salvador to transfigure in the same way the rich potential of this people with whom he has chosen to share his name. To be his instrument for bringing about this transformation in his people is the reason for the church's existence. That is why we have tried to reaffirm its identity and mission in the light of Christ. Only by being what he wants it to be will the church be able to give more intelligent and effective service and support to the just aspirations of the people.

This Is My Beloved Son: Listen to Him

The voice of the Father on Mount Tabor is the best guarantee there is for the church's mission among women and men, which is to point out Christ as the beloved Son of God and only Savior, and to remind them of the supreme duty of listening to him if they want to be truly free and happy.

Let us listen to him! He has much to say to Salvadorans who look to him with confidence at one of the most tragic and uncertain moments of our history.

We believe we are interpreting his divine word as we now, at the end of this pastoral letter, address ourselves to our compatriots:

To all Catholics, to our brothers and sisters of other churches, and to all persons of good will, we tell you that the Lord is present and that his voice speaks to us also from the misery of our people. Let us hear him: "In so far as you did this to one of the least of these brothers of mine, you did it to me" (Matt. 25:40).

To those who hold economic power, the Lord of the world says that they should not close their eyes selfishly to this situation. They should understand that only by sharing in justice and with those who do not have such power can they cooperate for the good of the country, and will they enjoy the peace and happiness that cannot come from wealth accumulated at the expense of others. *Listen to him!*

To the middle class, who have already assured a minimum of dignity for their lives, Jesus points out that there remain the masses who still do not have enough to live on. He urges them to support the poor and not to be content with simply making their own gains secure. *Listen to him!*

To the professional associations and to the intellectuals, the divine Master, who is the light of all understanding, says that they should use their scientific and technical expertise to investigate the problems of our country and fulfil their professional obligations by looking for solutions to them. They should publicly declare their interest in the welfare of the country and not take refuge in an uncommitted knowledge and science, in a calm seclusion remote from the suffering of the people. *Listen to him!*

To the political parties and popular organizations that have been the main concern of this pastoral letter, Christ, the guide of nations and of history, proclaims that they should learn to put their concern for the poor majority before their own interests, that they should use the political system effectively and with justice, and press honorably and boldly for the beginning of the transformation for which we long. *Obey him!*

To the public authorities, who have the sacred duty of governing for the good of all, Christ, the King of kings and Lord of lords, addresses a call for a sense of truth, justice, and of sincere service to the people. Therefore:

1) Let them pass laws that take into account the majority of Salvadorans who live in the countryside where there are serious problems about land, wages, and medical, social, and educational facilities.

2) Let them genuinely widen the narrow area of political discussion and give formal and real hearing to various political voices in the country;

3) Let them give an opportunity to organize legally to those who have been unjustly deprived of this human right, especially the rural poor.

4) Let them take notice of the people's rejection of the Law for the Defense and Guarantee of Public Order and in its place let them promulgate other laws that in fact guarantee human rights and peace; let them establish adequate channels for civil and political dialogue, so that no one need be afraid to express ideas that may benefit the common good, even if they imply a criticism of the government.

5) Let them stop the terrorization of the rural poor and put an end to the tragic situation of confrontation between *campesinos,* exploiting their poverty to organize some under the protection of the government and persecuting others just because they have organized themselves independently of the government to seek their rights and a reasonable standard of living.

6) Let them win the confidence of the people with such intelligent and generous initiatives as the following: amnesty for all those prisoners who are accused of having violated the Law of the Defense and Guarantee of Public Order; liberty for the great number who have been imprisoned for political reasons, yet who have not been brought before any court, or have disappeared after being captured by the security forces; and a safe return home for all those who have been expelled from the country, or who are unable to return to it, for political reasons.

We believe that all this is the will of the divine Savior of the world and that the Father's command is: *Listen to him!*

The Church Promises to Work and Pray

For its part the church, which in this letter has reasserted its identity and explained its mission, promises to contribute to the general well-being of the country, and pledges its faith in Jesus Christ and its collaboration with all who are ready to make justice reign as the basis of a peace that will bring us real progress.

We turn with filial confidence to the intercession of our queen and mother, the Blessed Virgin of Peace, who is also a Patron of El Salvador. May she obtain for us from the divine Savior of the world an abundance of grace and good will for the transfiguration of our people.

NOTES

1. Medellín, "Peace," §1.
2. See *Evangelii Nuntiandi,* §12.
3. *Gaudium et Spes,* §43.
4. §4.
5. *Gaudium et Spes,* §11.

6. §23.
7. *Gaudium et Spes,* §68.
8. "Justice," §12.
9. *Gaudium et Spes,* §74.
10. §22.
11. *Mater et Magistra,* §125.
12. Ibid., §146.
13. *Gaudium et Spes,* §9.
14. August 1968.
15. See "Justice," §§11-12.
16. Medellín, "Peace," §§20, 27.
17. *Gaudium et Spes,* §42.
18. §§13, 23.
19. *Lumen Gentium,* §1.
20. *Evangelii Nuntiandi,* §58.
21. Ibid.
22. *Gaudium et Spes,* §75.
23. Ibid., §42.
24. "Peace," §27.
25. See *Evangelii Nuntiandi,* §§29-36
26. Ibid., §30.
27. See ibid., §§33-37.
28. Ibid., §32.
29. Ibid., §38.
30. See ibid., §§30, 31.
31. "Peace," §§15, 19.
32. Ibid., §16
33. Ibid., §§17,18.
34. Bogotá, Aug. 23, 1968, quoted in Medellín, "Peace," §17.
35. "Peace," §15.
36. June 23, 1978.
37. "Peace," §19.
38. *Osservatore Romano,* loc. cit.
39. "Peace," §15.

The Church's Mission
amid the National Crisis

Fourth Pastoral Letter of Archbishop Romero,
Feast of the Transfiguration, August 6, 1979

To my beloved brothers and sisters, the priests, religious, and laity of the archdiocese of San Salvador, and to all other Salvadorans of good will: the peace of Jesus Christ, our divine Savior.

A PROVIDENTIAL FEAST

To call ourselves "the Republic of the Savior" (*República de El Salvador*), and each year to celebrate, as our titular feast, the mystery of the transfiguration of our Lord is, for us Salvadorans, a true privilege. It was not only through the piety of Don Pedro de Alvarado that we were baptized with so majestic a title, as the servant of God, Pope Pius XII, reminded us in his outstanding address to our Eucharistic Congress of 1942. It was the providence of God that baptized us, the providence that gives each people its own name, its own place, and its own mission.

To hear each August 6 the voice of the Father in our church's liturgy proclaiming that our patron is none other than "My Son, the beloved," and that our duty is "to listen to him," constitute our most precious historical and religious legacy, and the most effective motivation for our hopes as Christians in El Salvador.

That is why I feel it one of my most important pastoral duties to make real here and now, for the archdiocese that the Lord has given into my charge, this legacy, and to revitalize that motivation in line with the new circumstances in which, each August 6, we find ourselves. In these new circumstances there is one constant: the challenge, made in love, of Christ's transfiguration, which should lead to the transfiguration of our people. This is the traditional challenge of the divine Savior to our homeland and to the church. It is unchangeable—as unchangeable as the truth and revelation of God. It ought to enlighten the changing realities of our history. We must learn to express it in the language spoken by persons of today, as their new needs and their new hopes demand it.

My Three Earlier Pastoral Letters

My first two pastoral letters, in 1977, were inspired by the new situation of the archdiocese of San Salvador. I wrote the first when I replaced the distinguished Archbishop Luis Chávez y González, and it was my letter of introduction. It was a profession of faith, of confidence in the Spirit of the Lord who builds up and encourages, who gives unity and progress to the church even when the human beings who are its members and who direct it change. Under the title "The Easter Church," I wanted to dwell on the circumstances, both liturgical and actual, of lent, passiontide, and Easter that marked that "moment of replacement." In "The Church, the Body of Christ in History" I tried to deepen that same idea of the church and of its service to the world as a prolongation of the mission of Christ. I wrote it for August 6, 1977. I recalled the history—intense, tragic, but also paschal—of my first six months in this beloved see.

And once again for August 6, Bishop Arturo Rivera y Damas of Santiago de María and I last year wrote the pastoral letter "The Church and Popular Political Organizations." We had together made an *ad limina* visit to the unforgettable Pope Paul VI. Our contact with that outstanding pontiff, who so well understood the modern world, had been illuminating, and it inspired us to give a response in faith to the highly unusual political anxieties of our people.

I bless the Lord for the good that that letter brought about. And it goes on bringing it about, for some of our Christian communities have taken it as an outline for reflection. I bless God, too, for the generous, enthusiastic welcome that communities, institutions, and publications elsewhere on this continent and also in Europe have given it. Annnexed to that third letter and published in a separate section there were three studies: "The National Situation in Which the Church Develops Its Mission," "The Word of God and Human Misery," and "The Most Recent Teaching of the Church." I believe that they have fulfilled their purpose by enriching your reflection on the letter.

So I ask you now, keep the three previous letters in mind when studying this one. I will not repeat myself here, but I will take for granted many concepts that have been examined in the earlier ones.

The Reasons for This Fourth Pastoral Letter

On this new celebration of the transfiguration of our Lord, the light of this feast day illumines the new situation in which the country and the archdiocese find themselves. It is right to think of our life in that light.

In El Salvador new kinds of sufferings and outrages have driven our national life along the road of violence, revenge, and resentment. As Puebla describes them, these are the "anxieties and frustrations" which "have been caused by sin, which has very broad personal and social dimensions." But, thanks be to God, we also feel that there are in our nation those "hopes and expectations of our people [that] arise from their deeply religious sense and their richness as human beings."[1]

For its part the church has this year lived through new situations that have made it better able, in accordance with its own nature, to identify with the people in its "anxieties and frustrations, hopes and expectations."

Outstanding among these new events was the Third General Conference of the Latin American Bishops, which took place at Puebla, Mexico, at the beginning of the year. Under the overall theme of "evangelization at present and in the future of Latin America," that "new pentecost" of our continent brought together the rich heritage of our history and urged the church onward into the century to come. At Puebla we were able to call upon "the unique inheritance left to the church by Popes John XXIII and Paul VI," as his holiness Pope John Paul II called it in his first encyclical, *Redemptor Hominis*, when he was discoursing on the new era of "John Pauls." Like the one at Medellín ten years before, the assembly at Puebla was a new step forward for the church on our continent. It was an effort to follow the policy for renewal that Vatican Council II spelled out, and which those two immortal pontiffs of our time brought to a happy conclusion.

In Memory of Paul VI and John Paul II

It is fitting to recall here again, as I did last year, "the eloquent coincidence of Paul VI's death and our own titular feast of the transfiguration." Since his holy death on August 6 last year, how many signs during the pontificates of his successors have drawn attention to the evangelical grandeur of the church! The very tomb of Paul VI, which I visited this year with devout admiration and filial affection and gratitude, highlights a new style of simplicity and humility in the service of the church. I recalled there beside the tomb the warmth of his two hands grasping mine scarcely a year ago, as he told me of his concern and love for our homeland. He recommended that I stand with my people in their demand for justice, so that they might not turn aside into paths of hatred and violence.

And in Rome I likewise received from his holiness John Paul II both understanding and guidance for my difficult pastoral labor, as well as a ratification of my hierarchical communion with him and of my commitment to the people God has entrusted to me. The new pope's attitude, and what he said, pointed to Christ as the only force for complete liberation, for in his name is demanded the highest respect for the dignity and for the freedom of men and women.

Commitment to Puebla and to My Archdiocese

From this bountiful source of the papal magisterium, of the council, and of the Latin American bishops has sprung forth "the spirit of Puebla."

This pastoral letter is intended to be a solemn witness of my acceptance of, and personal commitment to, that spirit. At the same time it will be a call—an urgent call, as the pope wished—to all priests, religious communities, and laity "that in a short time all your ecclesial communities will be informed and suffused with the spirit of Puebla and the guidelines of this historic conference."[2]

Archdiocesan Survey

But "the holy people of God shares also in Christ's prophetic office . . . under the guidance of the sacred teaching authority."[3] And Paul VI of happy memory counseled us "with the help of the Holy Spirit . . . in dialogue with other Christians and all men and women of good will, to discern the options and commitments that are called for in order to bring about the social, political, and economic changes seen in many cases to be urgently needed.[4]

Taking account of the charism of dialogue and consultation, I wanted to prepare for this pastoral letter by undertaking a survey of my beloved priests and of the basic ecclesial communities of the archdiocese. I have been struck yet again by the maturity of the reflection, by the evangelical spirit, by the pastoral creativity, by the social and political sensibility expressed in the large number of replies. I have read them with great care.

Notwithstanding their occasional inaccuracies or doctrinal and pastoral impetuosity, they have served to stimulate that charism of teaching and of discernment with which the Lord has entrusted me. All the disquiet, all the suggestions made, have been taken into account. In thanking you very cordially, I want to repeat my invitation to continue this dialogue and reflection in the way that I began it a year ago when, fully conscious of my limitations, I made "a call to the whole people of God to reflect on these matters in their local churches, with their pastors, and with the universal church, in the light of the gospel and in fidelity to the true identity of the church."[5]

To sum up, then, this pastoral letter is meant to be, as the title suggests, a formal consignment to the archdiocesan church of the Final Document of Puebla. And it is also an attempt, in the light of the theological and pastoral teaching contained in that document, to face up to the disquiet expressed by our local church in the present situation in our country. Backed by the universal magisterium of the church, and by the magisterium of the church on this continent, I believe it possible to give expression to the views of the church of this archdiocese. At a time when it is a serious obligation in conscience on the part of every Salvadoran to contribute ideas and guidelines from within his or her special competence, the views of the church are its specific response, and contribution, to the country in its hour of crisis.

I shall develop my thinking in four parts: (1) the national crisis seen in the light of Puebla; (2) the church's contribution to the liberation of our peo-

ple; (3) light on some concrete problems; (4) Puebla's pastoral approach
applied to the archdiocese.

PART ONE
THE NATIONAL CRISIS IN THE LIGHT OF PUEBLA

Pastoral Criteria

"Pastoral Overview of the Reality that is Latin America" is the title of
the first part of the Puebla Final Document. From the very beginning,
therefore, one is made to understand what are the criteria it uses to analyze
the situation of the world that the church is to evangelize. Pastoral criteria
have also guided the first point in our survey of the archdiocese: the country's present crisis, and prospects for the future.

It is never to be forgotten that the church's mission is in the realm of
religion. It is not in the political, social, or economic realms. But nor is it to
be forgotten that "out of this religious mission itself came a function, a
light, and an energy which can serve to structure and consolidate the human
community according to divine law."[5]

With the Backing of Puebla

Many would have liked Puebla to speak out more concretely on certain
particular situations in Latin American countries. But in its analysis of, and
evangelical judgment on, the situation in Latin America, there is enough to
be found to allow each country or each pastor to draw material relevant to
their own situations, and hence to speak with the collective voice of all the
continent's pastors.

In this pastoral letter, therefore, I want to back up the advice given by the
archdiocese about the crisis in this country with the judgments approved at
Puebla for the whole of Latin America.

Limits of This Analysis

It is not my intention to undertake an exhaustive analysis of the
economic, political, and social structure of El Salvador. A brief survey was
offered last year as a leaflet appended to my third pastoral letter. Nor am I
trying to offer a complete account of what has happened in this country—
the events that have so much preoccupied us this year. I have been required,
in my service to the word of God, to be faithful to the truth and to justice
when I was faced with these events in the course of an event-filled year of
our history. It has also been a great satisfaction to me to have had the opportunity to offer a pastoral service by means of the Legal Aid Bureau and
the Secretariat for the Means of Social Communication of the Archdiocese
in the difficult ups and downs of our communities and families, and of
individuals.

One more observation. Even during the crisis in our country there are
many positive signs, and it would be wrong not to recognize that fact. They

give us solid ground for coming to see that we Salvadorans are capable, by using our intelligence, of finding a peace based on justice. It is not necessary to pay the high price of violence and of blood spilt for the liberation of our people. I give these hopeful signs due credit. They have my admiration. I am encouraged by them. But today it is not my intention to dwell upon them.

Here I am going to emphasize only the negative aspects of our country's crisis which have been pointed out and remarked upon by our communities, because it is these that require our attention. To them I will apply the evangelical judgment that Puebla formulated for such situations.

At the Root of Social Injustice

What Puebla asserted about social injustice throughout the continent is true of El Salvador. It has here a very tragic aspect, and it makes urgent Christian demands: there are today more people than ever living under conditions of great injustice. That "muted cry" of wretchedness that Medellín heard ten years ago, Puebla now describes as "loud and clear, increasing in volume and intensity, and at times full of menace."[6] It calls the characteristics that delineate this situation of injustice "the most devastating and humiliating kind of scourge."[7] They are infant mortality, the housing shortage, health problems, starvation wages, unemployment, malnutrition, no job security, and so on:

This situation of pervasive extreme poverty takes on very concrete faces in real life. In these faces we ought to recognize the suffering features of Christ the Lord, who questions and challenges us. They include:
—the faces of young children, struck down by poverty before they are born, their chance for self-development blocked by irreparable mental and physical deficiencies; and of the vagrant children in our cities who are so often exploited, products of poverty and the moral disorganization of the family;
—the faces of young people, who are disoriented because they cannot find their place in society, and who are frustrated, particularly in marginal rural and urban areas, by the lack of opportunity to obtain training and work;
—the faces of the indigenous peoples, and frequently of the Afro-Americans as well; living marginalized lives in inhuman situations, they can be considered the poorest of the poor;
—the faces of the peasants; as a social group, they live as outcasts almost everywhere on our continent, deprived of land, caught in a situation of internal and external dependence, and subjected to systems of commercialization that exploit them;
—the faces of laborers, who frequently are ill-paid and who have difficulty in organizing themselves and defending their rights;
—the faces of the underemployed and the unemployed, who are dis-

missed because of the harsh exigencies of economic crises, and often because of development-models that subject workers and their families to cold economic calculations;

—the faces of marginalized and overcrowded urban dwellers, whose lack of material goods is matched by the ostentatious display of wealth by other segments of society;

—the faces of old people, who are growing more numerous every day, and who are frequently marginalized in a progress-oriented society that totally disregards people not engaged in production.[8]

Deterioration of the Political Situation

Together with Puebla we must also denounce the serious deterioration of a political situation that institutionalizes injustice. "The participation of citizens in the conduct of their own affairs and destiny" has declined.[9] Governments "look askance at the organizing efforts of laborers, peasants, and the common people; and they adopt repressive measures to prevent such organizing. But this type of control over, or limitation on, activity is not applied to employer organizations, which can exercise their full power to protect their interests.[10]

The graph of violence presented by the Legal Aid Bureau is very striking.[11] Simply from January to June of this year the number of those murdered by various sections of the security forces, the armed forces, and the paramilitary organizations rose to 406. The number of those arrested for political reasons was 307. The discrimination to which Puebla drew attention is borne out, and that makes the statistics even more scandalous. Not a single victim comes from the landowning class, whereas those from among the *campesino* population abound.

Faced with this oppression and repression, there arises naturally what Medellín called the "explosive revolutions of despair."[12] To date, it has accounted for more than 95 victims in this country.[13]

The "spiral of violence" is racing toward hitherto unsuspected levels of cruelty. It is making increasingly problematic the likelihood of resolving the structural crisis peacefully. It has reached the stage where it seems we are engaged in a real civil war. It may be informal and intermittent, but it is nonetheless pitiless and without quarter. It tears apart normal, everyday life, and brings terror into every Salvadoran home.

A special section of the third part of this letter will be devoted to a consideration of the problem of violence.

The Government's Attitude

The government shows itself quite incapable of arresting this country's escalating violence. One suspects, in fact, that it tolerates the bands of armed men who, because of their implacable persecution of opponents of the government, can be regarded as creatures of the government. This contradicts in practice the government's emphatic statements against any sort of violence. It seems to demonstrate, on the contrary, the repression of any political opposition and of any organization of social protest.

The state of siege, which was imposed on May 23 and lasted until July, served in no way at all to allay political murders. Facts and figures about the murdered and those who have disappeared reveal an environment of impunity that favors the proliferation and activities of right-wing gangs of assassins who have worsened the picture of violence in this country.

Puebla's judgment on all this is very eloquent. It denounces "countries . . . where there is frequently no respect for such fundamental human rights. . . . [They] are in the position of permanently violating the dignity of the person."[14] The Latin American bishops mentioned by name these "abuses of power, which are typical of regimes based on force."[15] They put themselves in solidarity with "the anxieties based on systematic or selective repression; it is accompanied by accusations, violations of privacy, improper pressures, tortures, and exiles. There are the anxieties produced in many families by the disappearance of their loved ones, about whom they cannot get any news. There is the total insecurity bound up with arrest and detention without judicial consent. There are the anxieties felt in the face of a system of justice that has been suborned or cowed."[16]

Faced with this worrisome situation, Puebla recalls, in the name of the supreme pontiffs, that "the Church, by virtue of 'an authentically evangelical commitment,' must raise its voice to denounce and condemn these situations, particularly when the responsible officials or rulers call themselves Christians."[17]

Economic and Ideological Bases

Analysts of our economy point out that, if it is to function well, it needs a large and cheap labor force. Producers of coffee, sugar cane, and cotton, which go to make up the agricultural export trade, need unemployed, unorganized *campesinos*. They depend on them for an abundant and cheap labor force to harvest and export their crops.

On the other hand, the agricultural and cattle-raising sector of the economy is the one that pays the most taxes to the public treasury—which is one of the reasons why it has the greatest influence upon the government.

And still today many industrial or transnational corporations base their ability to compete in international markets on what they call "low labor costs," which in reality means starvation wages.

All of this explains the firm opposition of important sectors of capital to initiatives, whether of the people or of the government, that, through trade union organizations, seek to improve the living conditions, or to raise the wages, of the working class. The ruling class, especially the rural elite, cannot allow unions to be organized among either rural or urban laborers so long as, from a capitalist point of view, they believe their economic interests are at risk. This viewpoint makes repression against popular organizations something necessary in order to maintain and increase profit levels, even though it is at the cost of the growing poverty of the working class.

And if we add to this the country's population explosion and its high cost of living, then the growing unrest among workers and the unemployed can be easily understood. Repression of late has been the only kind of answer to protest against "institutionalized violence," and hence it feeds the spiral of violence.

The Puebla document backs up this analysis when it refers to the right to form trade unions:

> In many places labor legislation is either applied arbitrarily or not taken into account at all. This is particularly true in countries where the government is based on the use of force. There they look askance at the organizing efforts of laborers, peasants, and the common people; and they adopt repressive measures to prevent such organizing. But this type of control over, or limitation on, activity is not applied to employer organizations, which can exercise their full power to protect their interests.[18]

This is the right place to draw attention also to the ideology that underlies this unjust repression. I am speaking of the "ideology of national security," which the Puebla document firmly denounces on many occasions. This new political theory and practice lies at the root of this situation of repression and of repressive violence against the most basic rights of the Salvadoran people. But because it is an "absolutization" or idolatry of power, I shall speak of it in the next part of this letter when I explain, as the church's specific contribution to the crisis in this country, its mission of unmasking idolatries and of denouncing false absolutes.

Moral Deterioration

There is an eloquent coincidence between Puebla's thinking and the replies that our communities gave to the survey. Both singled out moral deterioration as the origin of our fearsome decline in social, political, and economic life.

Puebla says explicitly: "Recent years have seen a growing deterioration in the sociopolitical life of our countries. They are experiencing the heavy burden of economic and institutional crises, and clear symptoms of corruption and violence."[19]

As particular causes and expressions of this scandalous moral deterioration in Latin America, Puebla mentions:

> —Individualistic materialism, the supreme value in the eyes of many of our contemporaries . . . and collectivist materialism [which] subordinates the person to the State.

—Consumptionism, with its unbridled ambition to "have more," [which] is suffocating modern human beings in an immanentism that closes them off to the evangelical values of generosity and austerity. . . .

—The deterioriation of basic family values [which] is disintegrating family communion, eliminating shared and responsible participation by all the family members and making them an easy prey to divorce or abandonment. In some cultural groups the woman finds herself in a position of inferiority.

—The deterioration of public and private integrity. . . . We also find frustration and hedonism leading people to such vices as gambling, drug addiction, alcoholism, and sexual licentiousness. . . .

—Information is manipulated by various authorities and groups. This is done particularly through advertising, which raises false expectations, creates fictitious needs, and often contradicts the basic values of our Latin American culture and the Gospel. The improper exercise of freedom in these media leads to an invasion of the privacy of persons, who generally are defenseless.[20]

Our country is, sadly, no exception to these painful symptoms to be found throughout Latin America. Our survey produced an even more horrific inventory of infidelities to, and betrayals of, ethical and Christian values, and even of our political Constitution itself. For example:

In Public Administration
• The infidelity of the Supreme Court and of other courts of justice to their noble mission of fulfilling, and ensuring the fulfillment of, the constitution of a democratic country, showing themselves, on the contrary, to be feeble instruments at the beck and call of a regime based on the use of force.
• As a result, the prostitution of justice and the destruction of the freedom and the dignity of men and women.
• The fact that so many fearful crimes go unpunished, a good number of them carried out either openly or, it is popularly reported, in civilian disguise by the security forces.
• Indifference to the anguish of so many families who seek liberty for, or, at least, news of, their loved ones who have disappeared into the power of civil authorities.
• The ineffectiveness of so many constitutional appeals for the right of habeas corpus, a tragic mockery of the guarantees of such an appeal.
• Silent connivance at so many breaches of the constitution or at other administrative maneuvers that promote the interests of privileged groups or individuals, despite the fact that these interests are harmful to the interests of the common good.
• Manipulation of the popular will in the democratic electoral process.
• Discreditable propaganda for, and imposition of, antibirth policies that

are practically "castrating" our people and are undermining their reserves of morality.

In Private Life

• Maneuvers by which many employers repress the rights of their workers, or buy the impartiality of trade union leaders.
• Unjust handling of some strikes or of the rightful demands of trade unions or workers.
• The low, even nonexistent, output by some employees and workers neglectful of their duties; or the demand for further payments ("tips" or "bribes") for services, or for work that has already been paid for in wages.
• Taking advantage of administrative positions either for one's own benefit or for the benefit of one's relatives and friends.
• The salting away, or misuse, of public or private funds by means of fictitious reports and expenses, and other pretexts.
• Indecent bargaining with the dignity of another by a variety of means, such as demanding sexual favors in return for providing work, or by setting up lucrative centers for vice, such as cafés, "motels," "guest houses," and every kind of disguised brothels for the human slave traffic in prostitution and illegal drug-taking.
• Manipulation of the means of social communication by way of pressure or by bribes to defame persons, or pervert the truth in other ways.
• Modern forms of blackmail, such as kidnapings, threats from real or imaginary secret organizations—sometimes with the suspicion of official complicity.

Our moral decline is self-evident. On every side we find that what our Lord called "the mystery of iniquity" has taken over. It is the church's pastoral duty not to cease in denouncing this reign of sin, and urgently to appeal to the personal responsibility of each of us, and to each social and family group, and especially to individuals or groups in authority who, directly or indirectly, benefit from this state of affairs. For it is these last who have in their hands the most effective means of remedying this situation.

The Crisis within the Church

In my earlier letters I drew attention to many of the positive things one might say about the church. It is therefore unnecessary to insist upon them here, but rather to encourage perseverance and strenuous efforts for improvement. Furthermore the fourth part of this letter will offer pastoral approaches for us to go on building up our archdiocese in line with the suggestions and the ideals of Vatican II and of the Medellín and Puebla assemblies of the Latin American Episcopal Council.

It is, however, necessary to recall today—also in the light of Puebla—the denunciations and criticism that draw attention to our own failings as the human components of the church. For at a time of national crisis those of us who feel it our duty to denounce the sin that lies at the root of the crisis ought also to be ready to be criticized so as to bring about our own conversion and to build up a church that can be, for our own people, what Vatican II defines as "the national sacrament of salvation."[21]

The same council guides us in this examination of our consciences when it states frankly, and with all humility, that "the Church, embracing sinners in her bosom, is at the same time holy and always in need of being purified, and incessantly pursues the path of penance and renewal."[22]

According to the reflection undertaken in our communities, there are three main failings within the church that call for conversion. They are: disunity; failure of renewal and adaptation; disregard for the criteria laid down in the gospel.

Disunity

The most obvious of the sins to which our survey drew attention is the disunity within a church that ought to have unity as a mark of its authenticity. Our communities pointed out that when this disunity affects the hierarchy itself and the clergy, there results even greater confusion among the people of God. This is indeed true, and faced with this evidence one can only be repentant, reflect, and exhort.

What is needed is a confession of guilt and a plea for forgiveness, together with the sincere intention to seek out, with each other's help, ways toward unity, and the supernatural courage to follow them.

The way to explain this sad phenomenon of disunity, and to establish a basis for conversion to unity, is to consider that the lack of unity within the church is nothing else than an echo of the division that exists all about it— the division within the society in which it lives and works. It is the human element in the church. In today's society there is a polarization of political forces from the extreme right to the extreme left. Groups and organizations either support one another, or reject one another totally.

Church members, not excluding the hierarchy, are forced to operate in this environment. They run the risk of siding with one or other polarization if they fail to keep in mind their vocation, and their evangelical mission, defined by Puebla as "a preferential option for the poor."

This preference for the poor, which the gospel imposes upon Christians, neither polarizes nor divides. It is a force for unity because it does "not propose to exclude the other representatives of the social corpus in which we live . . . we invite all, regardless of class, to accept and take up the cause of the poor as if they were accepting and taking up their own cause, the cause of Christ himself: 'I assure you, as often as you did it for one of my least brothers, you did it for me.' "[23]

This preferential option for the poor, understood in the sense of the gospel, can alone be the key to this crisis of our unity. The Puebla document here draws attention to the cause of our internal divisions: "Not all of us in the Latin American Church have committed ourselves sufficiently to the poor. We are not always concerned about them, or in solidarity with them. Service to them really calls for constant conversion and purification among all Christians. That must be done if we are to achieve fuller identification each day with the poor Christ and our own poor."[24]

Out of this reflection on our own sin of disunity flows the exhortation that we should make the effort to convert ourselves to that common ideal. But an interior conversion would be pointless were there not at the same time, as Puebla teaches, "a radical conversion to justice and love . . . transforming from within those structures of a pluralistic society that respect and promote the dignity of the human person, and that provide persons with the possibility of achieving their supreme vocation: communion with God and with each other."[25]

Inasmuch as we have not yet achieved this beautiful unity among all within the church, it is only proper to exhort everyone to maintain a calm Christian maturity so that we are not scandalized by the sin within the church, and so that all will do what they can in their Christian lives even though others do not do likewise. As far as our archdiocese is concerned, we are ready to continue structuring our pastoral life along the lines Puebla put forward as the authentic way to this unity: the preferential option for the poor. This is the demand the gospel makes upon us, and unity is authentic only when it is built up on the basis of the gospel. This will also be the best contribution the archdiocese can offer to the changes needed in the country.

Failure to Renew and Adapt

Both at Medellín and at Puebla the bishops of Latin America tried to interpret for our continent the concern the council expressed about the age in which we live: to bring the church up to date, and to learn today's language in order to pass its message on. Even more, Puebla's theme looks towards the future: "evangelization at present and in the future of Latin America." It frankly states:

> Until recently our continent had not been touched or swallowed up by the dizzying flood of cultural, social, economic, political, and technological changes in the modern age. At that time the weight of tradition helped the communication of the Gospel. What was taught from the pulpit was zealously welcomed in the home and the school; and it was safeguarded and sustained by the social pressure of the surrounding milieu. Today nothing like that happens. The faith proposed by the Church is accepted or rejected with much more freedom and with a notably critical-minded sense. Even the peasants, who previously were isolated from contact with civilization to a large extent, are now acquiring this same critical sense. This is due to the ready contact with the present-day world that is afforded them . . . it is also due to the consciousness-raising efforts of pastoral agents.[26]

With an identical point of view and conviction, several communities in the archdiocese lament the difficult, anti-apostolic attitude displayed by some priests, religious communities, and other pastoral workers who reject the efforts toward renewal and adaptation that our pastoral strategy is promoting in obedience to the guidelines mentioned above.

Several of the answers to the survey analyze the high levels of unrest and agitation that move our people in the direction of social and political changes in the country. "The church," to quote one of them verbatim, "has to interpret for, and to accompany, this people as it struggles for freedom; if not, in the course of time it will be marginalized. With or without the church the changes will take place, but by its very nature its duty is to be present in the midst of these changes, which are delineating the kingdom of God."

This criticism of the internal workings of the church draws the attention of pastoral workers to another serious motive for reflection and conversion. It urges upon all of us who work in the apostolate, and especially upon priests and religious communities who, by their vocation, profession, and mission, most intimately belong to the life and mission of the church, to make determined efforts toward our own improvement so that we can always be abreast of the modern church. It is in this spirit, most recently expressed at Puebla, that we are trying to conduct the apostolate in our own archdiocese. The inexplicable opposition or lack of comprehension—an object of criticism—results, in our present circumstances, in a regrettable lack of that "communion and involvement" that the spirit of Puebla so much insists upon.

Adulteration of Gospel Criteria

To lose sight of, or to alter, Christian principles constitutes another sin or danger within the church. When making a noble effort to renew or to adapt our church for a membership now highly politicized, one can fall into the sin that is at the opposite extreme from the one we have just pointed out— namely, the political or ideological adulteration of the faith and of Christian criteria. Those Christians who, motivated by the faith, take up concrete political options are in particular danger of this sin.

I am not going to develop further this topic, which is of enormous interest for Christian communities, because I have already treated it sufficiently in my third pastoral letter. That letter focused precisely upon the relationship between the church and popular organizations. I recommend that those guidelines be kept well in mind. Far from losing their pertinence, they are daily more necessary for a Christian in El Salvador.

For the rest, there will be two places in this fourth pastoral letter where guidelines will be offered on this subject: when treating, in part three, the danger of "absolutizing" an organization and, in part four, on the need for an "apostolate of following," to accompany Christians in their political options—without the church thereby losing its identity and Christians their faith.

PART TWO
THE CHURCH'S CONTRIBUTION
TO THE PROCESS OF LIBERATING OUR PEOPLE

If the Puebla document, which is the basis of our reflection, supports the pastoral focus upon the situation here in El Salvador, it invites us also to search out, in a sincere spirit of service to the nations of Latin America, the specific contribution our local church can offer El Salvador at this time of crisis. Here I am also taking into account the valuable suggestions made by our Christian communities.

What, then, is the contribution which, in the spirit of Puebla, the arch-diocese can offer to the process of liberating our people? I think it can be understood under the following headings. I shall develop them in the course of this part two: the Church's own identity; integral evangelization; a solid doctrinal orientation; denunciation of error and sin, with a view to conversion; unmasking the idolatries of society; promoting integral liberation; pressing for far-reaching structural changes; sharing life and the gospel with both the ordinary people and the ruling class.

The Church's Own Identity

This is the prime contribution our church ought to make to the life of this country: to be itself. This is what I call its own identity.

I have said, over and over again, that the whole effort of the apostolate in this archdiocese ought to be turned to this before all else, to building up our church. Despite all the clashes and all the opposition, the church is not looking for opposition. It does not want to clash with anybody. It wants only to build up toward the great affirmation of God and his kingdom. It will clash only with those who oppose God and his kingdom.

The church wants to offer no other contribution than that of the gospel. It has no purely political contribution to make, nor any merely human skill to offer. Quite truthfully, the church is interested only in offering the country the light of the gospel for the full salvation and betterment of men and women, a salvation that also involves the structures within which Salvadorans live, so that, rather than get in their way, the structures can help them live out their lives as children of God.

The church is well aware that anything it can contribute to the process of liberation in this country will have originality and effectiveness only when the church is truly identified as church—that is to say, only when it is most clearly that which Christ wants it to be at this particular hour of the nation's history.

It is in this sense that one has to understand the ceaseless exhortation of John Paul II: the church has no need to politicize itself in order to make its saving contribution to the world. It is also in this sense that I believe one ought to interpret certain fears expressed at Puebla, when there was talk of misinterpretations of Medellín, and concepts were pointed to that could make a theology of liberation ambiguous.

Because it is not turning itself into a political power, and because it is not doing anything else that might be alien to its nature and to its mission, the church as church can contribute something fundamental to the betterment of this country. As Paul VI warned, should the liberation the church is preaching and promoting be reduced "to the dimensions of a simply temporal project . . . to a man-centered goal . . . its activity . . . would become initiatives of the political or social order. But if this were so, the Church would lose its fundamental meaning. Its message of liberation would no longer have any originality and would easily be open to monopolization and manipulation by ideological systems and political parties. It would have no more authority to proclaim freedom as in the name of God."[27]

But neither can we call wrong—a sin of the church against its own identity—the effort it makes to come close to the real problems that affect human beings and that drive it to commit itself to them. The contrary would be sinful: to be so concerned with its own identity that this preoccupation gets in the way of its closeness to the world. As Pope John Paul II has insisted, men and women are the pathways on which the church seeks to fulfill its mission.

The church's mission is transcendent. As Vatican II teaches, it "is not identified in any way with the political community nor bound to any political system. It is at once a sign and a safeguard of the transcendent character of the human person."[28] But this is not a transcendence that loses hold of what is human. It is by transcending the human being from within that the church finds, and brings into being, the kingdom of God that Jesus promised, and which he continues to proclaim by means of the church's work.

Integral Evangelization

In order to safeguard its own identity, the church offers first and foremost, as its specific service to the world, its work of evangelization. That is why we pastors, when we were gathered together at Puebla, said to Latin America that we would concentrate our deliberations on "evangelization at present and in the future of Latin America."

At the root of our reflection there was always that Magna Carta of modern evangelization, the apostolic exhortation *Evangelii Nuntiandi* of his holiness Pope Paul VI, which was, in its turn, the fruit of the 1974 world synod of bishops. "We want to confirm," said the fathers at that synod, "once again, that the task of evangelizing all men and women constitutes the essential mission of the church."

And this is the case because at the root of evangelization is the person and the mission of Jesus himself. He himself is "the gospel of God" and the "first and greatest preacher of the gospel." From him sprang the church evangelized, which in turn became the church evangelizing when he sent it out, identifying himself with it so that it might carry his salvation to all peoples.[29] "Evangelizing is in fact the grace and vocation proper to the Church, its deepest identity. It exists in order to evangelize, that is to say in order to preach and teach, to be the channel of the gift of grace, to reconcile sinners with God, and to perpetuate Christ's sacrifice in the Mass, which is the memorial of his death and glorious Resurrection."[30]

Complex Mission

Evangelization, then, taken in its full sense, is the whole of the divine mission of Jesus and his church. Given the complexity of this mission, there is a danger of reducing it simply to some elements "of preaching, of catechesis, of conferring baptism and the other sacraments." But "any partial and fragmentary definition which attempts to render the reality of evangelization in all its richness, complexity, and dynamism does so only at the risk of impoverishing it and even of distorting it."[31]

In evangelization, therefore, there is "the essential content, the living substance, which cannot be modified or ignored without seriously diluting the nature of evangelization itself." But "there are certainly many secondary elements" in evangelization, and "their presentation depends greatly on changing circumstances."[32]

In keeping with that rich modern theology of evangelization, and adapting it to our continent, we bishops gathered at Puebla proclaimed that, "evangelized by the Lord in his Spirit, we are sent out to bring this Good News to all our brothers and sisters, especially to the poor and the forgotten. This evangelizing task leads us to complete conversion and communion with Christ in the Church. It will impregnate our culture. It will incite us to the authentic improvement of our communities. And it will make us a critical-minded, guiding presence in the face of the ideologies and policies that condition the fate of our nations."[33]

Liberating Evangelization

What, then, will be the evangelization our archdiocese ought to offer this country so that, through it, the full force for liberation with which our divine Redeemer has endowed it may run its course? As has been said, to limit it to just a few elements would be to betray this mission of our church at a time when its contribution ought to open up a unique hope for the entirety of our people.

Generally speaking, in our circumstances this danger of reductionism as far as evangelization is concerned can take two forms. Either it can stress only the transcendent elements of spirituality and human destiny, or it can go to the other extreme, selecting only those immanent elements of a kingdom of God that ought to be already beginning on this earth.

The evangelization our archdiocese has to offer, as the church's specific contribution to our homeland in its crisis, must not fall victim to either of those two forms of reductionism. It ought to be inspired by the balanced guidelines laid down this century by Vatican II, so clearly presented and lived out by our modern popes, and adapted to our continent by the two great meetings of bishops at Medellín and Puebla.

Seen in that light, the suggestions put forward by our Christian communities have stressed certain aspects of evangelization of which our people stand in most need. With the cooperation of all, this archdiocese is ready to offer its help, with great pastoral love, and despite persecution and misunderstanding. These aspects of evangelization are treated in the remaining six major subsections of part two of this pastoral letter.

A Sound Doctrinal Orientation

The first element in evangelization is its content: "We now wish to shed the light of the truth that makes us free (John 8:32) on our compelling pastoral concern. It is not a truth that we possess as something of our own. It comes from God."[34]

And so at Puebla we laid down the criteria that are to guide us as pastors and teachers of the church when we are addressing the peoples of Latin America. The content of evangelization is the truth that God has revealed, and that we human beings accept through faith. How necessary this "pillar of truth" is in an atmosphere of lies and insincerity, where the truth is itself enslaved to the interests of wealth and of power. "But the word of God is not in chains," and so long as we believe in that truth we are free.

To teach the truths of the gospel, and by means of them to cast light on our own situation so as to bring it closer to God's truth and not to human sophistries, is the most important service that the church can render to this country. Hence it is important that not only our pastoral ministers but all who have influence upon society and upon the family should know this truth well, and spread its light about them.

The Truth about Christ, about the Church, and about Humankind

Applying to Latin America the wide content of evangelization, his holiness John Paul II drew attention to the threefold doctrinal synthesis incorporated in the Puebla document. These are the three "central truths of evangelization": the truth about Christ, about the church, and about humankind.

Christ, our hope, is in our midst as the Father's envoy, animating the Church with his Spirit and offering his word and his life to people today in order to lead them to full and complete liberation.

The Church, a mystery of communion, the People of God in the service of human beings, continues to be evangelized through the ages and to bring the Good News to all.

For the Church, Mary is a cause for joy, and a source of inspiration

because she is the star of evangelization and the Mother of the Latin
American peoples.

Human beings, by virtue of their dignity as the image of God, merit a
commitment from us in favor of their liberation and their total fulfillment in Christ Jesus. Only in Christ is their more intimate reality fully
known. Hence we, being pastors, speak to human beings and proclaim to
them the joyful news that humanity has been assumed and exalted by the
very Son of God. For he chose to share with human beings the joys, labors, and sufferings of this life and the heritage of eternal life.[35]

Social Teaching

The pope also reminded us at Puebla of the importance that the study of
the church's social teaching ought to have for us today: "When injustices
increase and the gap between rich and poor widens distressingly, then the
social doctrine of the Church—in a form that is creative and open to the
broad areas of the Church's presence—should be a valuable tool for formation and action." He counseled us "to place responsible confidence in this
social doctrine, even though some people try to sow doubts and lack of
confidence in it; to study it seriously; to try to apply it; to teach it and be
loyal to it; in children of the Church, all this guarantees the authenticity of
their involvement in delicate and demanding social tasks, and of their efforts on behalf of the liberation or advancement of their fellow human
beings."[36]

Denunciation of Error and of Sin

As a logical consequence of the proclamation of truth, love, and the holiness of the kingdom of God, evangelization has the mission of denouncing
every lie, every injustice, every sin that destroys God's plan. The purpose of
this denunciation is not negative. It has a prophetic character. It seeks the
conversion of those who commit the sin. "God does not want the death of
the sinner but that he be converted and live." The church itself cannot stand
aside from this need for denunciation and conversion. We preach it and we
want it for ourselves as church, in order to demand it of society. For the
"faith denounces everything that is opposed to the construction of the
Kingdom. This entails necessary and sometimes painful breaks"[37] and persecution.[38]

John Paul II has again reminded us of this inescapable mission of the
church:

This service of truth as a participation in the prophetic service of Christ is
an obligation upon the church. It finds itself fulfilling it in very diverse
historical contexts. It is necessary that injustice be given its correct desig-
nation: the exploitation of some human beings by others, the exploitation of a people by the state, by institutions, by the structure of economic

systems, or of regimes that sometimes operate callously. It is necessary to give the correct name to every social injustice, to every act of discrimination or violence inflicted on human beings, whether on persons themselves, or their spirit, or their consciences, or their convictions.[39]

Unmasking the Idolatries of Our Society

Adhering to the demands of the same prophetic denunciation and conversion, the church reminds us that making any created thing into an absolute is an offense against the one Absolute and Creator, because it erects and serves an idol, which it attempts to put in the place of God himself.

As well as offending God, every absolutization disorients, and ultimately destroys, human beings. It is the vocation of human beings to raise themselves to the dignity of the children of God and to participate in God's divine life. This transcendence of human beings is not an escape from problems here on earth, still less is it an opium that distracts them from their obligations in history. On the contrary, by virtue of this transcendent destiny people have the capacity to always remain critical vis-à-vis the events of history. It gives them a powerful inspiration to reach out to ever higher goals. Social forces should harken to the saving voice of Christ and of true Christians, cease their questioning, and open themselves to the values of the one and only Absolute. When a human value is turned into an absolute and endowed, whether in theory or in practice, with a divine character, human beings are deprived of their highest calling and inspiration. The spirit of the people is pushed in the direction of a real idolatry, which will only deform and repress it.

Among the evils that afflict El Salvador, I find that there are three idolatries, or absolutes, that the church ought to unmask in the name of the one God and Lord.

The Absolutization of Wealth and Private Property

The absolutization of wealth holds out to persons the ideal of "having more" and to that extent reduces interest in "being more," whereas the latter should be the ideal for true progress, both for the people as such and for every individual. The absolute desire of "having more" encourages the selfishness that destroys communal bonds among the children of God. It does so because the idolatry of riches prevents the majority from sharing the goods that the Creator has made for all, and in the all-possessing minority it produces an exaggerated pleasure in these goods.

As for the absolutization of private property, John Paul II, speaking at Puebla, gave voice to the contrary opinion of the traditional and of the modern teaching of the church. For "this voice of the Church, echoing the voice of human conscience, . . . deserves and needs to be heard in our own day as well, when the growing affluence of a few . . . parallels the growing poverty of the masses. . . . The Church's teaching [is] that there is a *social mortgage* on all private property. . . . This Christian, evangelical principle will lead to a more just and equitable distribution of goods."[40]

Absolutizing wealth and private property brings about the absolutizing of political, social, and economic power, without which it is impossible for the rich to preserve their privileges, even at the cost of their own human dignity. In our country this idolatry is at the root of structural and repressive violence. In the final analysis, it is the cause of a great part of our economic, social, and political underdevelopment.

This is the capitalism condemned by the church at Puebla, following the teaching of recent popes and of Medellín. Whoever reads these documents would say that they are describing a situation in our country that only selfishness, ignorance, or servility could defend.

The Absolutization of National Security

I have already drawn attention in the first part of this letter to the doctrine or ideology of national security as the ideological foundation for repression. Puebla frequently denounced this new form of idolatry, which has already been installed in many Latin American countries. In this country it has its own particular way of working, but substantially it is identical with that described at Puebla: "In many instances the ideologies of National Security have helped to intensify the totalitarian or authoritarian character of governments based on the use of force, leading to the abuse of power and the violation of human rights. In some instances they presume to justify their positions with a subjective profession of Christian faith."[41]

By virtue of this ideology, the individual is placed at the total service of the state. His or her political participation is suppressed, and this leads to an unequal participation in the results of development. Peoples are put into the hands of military elites, and are subjected to policies that oppress and repress all who oppose them, in the name of what is alleged to be total war. The armed forces are put in charge of social and economic structures under the pretext of the interests of national security. Everyone not at one with the state is declared a national enemy, and the requirements of national security are used to justify "assassinations, disappearances, arbitrary imprisonment, acts of terrorism, kidnapings, acts of torture . . . [all] indicate a complete lack of respect for the dignity of the human person."[42]

The interests and advantages of the few are thus turned into an absolute. This absolutization becomes a mystique—as if the national security regime, which attempts to give itself a good public image by "a subjective profession of Christian faith,"[43] were the only, or the best, "defender of the Christian civilization of the West."[44] This perverts the noble function of the armed forces. Instead of serving true national interests, they become the guardians of the interests of the oligarchy, thus furthering their own ideological and economic corruption. Something similar is happening to the security forces. They, instead of caring for civil order, have turned themselves basically into an organization for repressing political dissidents. And

finally, the high command unconstitutionally changes the political procedures that ought to decide democratically the country's course.

The judgment merited by the ideology of national security has, for Christians, been clearly expressed at Puebla: it is "not compatible with the Christian vision of the human being as responsible for carrying out a temporal
project, and to its vision of the State as the administrator of the common
good."[45]

The omnipotence of these national security regimes, the total disrespect
they display towards individuals and their rights, the total lack of ethical
consideration shown in the means that are used to achieve their ends, turn
national security into an idol, which, like the god Molech, demands the
daily sacrifice of many victims in its name.

The legitimate security that the state ought to seek for its members is
cruelly perverted, for in the name of national security "the insecurity of the
individual becomes institutionalized."[46]

The Absolutization of Organizations

There is a third absolute, typical of the present situation in this country. I
am speaking of the absolutization of an organization. This is a trap into
which many members of popular organizations fall. They make their own
organization the supreme value, and subordinate everything else to it.

This organizational absolutization differs from the other two just mentioned. They are fundamentally evil, as has been indicated. The absolutization of an organization, on the other hand, has a good side to it because it
arises from among the people, as it puts to use its right of forming organizations for the purpose, at least in theory, of attaining the good of that same
people. But in practice they become so fanatical that the interests of the
people are no longer their chief concern, but the interests of the group
or organization. Here are some of the evils that flow from this new idolatry:

• Their activities become too political, as if the political dimension were the
only, or even the main, element in the lives of *campesinos*, workers, teachers, students, and other members who go to make them up.

• They try to subordinate the specific mission of trade union, social, and
religious organizations to their own political objectives. They try to manipulate the church, its worship, its magisterium, its teaching mission, and so
on, so that they serve the political and strategic aims of a political organization.

• The leaders of an organization, by making an absolute out of the political
problem of achieving power, can in practice lose interest in other real problems, and can misunderstand the ideological criteria that underlie them,
despite the fact that these are the very problems and criteria that concern the
majority of the people—for example, some of their more immediate socio-
economic needs, or the Christian principles of the members of the organizations. Another example would be the choice of a strategy that could

needlessly offend religious sensitivities (taking over churches, for example).
• They can become so highly sectarian that their partisanship gets in the
way of establishing dialogue or alliances with another type of organization
also fighting for justice.
• The most serious kind of this fanaticism is that which changes what might
be a force for the good of the people into an obstacle in the way of achieving
that same good, and into an obstacle to profound change.

I put forward a more detailed account of the evangelical service the
church could offer to popular organizations in my third pastoral letter.
They included defense of the right to organize, support for what was just in
their demands, support of Christians who joined them, and denunciation of
their possible mistakes and injustices, such as the mistake of turning them
into absolutes, as I have just been saying. And above all, the church turns
its entire effort for the liberation of the people toward the sole absolute,
that definitive liberation toward which all strivings for justice ought to converge: the liberation in Christ, which sets sin aside and, while promoting
liberation on earth, does not lose sight of the people's final vocation to the
one and only Absolute.

An organization runs the risk of turning itself into an absolute and of
becoming an idol when atheistic ideologies, or the limited interests of the
group, cause it to lose sight of those wide, transcendent perspectives, and
lose hold of the ideal of the country's common good.

In this context guidance has to be given about the possible presence, or
infiltration, of Marxism in El Salvador's popular organizations. But I prefer to defer this topic until I discuss some special problems in the third part
of this pastoral letter.

Promoting Integral Human Liberation

Another contribution that our archdiocese, in the name of evangelization, is offering to this country is its teaching on human nature and the drive
for integral human advancement. Pope Paul VI explicitly taught that there
is an inseparable link between evangelization and human advancement.[47]
The pope based the inseparability of these two tasks upon anthropological,
theological, and evangelical arguments.

These arguments guided us at Puebla in urging that the exigencies of the
integral betterment of human beings be observed. Thus Puebla added its
weight to the teaching of John Paul II when we recalled that as bishops we
were "defenders and promoters of dignity," because, as he said, the church
"does not have need to have recourse to ideological systems in order to
love, defend, and collaborate in the liberation of the human being. At the
center of the message of which the Church is the trustee and herald, it finds
inspiration for acting in favor of brotherhood, justice, and peace, and
against all forms of domination, slavery, discrimination, violence, attacks
on religious liberty, and aggression against human beings and whatever
attacks life."[48]

The Truth about Humankind

This difficult, little understood task of the integral advancement of human beings has its basis in "the truth about humanity" that Puebla, guided by the pope, saw as one of the three theological foundations of the evangelization of Latin America.

Humanity, seen from the perspective of Christ and of the church, could be wholly summed up in that rich message of John Paul and of the Puebla assembly: "With what veneration an apostle of Christ ought to pronounce the word 'man,' " exclaimed the present pontiff when, on October 22, 1978, he began his worldwide pastorate. According to his first encyclical, "this human being is the primary route that the church must travel in fulfilling its mission: the human being is the primary and fundamental way for the church."[49] He discussed human beings concretely, in history, as they live out their lives today,[50] a life and existence that are threatened,[51] whose "situation in the modern world [is] far removed from the objective demands of the moral order, from the exigencies of justice and, still more, from social love."[52]

The Peoples of Latin America

We, the bishops gathered at Puebla, looked toward the people of Latin America. We wanted to begin our evangelical and ecclesial reflections by taking account of the actual situation of millions of our compatriots so that we might find, in that situation, what it was that God and the people are asking of the church today. "The truth is that there is an ever increasing distance between the many who have little and the few who have much. The values of our culture are threatened. Fundamental human rights are being violated."[53]

This is the primary fact about the situation of the peoples in Latin America. The church must direct and convert itself to this, if it is to fulfill its mission of evangelization. And what it offers to its Latin American brothers and sisters is that which is most typically its own, that which is most in accordance with the gospel: it offers them human betterment and plenary liberation in Christ: "We have neither silver nor gold, but what we have we give you! In the name of Jesus of Nazareth, rise and walk."[54]

This is the integral evangelization for which the church goes on striving, in the bitter context of a people which suffers, which lives under constant threat, yet in the hope of the liberation that the divine Savior wants for all, and for which he lived, worked, died, and rose again. That is what our archdiocese understands as proclaiming and building the kingdom of God among the Salvadoran people.

Faith with a Historical Dimension

This ideal brings together all the dimensions of human reality, excluding none, and it does not reduce the faith merely to the improvement of the social or political order. Today, however, we should stress the social and historical dimensions of this liberation, as Puebla requested:

Confronted with the realities that are part of our lives today, we must learn from the Gospel that in Latin America we cannot truly love our fellow human beings, and hence God, unless we commit ourselves on the personal level and, in many cases, on the structural level as well, to serving and promoting the most dispossessed and downtrodden human groups and social classes, with all the consequences that will entail on the plane of temporal realities.[55]

The church, then, would betray its own love for God and its fidelity to the gospel if it stopped being "the voice of the voiceless," a defender of the rights of the poor, a promoter of every just aspiration for liberation, a guide, an empowerer, a humanizer of every legitimate struggle to achieve a more just society, a society that prepares the way for the true kingdom of God in history. This demands of the church a greater presence among the poor. It ought to be in solidarity with them, running the risks they run, enduring the persecution that is their fate, ready to give the greatest possible testimony to its love by defending and promoting those who were first in Jesus' love.

This preference for the poor, I must repeat, does not mean an unfair discrimination between the various classes of society. It is an invitation to all "regardless of class, to accept and take up the cause of the poor as if they were accepting and taking up their own cause, the cause of Christ himself: 'I assure you, as often as you did it for one of my least brothers, you did it for me.' "[56]

The basic ecclesial communities are a very effective pastoral method for achieving this evangelical presence of the church among our people and to bring about this integral betterment of human beings. I mention this providential instrument here only to recommend it to pastoral ministers, for I shall spend more time on it in the fourth part of this letter.

The Need for Profound Structural Changes

To preach and to encourage the urgent need for profound structural changes in the social and political life of our country is another contribution that the pastoral mission of the church can make. The church sincerely believes that without such changes the structural bases of our whole malaise will remain. The full liberation of the Salvadoran people, not to mention personal conversions, demands a thorough change in the social, political, and economic system. The government has itself recognized this, and has said so many times. It is the continued demand of political groups—those recognized by law, and those not. The perspective of the church is naturally one that stems from its own evangelical identity, and in line with the documents both of the universal magisterium and the magisterium of the bishops on this continent.

A Healthy Unrest

I realize that it is difficult, that it gives rise to conflict, to talk about structural changes with those who benefit from the old structures. It is perfectly true that there is a reactionary, extreme-right wing. But there are also men and women aware of the need for change, groups actively committed to working for change, working for a situation that favors the whole population of El Salvador. There is, then, a healthy unrest. But this itself requires of the church a greater subtlety in its judgments. The means of bringing about change are many and varied, and the Christian must take great care in choosing critically from among them, because not all merit the same judgment.

There are groups that would be content with small steps forward or minor reforms. There are other groups that want to bring about change rapidly, radically, and violently. There are differences in detail among these last mentioned groups, but in general their tactic is to sharpen the contradictions in society so as to bring on an intolerable situation.

Profound, Urgent, but Nonviolent Changes

The church favors urgent and profound social changes. But as it was also said at Medellín, "violent changes in structures would be fallacious, ineffectual in themselves and not conforming to the dignity of men."[57] The church therefore invites all who put their trust in violent means of change to reflect on the following points:

• Before any violent defense of the common good, or of human rights, can be undertaken, all nonviolent methods must be tried. The church urges, therefore, that every effort be made for dialogue, reasoning, and persuasion.

• It has to be remembered that many violent political acts serve only to provoke an overwhelming response from the state's repressive machinery, thereby generating great harm and suffering for the innocent, and for those unable to look after themselves.

• Therefore, instead of simply criticizing and rendering ineffective others' efforts to bring about peaceful change, it is better that group fanaticism— the belief that one group alone has the capacity to bring about all the changes we need—be overcome. Groups would then open themselves up to the possibility of dialogue and political negotiation so as to achieve the hoped for common objective by rational means. When our homeland is in danger, its needs must come before every party or group interest.

Sharing with the People

Without denying its own identity—on the contrary, being most itself— the church offers the country the service of companionship and guidance in its aspirations to be a free and liberating people. In this way it can carry out the mandate that Jesus gave it to be light, salt, leaven, becoming more and more part of the people's history, of its sorrows and hopes.

Liberating evangelization will be adapted differently when it is directed to the masses and when it is directed to the classes that run the country.

The Masses

It is a defamation of the church when its "preferential option for the poor" is interpreted to mean blind partiality in favor of the masses and disrespect for the powerful classes. The church does not approve of the poor and the oppressed simply because they are poor and oppressed—though it cannot forget that the Redeemer himself offered the grace of redemption to them first of all. The church knows perfectly well that among those who lack material goods there is a great deal of sinfulness. It therefore makes every effort to see that persons are saved from their inveterate vices, many of which are fomented by our historical situation. In the name of the preferential option for the poor there can never be justified the machismo, the alcoholism, the failure in family responsibility, the exploitation of one poor person by another, the antagonism among neighbors, and the so many other sins that our survey pointed to strongly as being concurrent roots of this country's crisis and violence.

Without rationalizing that clearly wrong behavior of the masses, the survey also drew attention to great human and Christian values. The church holds these in high regard, and believes it to be its duty to strengthen and guide them in the spirit of the gospel and in the light of faith. One might single out among these values the spirit of service, of solidarity, of responsibility, the experience of love, of toil, of courage. . . . One of the most basic of these values is that sense of community by which Salvadorans can overcome their selfishness and their sterile divisions.

In the present social and political conditions of this country, the evangelizing of the Salvadoran people cannot simply continue the tradition of preaching and encouraging en masse, or in a moralizing fashion. It has to pursue a personalizing education in the faith, one that forms, by means of small groups meeting for reflection, persons who take a critical stance vis-à-vis the world about them with criteria drawn from the gospel.

Evangelization, here and now, has to defend and encourage the political and social organization of the great mass of rural and urban workers and their families. I thank God that in this task the church can already count upon well-qualified lay Christians to whom it offers, as Pope Paul VI said, "the inspiration of faith, the motivation of fraternal love, a social teaching . . . [as] the foundation of [their] wisdom and [their] experience."[58]

In my third pastoral letter I defended, by means of the church's teaching, the right to form organizations, a right made sacred for Salvadorans in their country's Constitution. It is not only a matter of rights. It is a necessity and an obligation if there is to come about a more just order that takes real account of the majority of the people of this country.

The church does not, therefore, regard it as a crime but rather as a duty to encourage and to guide Christians who have the ability to organize themselves, drawing members from the people and acting for the people. By reason of the same duty the church also denounces the sin of those organizations that turn politics into an absolute, thereby hindering the full development of the human person and showing disrespect for those Christian values that were the inspiration of many of those who belong to various organizations.

The experience of recent years shows both the power of Christian values to animate popular organizations and the danger that organizations risk when they cease being animated by those same values. It is possible that popular organizations, with their political alliances, come to think that Christian values are no longer necessary for them, that they are self-sufficient in their task of giving the great mass of the people, and especially the *campesinos*, all that they need. It is even possible that they come to believe that they have the right to manipulate the church, the gospel, the faith, for the benefit, not of the ordinary people, but of their organizations. By so doing, however, they rob the salt and the leaven of the power that the gospel portions out so that the whole be not corrupted, and they display little respect for the deeply-held beliefs of many members of their organizations. It would be a mistake to oppose the driving force of political organizations to the driving force of the church. This would be to subordinate to the absolutization of a human organization the bringing into being in history of the kingdom of God.

The church, I must repeat, is pleased that in this country there are lay persons who are capable of politically organizing the masses. Vatican II itself recognizes the autonomy of temporal undertakings and values, such as political and organizational activities. The church therefore also reminds all of, and demands, its own proper independence and its transcendent identity, its apostolic mission in the midst of the temporal activities of men and women. It must not allow itself to be manipulated for any political purpose, although its apostolic mission obliges it not to abandon its specific mission as church to the political organizations. It will support them in what is just in their demands and, above all, it will defend their right to exist, which is based upon the legitimate human right to organize—a right so vulnerable to attack in our repressive environment.

The Elites

With respect to the classes that have social, political, and economic power, the church calls upon them, before all else, to be converted, to remember their very grave responsibility to overcome disorder and violence not by means of repression but through justice and the participation of ordinary people.

In a society such as ours, in which the majority have hardly anything, the privileged minority, separated as if by an abyss from all the rest, enjoys a standard of living similar to that which a few enjoy in the richest countries. They have, moreover, enormous power simply because our political organization is undemocratic. Would that they should favor social change rather than impede it, or violently resist it! They could do so out of self-interest, but especially because charity demands it. Charity consists not only in giving others what is their due, but even in giving them something that is one's own. Would that they might honestly judge that this would be the best for everybody—including, in the long run, themselves and their children! Would that they might remember those words of Jesus, that they will be dealt with both in this life and the next according to the measure they have dealt out to others!

I realize that some terrorist activities induce a state of mind in the powerful that hardly favors serenity and reflection. But they ought to overcome that preoccupation and generously lay down the basis for a democratic evolution, so that the majority of the population may participate equitably in the national resources that belong to all. Thus the root cause of terrorist, and all other unjust, violence would be eradicated.

Puebla states:

It is of the utmost importance that this service to our fellow human beings take the course marked out for us by Vatican II: "The demands of justice should first be satisfied, lest the giving of what is due in justice be represented as the offering of a charitable gift. Not only the effects but also the causes of various ills must be removed. Help should be given in such a way that the recipients may gradually be freed from dependence on others and become self-sufficient."[9]

PART THREE
LIGHT ON SOME SPECIAL PROBLEMS

In this third part I am going to propose clarification and guidance on violence, Marxism, and national dialogue.

Undoubtedly there are other problems that disturb consciences at this time of national crisis. But these three, together with the others upon which I have tried to throw light elsewhere in this letter, stand out in the reflections of our Christian communities. This reflection ought to continue in a dialogue between pastors and Christian communities because only in that way can we progress in throwing light, and guidance, on the many and varied subjects under discussion.

I beg those who are learned in these matters to study them and to pass on their thinking about them to others, so that they too may offer, at this critical period of research, a valuable service not only to the members of the church but to all persons of good will. It should help them clarify their own thinking, and to adopt positions that are tenable.

Violence

I have spent a good time already, in the third part of my third pastoral letter, on the judgment of the church on violence. Here I am going to presuppose that summary of the church's traditional moral teaching on violence. I only want to dig a little deeper, to bring those ideas up to date, given the escalation of the violence that casts a shadow over so many families in our homeland. Would that this reflection might persuade Salvadorans to lay unjust attitudes aside, and to get them, with sincere change of heart, to wash clean so many hands and consciences stained by social injustice and human blood!

Inspired by the gospel, the church feels itself driven to seek peace before all else. But the peace that the church urges is the work of justice (*opus justitiae pax*). Therefore its judgments on the violence that disturbs the peace cannot ignore the demands of justice. There are many different judgments, just as there are many different forms of violence. The church cannot state, in a simplistic fashion, that it condemns every kind of violence.

Structural Violence

The church condemns "structural" or "institutionalized violence," "the result of an unjust situation in which the majority of men, women, and children in our country find themselves deprived of the necessities of life."[60] The church condemns this violence not only because it is unjust in itself, and the objective expression of personal and collective sin, but also because it is the cause of other innumerable cruelties and more obvious acts of violence.

More and more Salvadorans are learning the point that the deepest root of the serious evils that afflict us, including the renewed outbreak of violence, is this "structural violence." It takes concrete form in the unjust distribution of wealth and of property—especially insofar as it includes landownership—and, more generally, in that amalgam of economic and political structures by which the few grow increasingly rich and powerful, while the remainder grow increasingly poor and weak.[61]

Arbitrary Violence of the State

The church likewise condemns the arbitrary and repressive violence of the state. We in El Salvador well know, as did Puebla, how any dissent against the present form of capitalism and against the political institutions that support it is repressed with ever increasing violence and ever greater injustice—inspired by the theory of national security. We also know how the majority of the *campesinos*, the laborers, slum dwellers, and others who have organized themselves to defend their rights and to promote legitimate structural changes are simply declared to be "terrorists" or "subversives." They are therefore arrested, tortured, murdered, or they simply disappear—and all without reference to the law or to any judicial institution that might protect them or give them the chance to defend themselves and prove their innocence. Faced with this prejudicial and unjust situation, many have decided that they had no alternative but to defend themselves with violence. And recently they have encountered, in response, the arbitrary violence of the state.

Public authority certainly has the right to punish social disorder. But in order to do so there must be the intervention of a court of justice that gives the accused the chance to defend themselves and can declare the guilty worthy of punishment. Any other kind of sanction—arbitrary and repressive—is an abuse of authority.

Violence of the Extreme Right

The church equally condemns the violence favored by right-wing gangs of terrorists. They go absolutely unpunished, which makes one suspect official connivance. They have cast their shadow over the country's teachers, over the popular organizations, over political parties, and even over the church itself. Their intention, which they clearly cannot sustain indefinitely, is to try to uphold the unjust social order to which I referred above. Therefore they, more than anyone else, are involved in the injustice of the system.

Terrorist Violence

The church also condemns the violence perpetrated by politico-military groups or individuals when they intentionally victimize innocent persons, or when the damage they do is disproportionate, in the short or medium term, to the positive effect they wish to achieve.

Insurrectional Violence

On the other hand, Pope Paul VI's encyclical *Populorum Progressio*, quoted at the Medellín assembly, takes up again the classic teaching of Catholic theology, according to which insurrection is legitimate "in the very exceptional circumstances of an evident, prolonged tyranny that seriously works against fundamental human rights and seriously damages the common good of the country, whether it proceeds from one person or from clearly unjust structures."[62]

In addition, our own national constitution recognizes the right of just insurrection.

Violence of Legitimate Defense

In the same class as legitimate insurrectional violence, we can place the violence of legitimate defense. This occurs "when a person or a group repels by force an unjust aggression that they have suffered" (Third Pastoral Letter).

These are the dangerous, violent forces that are aroused when changes in the structures of oppressive violence are delayed, and when it is believed that the structures can be kept in being through repressive violence.

Conditions for Legitimate Violence

We must not forget the necessary conditions, which I recalled, in line with the church's theology, in my third pastoral letter already quoted. For the violence of insurrection or of defense to be legitimate, it is required:

1) that the violence of legitimate defense not be greater than the unjust aggression (for example, if it is enough to defend oneself with one's fists, then it is not permitted to shoot an aggressor);

2) that one resort to a form of violence, in proportion to the need, only after every other possible peaceful means has been tried;

3) that the violence used in defense not bring in retaliation an even greater evil than that being resisted.

In practice it is very difficult to take account of all these theoretical measures for the justification of violence. History has taught us how cruel and painful is the price of blood, and how difficult it is to repair social and economic damage caused by war. This is an opportune moment to recall that celebrated phrase of Pope Pius XII on war: "Nothing is lost by peace, everything may be lost in war."

The most reasonable and effective thing for a government to do, therefore, is to use its moral and coercive force not to defend the structural violence of an unjust order, but to guarantee a truly democratic state, one that defends the fundamental rights of all its citizens, based on a just economic order. Only in this way will it be possible to make those instances distant and unreal in which recourse to force, by groups or by individuals, can be justified by the existence of a tyrannical regime and an unjust social order.

The Christian Is Peaceful, but Not Passive

In this atmosphere of violence and of change in the country, how much to the point, and how valuable, have those guidelines become that Medellín expressed: "The Christian is peaceful and not ashamed of it. He is not simply a pacifist for he can fight, but he prefers peace to war. He knows that violent changes in structures would be fallacious, ineffectual in themselves, and not conforming to the dignity of man."[63]

Marxism

The problem of Marxism is very complex. It is not dealt with simply by condemning it. Puebla itself teaches us to distinguish between Marxism as a dominant ideology for the whole of behavior, and collaboration with groups who share this ideology. Naturally if one understands by Marxism a materialistic, atheistic ideology that is taken to explain the whole of human existence and gives a false interpretation of religion, then it is completely untenable by a Christian. A Christian's faith must guide his or her whole life, starting from the existence of God, toward a spiritual and eternal transcendence made possible in Christ through the Holy Spirit. These are two diametrically opposed interpretations of life.

But Marxism can also be understood in other senses. It can be understood as a scientific analysis of the economic and social order. Many in El Salvador, as elsewhere in Latin America, use this analysis as a scientific tool because, they claim, it in no way affects their religious principles. The magisterium of the church (in *Octogesima Adveniens,* for example), although it recognizes the distinction between Marxism as an ideology and as a scientific method, prudently warns of possible ideological risks.

Understood in terms of political strategy, many use Marxism as a guide in the struggle for socio-political power. Perhaps this aspect has in practice greater hidden dangers. Marxist political praxis can give rise to conflicts of conscience about the use of means and of methods not always in conformity with what the gospel lays down as ethical for Christians. Such political praxis can lead to the absolutization of popular political organizations. It can dry up the Christian inspiration of their members, and even cut them off from the church, as if the church had no right to exercise, from the perspective of its own transcendent ideology, a critical function in relation to political activities.

So it is evident that we are here dealing with a complex concept. Many of our communities frankly admit that they have little knowledge about it, and ask for greater clarification. As a pastor, therefore, I beg all those skilled in this science to spread knowledge of it, along with Christian criteria. The topic is of absorbing interest to many, and worries a large number of Christians.

One could benefit in the meantime from studying sections 543–45 and 550–51 of the Puebla Final Document, and sections 69 and 71 of the conciliar constitution *Gaudium et Spes.*

Moreover, although there may be very little scientific understanding of Marxism, it must not be forgotten that some anti-Marxist declarations and courses of action that Christians may make can turn into support for capitalism. Such is the situation in this country. And in concrete terms, capitalism is in fact what is most unjust and unchristian about the society in which we live. "Fear of Marxism," says Puebla, "keeps many from facing up to the oppressive reality of liberal capitalism. One could say that some people, faced with the danger of one clearly sinful system, forget to denounce and combat the established reality of another equally sinful system. We must give full attention to the latter system, without overlooking the violent and atheistic historical forms of Marxism."[64] The best way to defeat Marxism is to take seriously the preferential option for the poor.

National Dialogue

A realistic national dialogue is a necessity for this country if it is to find a way out of its crisis. It is therefore, I believe, the right time to throw some light on this topic. And I have to begin by regretting that the government's call for national dialogue has wasted a good opportunity, because it was not offered under acceptable conditions. From the start, therefore, that call met with a very cool public reception. There was criticism of the lack of confidence and of the lack of freedom to give voice to, on equal terms with the government, all the unrest and all the strong viewpoints held by Salvadorans.

For genuine dialogue as a means of guiding us out of our present crisis, the following points seem to me essential:

1) There must be involvement of all social forces, or at least all those that have not gone underground. All have the right to speak and to be heard in this dialogue, and it should, in principle, be possible to reach agreement with all. But national dialogue would, on the contrary, become nonsense if it were to be reduced to a forum where were welcome only the views of the government's friends and of those who, deep down, do not want profound change.

2) Another essential element of this dialogue is that an end be put to all kinds of violence. Dialogue searches for truth and justice by way of reason. It requires an atmosphere of confidence and serenity. This is especially pertinent to the government's attitude. So long as there is violent and disproportionate repression of all public protest; so long as the present level of politically motivated murder continues; so long as persons disappear and there are political prisoners; so long as political, social, and religious leaders are banned from the country—it is absurd to talk about a dialogue. On these issues there is no room for dialogue. They are preconditions for dialogue.

One cannot simplistically point to the existence of terrorist groups as an argument for excluding certain opinions from the dialogue. As has already been pointed out when talking about violence, terrorism originates in a context of institutionalized violence. This situation strongly influences many to act violently in response to the continual, systematic oppression exercised by the groups in power—or at least it gives them a pretext for doing so. And the purpose of dialogue is precisely to rid the country of this root cause of violence.

Naturally terrorists, and all other partisans of a violent situation, must lay their attitude aside when they come up against a serious and sincere wish for dialogue. They must cooperate to create the atmosphere of serenity that is needed for realistic dialogue with a view to changing profoundly this country's structures.

3) The chief topic of dialogue is to be reform and structural changes. I

have to say it again: in order for repression to be eliminated, the roots that feed the violence in the social sphere, and which thus provoke the temptation to further acts of violence, must be attacked. National dialogue cannot be effectively brought into being unless there is some sign of a desire and a determination to approve the changes that might guarantee a better standard of living for all Salvadorans.

4) Another important topic for dialogue ought to be freedom to organize. Our natural inclination and Christian sensitivity make us prefer methods of achieving social justice that are based on organization of the people, in line with the principles of our Constitution, and eminently peaceable. I believe that trade unionism is a definite gain for the working classes in all democratic countries, and that it neither can nor should be rejected in El Salvador.

When taking part in national dialogue, employers ought to understand the logic and the justice of trade unionism. It has not arisen to do harm to business. We all depend on the national economy for our livelihood. Trade unionism has arisen to achieve a more equitable distribution of what is produced by capital and labor working together.

On the other hand, in order to be worthy participants in such a dialogue, the trade unions and the workers themselves must be conscious of the effectiveness of their organized forces. They must not allow themselves to fall into that same sin that they complain of in others—letting themselves be manipulated by interests far removed from those of the workers. Nor must they abuse the power that solidarity gives them by making exorbitant demands.

As long as the national dialogue that we need does not come to pass, there is an even greater obligation upon citizens to contribute their opinions in the search for the guidance that our homeland needs, so that it may find once more the peace that it has lost. "To gain it is its greatest glory," as our national anthem says.

For its part, our archdiocese offers the general force of this pastoral letter as a voice of the church in national dialogue. It repeats the offer, made once before, to put its modest means of social communication at the service of constructive points of view.

PART FOUR
PUEBLA'S PASTORAL APPROACH
APPLIED TO THE ARCHDIOCESE

I turn now very especially to my beloved pastoral co-workers—to the priests, religious, and laity—because we have together to translate into real terms the valuable contribution the church offers the country at this time of crisis. Our situation, seen in the light of the church's teaching that I have just been putting forward, shows us that our people in El Salvador, together with all the peoples of Latin America, "are journeying amid anxieties and hopes, frustrations and expectations," as Puebla puts it.[65]

Sharing Puebla's concern, then, let us ask ourselves some questions. How has the church viewed this reality? How has the church interpreted it? Has the church been successful in finding some way to focus on it and clarify it in the light of the gospel? Has the church managed to discern which aspects of this reality threaten to destroy the human being, who is the object of God's infinite love, and which aspects have been developing in line with God's loving designs? How has the church been developing itself in order to carry out the saving mission that was entrusted to it by Christ, which is supposed to be implemented in concrete situations and reach out toward concrete human beings? What has the church done in the last ten years in the face of the changing reality around it?

Puebla says that "these are the great questions that we, as pastors, ask ourselves . . . keeping in mind that the fundamental mission of the Church is to evangelize in the here and now with an eye on the future."[66]

In response to this grave questioning, let us renew our apostolic generosity in the direction of those steps toward which the "spirit of Puebla" also inspires us and which, thank God, coincide with efforts already being made in this archdiocese.

Attitude of Searching

Here I am going to go back again over a problem already mentioned earlier in this letter: the pastoral need to adapt evangelization to the present circumstances of this country. Puebla notes the great changes in this sphere since only a short time ago:

> The weight of tradition helped the communication of the Gospel. What was taught from the pulpit was zealously welcomed in the home and the school; and it was safeguarded and sustained by the social pressure of the surrounding milieu. Today nothing like that happens. The faith proposed by the Church is accepted or rejected with much more freedom and with a notably critical-minded sense. Even the peasants, who previously were isolated from contact with civilization to a large extent, are now acquiring this same critical sense. This is due to the ready contact with the present-day world that is afforded them, chiefly by radio and means of transportation; it is also due to the consciousness-raising efforts of pastoral agents.[67]

Hence, without falling into the sin of infidelity to our mission, we cannot remain unmoved before the demands of a world in a state of flux.

There are two important factors in the apostolate: the gospel message we preach, and the changing reality of peoples, times, and places in which the church finds itself, and where it has to fulfill its mission. Therefore we have to shake off our laziness and bring ourselves up to date, as far as we are able, with current theological thinking. And those of us who can do so have to spread that thinking of the church as far as possible with all available means. It is also necessary that, together with the universal church, we should go on, as Puebla tells us, "acquiring an increasingly clear and deep realization that evangelization is its fundamental mission; and that it cannot possibly carry out this mission without an ongoing effort to know the real situation and to adapt the gospel message to today's human beings in a dynamic, attractive, and convincing way."[68]

In this attitude of search, let us recall that the church is historical, that it is moving forward. It is not something fixed and determined. It does not have a closed system for interpreting the gospel, applicable to each epoch and every circumstance. The church is a pilgrim. The word of God is inexhaustible; it forever discloses new facets that have to be more deeply understood. So the church goes on evolving in the way it presents the unique message of the gospel, in keeping with the particular period in which it is living. We believe in the Lord of history, and in his Spirit who makes all things new.

The Preferential Option for the Poor

Puebla continues:

The situation of injustice . . . forces us to reflect on the great challenge our pastoral work faces in trying to help human beings to move from less human to more human conditions. The deep-rooted social differences, the extreme poverty, and the violation of human rights found in many areas pose challenges to evangelization. Our mission to bring God to human beings, and human beings to God, also entails the task of fashioning a more fraternal society here. And the unjust social situation has not failed to produce tensions within the Church itself. On the one hand they are provoked by groups that stress the "spiritual" side of the Church's mission and resent active efforts at societal improvement. On the other hand they are provoked by people who want to make the Church's mission nothing more than an effort at human betterment."[69]

The church of this archdiocese, thank God, has taken many sure steps in keeping with this meaning of the preferential option for the poor. From the time of my honored predecessor Archbishop Luis Chávez y González, who led the archdiocese wisely and firmly, the foundations were laid for an apostolate that took shape with a preference for the great mass of the dispossessed, the rural poor above all. And as evidence of his great catechetical work there still remain the radio schools for adult literacy, the cooperatives, and so on.

It is a deep satisfaction to me that Puebla said we were right in our apostolic labors, for some at home and abroad had interpreted them negatively. Pastoral documents on social justice, the creation of organizations to express solidarity with those who suffer, the denunciation of outrages, the defense of human rights, stimulating priests and religious to opt for the poor, supporting them sometimes to death in testimony of their prophetic mission, are all aspects mentioned by Puebla of an ecclesial apostolate in Latin America concerned about its fidelity to Christ. And that is what we are doing here, even at the risk of being unjustly interpreted.

I realize nonetheless that there is still much to be done. But here the remedy that Puebla stressed for unity is apropos—to take seriously the preferential option for the poor:

• Striving "to understand and denounce the mechanisms that generate this poverty."[70]

• Uniting our efforts "with those of people of good will in order to uproot poverty and create a more just and fraternal world."[71]

• Supporting "the aspirations of laborers and peasants, who wish to be treated as free, responsible human beings. They are called to share in the decisions that affect their lives and their future, and we encourage all to improve themselves."[72]

• Defending "their fundamental right to freely create organizations to defend and promote their interests, and to make a responsible contribution to the common good."[73]

United in a Joint Apostolate

Different situations require different responses, but all responses ought to converge upon fundamental options and common objectives, thus moving toward a combined apostolate. We must never think that the various responses, to which one single Spirit gives rise, as being at odds with one another. They have to be seen as complementary, and all beneath the watchful overview of the bishop, the person responsible for the apostolate in the diocese. Let us remember that the apostolate ought to be a joint response, and if it is not, then it is neither a pastoral response nor a response of the church.

I realize that the apostolate, the apostolic spirit, is the fruit of the Spirit, to whom persons generously respond. But just as a river has to be channeled if it is to irrigate the land better, so too the apostolate, which the Spirit promotes through a variety of charisms, needs to be planned and carried out as a whole if it is to serve the well-being of the mystical body of Christ. An apostolate without the apostolic spirit is a technique devoid of inspiration. An apostolate without pastoral planning becomes ineffective, it wastes itself. A united apostolate is at the same time a technique and a mystique.

This is Puebla's guidance too: "We assume the necessity of an organic pastoral effort in the Church as a unified source of dynamism, if it is to be effective in an ongoing way. This would include, among other things, guiding principles, objectives, options, strategies, and practical initiatives."[74]

I want to refresh the memories of all pastoral ministers on options taken during the archdiocesan pastoral week, January 5 to 10, 1976, which have served to shape the pastoral approach during my episcopate, and which today can count on new backing from Puebla:

—The fundamental option for evangelization at every level; this is to be regarded as serious, urgent, and necessary.

—Renewal of all the means at our disposal for an adequate evangelization that will brook no delay, but neither will it tolerate superficiality.

—The urgent need to select, and adequately to form, pastoral workers, especially lay persons.

—Christian communities as the objective on the horizon, if we intend to revitalize the church.

—The creation and preparation of mechanisms to give dynamism to, and to put into execution, the options we have taken.

Pastoral Adaptation

When I reflect on the fruit of pastoral experience, the unrest to which Christian communities draw attention, and the creative richness shown by the many new ways found to embody the message, I am urged to put great emphasis on what I want to call "pastoral adaptation." To explain this I am going to distinguish between three types of apostolate:

1) The mass apostolate, which refers to extensive evangelization.

2) An apostolate for basic Christian communities or small groups, in the sense that they are sign, leaven, salt, and light. This refers to intensive evangelization.

3) An apostolate of companionship or following, which refers to a personal or group apostolate faced with the diversity of concrete options that Christians can take, as the faith demands for the urgent changes needed in society to make it more human and more Christian.

The Mass Apostolate

Nothing derogatory is meant by the idea of a mass apostolate. It envisions extensive evangelization. The masses do not have to go on being treated as faceless. The apostolate has to find precise ways of giving all Christians a critical outlook, an ability to value themselves as persons, made to the image of God, in control of their own destiny. The mass apostolate ought to be a liberating response by the church, helping the masses to be-

come a people, and helping a people to become the people of God.
As Puebla puts it:

> Like the Church as a whole, the religion of the people must be constantly
> evangelized over again. . . . Evangelization will be a work of pastoral
> pedagogy, in which the Catholicism of the common people is assumed,
> purified, completed, and made dynamic by the Gospel. . . . Guided by
> the light of the Holy Spirit and imbued with "pastoral charity," the
> agents of evangelization will know how to elaborate a "pedagogy of
> evangelization." Such a pedagogy demands that they love the people and
> be close to them; that they be prudent, firm, constant, and audacious.
> Only then can they educate this precious faith, which is sometimes in a
> very weakened state.[75]

The evangelization of the people is a slow, but forward-moving, process.
It demands in every pastoral worker creativity, imagination, respect in the
way things are put so as not to hurt others' feelings. But at the same time it
has to be staunch in its criticism of abuse. This apostolate takes great patience. Jesus himself compares the kingdom to a mustard seed. The sower
waits while it germinates, grows, flowers, bears fruit. It is not up to us to
accelerate the stages of this evangelization. God can do so if he thinks fit.
He can convert, in an instant, the persecutor Saul into the apostle Paul. But
we have to wait for the normal process. And this will not always be easy.

I therefore urge pastoral workers to evaluate, honestly and sincerely, all
the forms of mass apostolate that they use to embody the liberating message
of Christ among the people: the use of churches, processions of faith, slogans, and so on, so that they neither stagnate nor fall into abuses.

The Apostolate of Basic Christian Communities

One can say of the apostolate of basic Christian communities that it has
undergone modification and development according to the times and places
in which it operates. But the direction and the purpose remain the same: to
form groups of Christians committed to the church and committed, as is the
church, to their respective societies.

Puebla says of the basic Christian community:

> [It] brings together families, adults, and young people, in an intimate
> interpersonal relationship grounded in the faith. As an ecclesial reality, it
> is a community of faith, hope, and charity. It celebrates the Word of
> God and . . . it fleshes out the Word of God in life through solidarity
> and commitment to the new commandment of the Lord; and through the
> service of approved coordinators, it makes present and operative the
> mission of the Church and its visible communion with the legitimate
> pastors. It is a base-level community because it is composed of relatively
> few members as a permanent body, like a cell of the larger community.[76]

To live in community is not a matter of choice but of calling. Christianity demands, by its calling, the formation of community. Christianity cannot be thought of except in terms of relationships with other persons, brothers and sisters in whom we make real the comradely love that we preach. There is nothing in revelation about the de facto forms that communities should take. Canonical religious communities are not to be regarded as revealed models of community. It is the particular moment in history, the particular place in which they operate, that should give the precise shape to communities, as the occasion demands. This is where the theology of charisms fits in.

On the formation of Christian communities, moreover, one has to keep in mind what *Evangelii Nuntiandi* says to us, and what I myself had to say in my third pastoral letter:

1) Their encounter with Christ. There has to be a living out of the values of the gospel and of Christianity: faith, hope, love, prayer, the sacraments, the word of God—a living out that, at the moment when Christians realize what their options are, convinces them that evangelical virtues are true and effective.

2) Their encounter with the church. This entails a full understanding of the mission that they have as Christians and as church, and their relationship to other communities in the parish, in the vicariate, in the diocese. The basic Christian community is part of the church, it is not the whole church. The Christian community, the parish community, the diocesan community, the universal community—all these have Christ at their center, visible in the person of the pope, the bishop, the pastor.

3) Their encounter with the world. A basic Christian community is not an end in itself. If it were to become such, it would cease being leaven, cease being church, and become a sect. The purpose of the Christian community is to spread the kingdom of God. It cannot put itself forward to groups of Christians as a place of peaceful refuge that separates them off from the world. It is a deepening, and an intensification, of their commitment. That is what the gospel means when it uses the symbolism of leaven, salt, and light. One cannot imagine that yeast would fulfill its function if it were not within the dough it had to leaven, or if salt were not in the food to which it had to give flavor, or if light were not in the place it had to illuminate.

Let us not forget what Puebla says about giving dynamism to apostolic movements, to parishes, to basic Christian communities, and to active Catholics in general, so that they may be leaven more wholeheartedly.[77] We must give them a genuine missionary spirit.

On the other hand the dynamic to which Puebla drew attention—popular religion and the people's natural desire to achieve its own liberation—ought to find within the basic Christian communities its true worth and purification. The basic Christian communities, as Puebla says, "embody the Church's preferential love for the common people. In them their religiosity is expressed, valued, and purified; and they are given a concrete opportunity to share in the task of the Church and to work committedly for the transformation of the world.''[78]

We are well aware that when Christians assume their role of adults in the faith to a greater degree, and become coresponsible for the progress of the church, even more conflicts with parish priests and with ecclesiastical authorities will occur, because some officials will not want to move forward at the same pace as the church of today, and because they will see their authority questioned by the criticism and evaluations made of them. Even in these cases, of course, the good Christian has to be mindful of the supreme values of charity and unity.

The Apostolate of Companionship

By the apostolate of "companionship" or "following" I understand the personal evangelization of those individual Christians, or groups of Christians, who have made the concrete political option that, they believe in good conscience, represents the historical commitment of their faith. In this sense there are many options, charisms, and callings facing a Christian conscience, and a pastor has to respect, scrutinize, and guide consciences by the light of the Spirit.

In my third pastoral letter I spoke of the proliferation of popular political organizations as a new phenomenon to which the church must respond. We are now confronted, as a logical result of this proliferation, with the particular choices made by Christians and groups of Christians. It is not only that evangelization has a dimension that touches on politics; politicization is reaching out to our Christian communities, which often become standard bearers for political groups.

I am not speaking of a politicized apostolate but rather of an apostolate that has to guide, in accordance with the gospel, the consciences of Christians within a politicized environment. Political life, like all human activity, needs pastoral guidance. Our situation is made all the more difficult when many Christians, in an environment as politicized as the one in this country, choose their political options before finding their identity as Christians.

It is here, in order to respond to the challenge of the entirety of this complex situation, that the church requires a special kind of apostolate, one that I call an apostolate of "following" or "companionship," one that breaks out of the already well-known molds of the mass apostolate and of the apostolate of small groups. About this Puebla says:

Speaking in general, and without distinguishing between the roles that may be proper to its various members, the Church feels it has a duty and a right to be present in this area of reality. For Christianity is supposed to evangelize the whole of human life, including the political dimension. So the Church criticizes those who would restrict the scope of faith to personal or family life; who would exclude the professional, economic, social, and political orders as if sin, love, prayer, and pardon had no relevance in them. The fact is that the need for the Church's presence in the political arena flows from the very core of the Christian faith. That is to say, it flows from the Lordship of Christ over the whole of life. Christ sets the seal on the definitive brotherhood of humanity, wherein every human being is of equal worth: "All are one in Christ Jesus."[79]

There are several requirements for this apostolate—so urgently needed in our circumstances of political and social crisis—that are essential if it is to be effective. Some of them are:

• A great spirit of prayer and discernment before taking action.

• A great clarity and firmness about the criteria and the values of the gospel and a search for greater knowledge about more uncertain issues, such as the relationship between faith and politics, commitment in faith, commitment in history, Christianity and ideology, violence, and so on.

• A great respect for the diversity of choices and charisms that the one Spirit can give rise to so that human history itself becomes the history of salvation. A great mental and spiritual purity is needed if we are to rid ourselves of personal prejudices against individuals or institutions. I am not talking about pressuring persons to join political organizations, or about pressuring them to leave organizations or to abandon the choices they have made. Rather we want to help them evaluate and question their choices, from the perspective of gospel values. This evaluation and questioning can be about their own personal behavior, about the criteria of the group, about the consequences of their actions, about the very complexity of politics. For politics is much wider and more complicated than can be encompassed by one's personal or a group's options.

• A great spirit of commitment and sacrifice. I realize that this kind of apostolate will entail risks, criticisms, and false accusations. But I believe it is necessary because the times require it.

• A deep sense of hierarchical order and of teamwork. Although encouraging priests in this kind of apostolate, and pledging them my support and understanding, I beg them, for the honor of our church and the good of the people, never to take it up lightly, or for personal reasons, or by pure chance, letting themselves be dragged into it by the force of events, generously perhaps, but at times ingenuously or imprudently. They should rather associate themselves with an overall plan, in communion with their bishop, so that they can be part of the response of the church and as representatives of the church.

CONCLUSION

A Local Church in Communion with the Universal Church

I have tried to portray, from a pastoral point of view, the situation of crisis that exists in our beloved country. I have also tried to delineate the service that our church could and should render as part of the effort that all active forces in our homeland could and should render. Within the open and frank dialogue that this country needs with such tragic urgency, this pastoral letter, written under the guidance of the magisterium of the popes and of the Latin American church gathered at Puebla, and with valuable contributions made by our local communities, represents the sincere view of our archdiocese.

Whether it is heeded or not, as pastor of the archdiocese this pastoral letter gives me the satisfaction of having made an effort to unite in it the real purposes that inspire what is called the "pastoral approach of the archdiocese." To the universal church I offer it in filial devotion, as a contribution from one local church to the renewal that Vatican II began, and to which Medellín and Puebla gave concrete shape for the church in Latin America.

This gives me the opportunity of thanking persons for the many signs of support and solidarity that have come from different parts of Latin America, and from the world at large, support for the pastoral effort being made by our archdiocese from episcopal conferences, from cardinals, archbishops, bishops, priests, religious communities, and the laity, from ecumenical and secular organizations, and from individuals. I give thanks to the Lord, who is the only one who can comprehend the magnitude of this demonstration of the catholicity of the church and of universal human sentiment, which give proof of the authenticity of one local church.

Presentation of the Puebla Document to the Archdiocese

As I said at the beginning, the central purpose of this pastoral letter has been officially to present to the archdiocese the document of the third conference of Latin American bishops gathered at Puebla. And in presenting it, making it the basis for all my commentary, I am calling upon all priests, religious, and lay persons that we day by day assimilate it better, coming to know it more fully and putting it increasingly into practice, so that the holy father's desire, expressed in his letter of approbation, may be fulfilled in the archdiocese.

In the joint magisterium of the Puebla Final Document the experience of so many pastors who, in Latin America, live in circumstances similar to those of El Salvador teaches us how to analyze our situation and how to offer to this country in its hour of crisis the specific contribution of the church.

To be sure, these guidelines should not be thought of as closed to the creativity and originality of the various churches of Latin America. Their splendor is to be found in the different visages they present, deriving from the diversity of their own histories and problems. They offer us the surest path for our own creativity: they teach us to be always the one church of Christ within the unique framework of our own Salvadoran history.

The Divine Savior: Beginning and End of Our Apostolate

The foundation for all our work of evangelization is the mystery of Christ that we preach, the mystery that was so clearly revealed, in a way that can never be equalled, in the theophany commemorated by our titular feast. It has the certification of the Father, who presents Christ to us as the one and only Savior of the world. He alone is the way forward toward the true liberation of Salvadorans and of El Salvador: "Listen to him."

The church is his "body in history." We shall be more the church, and offer a better specific contribution from the church for the liberation of our people, the more we identify ourselves with him, and the more we are docile instruments of his truth and his grace.

The Final Ecstasy of Paul VI and the Point of Departure for John Paul II

It is opportune and pleasing to recall, exactly a year after his death, that this was the final testimony of his holiness Paul VI. This humble pope put his brilliant talents at the service of Christ. Therefore, during his pontificate, he was able to present to the world the shining glory of a church that, in the midst of today's formidable conflicts, did not lose its identity and continued to be a "pillar of truth." His last angelus message, which he was not able to recite in this world, was the final ecstasy of his life taken up by Christ in the theophany of that August 6. His successor John Paul II guides us along the same lines, and the title of his first encyclical, *Redemptor Hominis*, "Redeemer of Humankind," suggests an entire program for the modern apostolate.

Mary, Mother of the Church and Mother of America

I could not end this reflection on what the church can offer this country at its time of crisis without mentioning that most tender and most beautiful aspect of its involvement: Mary, mother of Christ, mother of the church, mother of America. Puebla, too, gave a rich interpretation of the role of Mary in the church's work of liberation, and of her providential presence in the devotion of our peoples.

The church, in its Latin American apostolate, has become increasingly convinced that it cannot ignore this devotion of the people to the Virgin Mary if it wants its apostolate among the people to be effective. Of this Marian devotion Puebla says that it is "a vital, concrete experience in the history of Latin America; it is part of the innermost 'identity' of the Latin American peoples."[80]

The evangelical service and the liberating force that the church, together with Mary, offers to our country was described by Paul VI "in words that find a timely echo." She is, he said, "a strong woman who knew poverty and suffering, flight and exile. Such situations can hardly escape the attention of those who wish to corroborate the liberating efforts of human beings and society with the spirit of the Gospel."[81] And John Paul II recalled how in the magnificat Mary is depicted as the model for all those "who do not passively accept the adverse circumstances of personal and social life and who are not victims of 'alienation,' as the expression goes today, but who instead join with her in proclaiming that God is 'the avenger of the lowly,' and will, if need be, depose 'the mighty from their thrones.' " [82]

A Blessing with Optimism and Enthusiasm

And so, with this Marian reflection, and in the midst of a crisis that brings despair to many and affliction to all, we feel that the feast of our Lord's transfiguration invites us to hope for the transfiguration of our homeland, placed as it is under the special protection of the divine Savior of the world.

With Puebla's filial optimism I can say, as I give my blessing to the archdiocese: "This is Mary's hour, the hour of a new Pentecost. She presides over this hour with her prayers as the Church, under the influence of the Holy Spirit, initiates a new stage on its journey. On this journey we pray that Mary may be 'the star of a continually renewed evangelization.' " [83]

NOTES

1. Final Document, §73.
2. Letter of Approval.
3. *Lumen Gentium*, §12.
4. *Octogesima Adveniens*, §4.
5. *Gaudium et Spes*, §42.
6. Puebla, Final Document, §89.
7. Ibid., §29.
8. Ibid., §§31–39.
9. Ibid., §46.
10. Ibid., §44.
11. See *Orientación*, July 22, 1979.
12. "Peace," §17, quoting Paul VI, homily, Bogotá, Aug. 23, 1968.
13. *Orientación*, July 22, 1979.
14. Puebla, Final Document, §41.
15. Ibid., §42.
16. Ibid.
17. Ibid.
18. Ibid., §44.
19. Ibid., §§507–8.
20. Ibid., §§55–62.
21. *Lumen Gentium*, §48.
22. Ibid., §8.
23. Puebla, Message to the Peoples of Latin America, §3.
24. Puebla, Final Document, §1140.
25. Ibid., §1206.
26. Ibid., §§76–77.

27. *Evangelii Nuntiandi*, §32.
28. *Gaudium et Spes*, §76.
29. See *Evangelii Nuntiandi*, §13.
30. Ibid., §14.
31. Ibid., §17.
32. Ibid., §25.
33. Final Document, §164.
34. Ibid., §165.
35. Ibid., §§166–69.
36. Opening Address, III, 7.
37. Puebla, Final Document, §358.
38. Ibid., §1138.
39. *Osservatore Romano*, Feb. 22, 1979.
40. Opening Address, III, 4.
41. Final Document, §49; see also §§314, 547, 549, 1262.
42. Ibid., §1262.
43. Ibid., §49.
44. Ibid., §547.
45. Ibid., §549.
46. Ibid., §314.
47. See *Evangelii Nuntiandi*, §31.
48. Opening Address, III, 2.
49. *Redemptor Hominis*, §23.
50. Ibid., §41.
51. Ibid., §46.
52. Ibid., §53.
53. Message to the Peoples of Latin America, §2.
54. Ibid., §3, quoting Acts 3:6.
55. Final Document, §327.
56. Message to the Peoples of Latin America, §3.
57. "Peace," §15.
58. *Evangelii Nuntiandi*, §38.
59. Final Document, §1146, quoting *Apostolicam Actuositatem*, §8.
60. Third Pastoral Letter, p. 106, above.
61. Puebla, Final Document, §1259.
62. Third Pastoral Letter, pp. 108–09, above.
63. "Peace," §15, quoting Paul VI, homily, Bogotá, Aug. 23, 1968.
64. Final Document, §92.
65. Ibid., §72.
66. Ibid., §75.
67. Ibid., §§76–77.
68. Ibid., §85.
69. Ibid., §90.
70. Ibid., §1160.
71. Ibid., §1161.
72. Ibid., §1162.
73. Ibid., §1163.
74. Ibid., §1222.
75. Ibid., §§457–58.

76. Ibid., §641.
77. Ibid., §462.
78. Ibid., §643.
79. Ibid., §§515–16, quoting Gal. 3:28.
80. Ibid., §283, quoting John Paul II's homily in Zapopán, §2.
81. *Marialis Cultus*, §37, quoted in the Puebla Final Document, §302.
82. Homily in Zapopán, §4, quoted in the Puebla Final Document, §297.
83. Puebla, Final Document, §303, quoting Paul VI, *Evangelii Nuntiandi*, §82.

Georgetown Address

Address of Archbishop Romero
on the Occasion of His Academic Investiture
as a Doctor of Humanities, Honoris Causa,
in the Cathedral of San Salvador, February 14, 1978

This evening the cathedral of San Salvador has been transformed into an auditorium of the renowned Georgetown University. Thus there is revived that ancient partnership between the faith and academic learning that was lived out in an earlier epoch by venerable cathedrals and famous universities. And I am reminded that it was in the shadow of those cathedrals that were born the centers of higher learning that today are the glory of all branches of scholarship throughout the world.

But there is something novel about this partly sacred, partly academic coming together of Georgetown University and our cathedral. I am the pastor and teacher of the faith in this archdiocese, and it is the university that comes to me, in my own cathedral, to confer on me its doctorate in humanities.

I wish to draw attention to the originality of this act as I express my gratitude and my welcome. This novel sign of a humble pastor, vested with the insignia of a university degree is, I believe, evocative of the prophetic and ecclesial dimension of the intentions both of Georgetown and of him who, filled with emotion and gratitude, receives this great honor.

At this solemn moment of my life I do not want to be anything more than a sign, a sign whose greatest glory and greatest satisfaction it is, as it was for John the Baptist, to decrease in notoriety so that the eternal word of the gospel may increase and triumph.

Georgetown's generous initiative has come to a climax here, in this cathedral, symbol of the university and of the teaching authority of the bishop. I wish, in accepting this honor, to identify it with the gospel message I preach in an intimate communion of ideals and affection with my beloved clergy, with all the selfless, dynamic men and women consecrated to the religious life, and with those of the people of God who have been entrusted to me.

For me, this generous and noble gesture of Georgetown University, this grant to me of their highest academic distinction, Doctor of Humanities honoris causa, has four aspects to it. And I, along with my church and my people, express my undying gratitude for them: (1) the act expresses solid support for the cause of human rights; (2) it is an act that gives recognition to all who have collaborated in this cause; (3) such an act of solidarity brings consolation and hope to all who have suffered the loss of their liberty and their dignity; (4) it is an echo of denunciation and a call to conversion.

SUPPORT FOR THE CAUSE OF HUMAN RIGHTS

The reason why (*honoris* causa) Georgetown University gives its approval to the modest labor of this archbishop is, first and foremost, to express solid support for that noble cause of Christian humanism that our church proclaims and defends. A celebrated university's giving to a member of El Salvador's hierarchy a doctorate of humanities indicates approval, in a way that will resound across the world, of the "new humanism" that the contemporary church teaches and practices. The church does so after much reflection—reflection that occurred mainly during two solemn convocations of its modern magisterium: the Second Vatican Council and the assembly of Latin American Bishops held in Medellín.

As he brought the council to a close, His Holiness Paul VI was able to challenge "modern humanisms that deny the transcendence of the highest things" to acknowledge the value of the council's "new humanism":

"We too, and more than anyone else, promote the betterment of the individual. . . . This council has recognized that the fundamental calling of men and women is to the attainment of the fullness of their rights and their transcendent destiny; their highest aspirations for life, for personal dignity, for an honorable freedom, for learning, for the renewal of the social order, for justice and for peace—these have all been purified and encouraged.[1]

This service to human dignity that the church cannot renounce was raised by the pope to its highest theological level when he recalled:

In the countenance of every individual, especially in a countenance made transparent by tears and suffering, we can and should recognize the countenance of Christ (Matt. 25:40), the Son of man; and in the countenance of Christ, moreover, we can and should recognize the face of the heavenly Father: "To have seen me is to have seen the Father," said Jesus (John 14:9). Our humanism becomes Christian; our Christianity becomes theocentric—so much so that we can also assert that, in order to know God, it is necessary to know human beings.[2]

It was also a theological, transcendent perspective that inspired the Latin American bishops at Medellín when they directed the evangelization of our continent toward the service of human rights and the betterment of human beings. They felt it to be an authentic summons of the Spirit, one from which the church could not turn away: "a muted cry pours from the throats of millions . . . asking their pastors for a liberation that reaches them from nowhere else."[3]

In this same evangelical context of service to humanity, Paul VI has acknowledged, and praised, the efforts being made by the people of El Salvador, stemming from that global vision of the individual and of humanity that is propounded by the church, to improve the conditions of human life.[4] Two months ago the pope clearly denounced to our ambassador at the Holy See the church's lack of freedom, the grief that results from the violence and repression, and the "manifest injustices that prevent created wealth from reaching everyone in an equitable fashion."[5]

This, then, is our church's "new humanism." The church has the same task as before—that of redeeming persons from sin and leading them to eternal life—but it starts from the situation in this world where there exists the duty of planting the kingdom of God now. This is the cause to which we want to be faithful, together with all that it entails. And Georgetown's homage is a great satisfaction to us not only because, in itself, it is an honor, but above all because it is an acknowledgement of the authenticity of our cause: the cause of Christian humanism.

RECOGNITION OF COLLABORATORS IN THE CAUSE

I cannot accept this honor for myself alone. I feel that, in justice, I must share it with the whole of our local church—and also with those who, though not belonging to the church, have made this cause their own through their sympathy, their support, and their collaboration. I am referring to countless priests, religious communities, lay Catholics, Protestants with a true sense of the gospel, and others of good will who have embodied this cause even to the heroic lengths of death and persecution.

I understand that being joined together in this honor does not so much mean taking pleasure in a duty performed in the service of a noble human cause; above all it means a call to a renewed commitment to the humanism of the gospel, the only humanism that can successfully humanize the relationships among persons in this world. Georgetown's presence in, and attitude toward our archdiocese indicates a God-given encouragement to the betterment of the human race. This is in keeping with the hopes expressed in the church's teaching:

> If further development calls for the work of more and more technicians, even more necessary is the deep thought and reflection of wise men and women in search of a new humanism that will enable modern human beings to find themselves anew by embracing the higher values of love and friendship, of prayer and contemplation. This is what will permit the

fullness of authentic development, a development that is for everyone the transition from less human to more human conditions.[6]

Vatican II highlights a valuable contribution to this fertile field of humanism that our poverty-stricken peoples can make: "The future of the world stands in peril unless wiser men are forthcoming. It should also be pointed out that many nations, poorer in economic goods, are quite rich in wisdom and can offer noteworthy advantages to others."[7]

SOLIDARITY IN HOPE

I also want to interpret this spiritual and cultural honor that Georgetown has made to our church as a gesture of solidarity, one that brings encouragement and hope to those who here suffer, in so many different and humiliating ways, from the violation of their fundamental rights. For the motivation that brought Georgetown here to render me this unforgettable homage had its beginnings there—in the tragic experience of those who have been abused, those whom the church has believed it its duty to defend, and to denounce the abuses. This voice raised in defense and denunciation has too often been silenced, distorted, or calumniated by those with vested interests, or naively misunderstood by some at home and abroad. But today this church knows that it has been clarified, strengthened, and encouraged by this act of a prestigious university, calmly thought out within its learned environment—and a university sufficiently distant not to be hurried into acting either by pressure or by passion.

The academic decision coincides and harmonizes with the apostolic attitude of our church, which, quite sincerely, wished only to live out the mission of the Servant of Yahweh: "sent to bring good news to the poor . . . to bind up hearts that are broken . . . to proclaim liberty to captives, freedom to those in prison . . . to comfort those who mourn" (Isa. 61:1–2).

Within the sphere for which our church is responsible, we wanted our human service to be a faithful echo of the noble voice of Paul VI speaking to the United Nations: "We feel we are making our own the voice of the dead and of the living," he said on that occasion, speaking of the tragic consequences of war.[8] Here we can think of the dead, victims of cruelty, and of those who continue to live, but in terror, under threat, bearing in their bodies the marks of torture, of outrages committed against them. "We also make our own," the pope went on, "the voice of the living who go forward confidently, the youth of the present generation, who legitimately expect a better human race. And we also make our own the voice of the poor, the disinherited, the suffering, of those who long for justice, for a life with dignity for freedom, for well-being, and progress."[9]

So I say that today, here with me, honor, respect, and admiration is being shown to the sufferings, the fear, insecurity, and marginalization endured by so many of my brothers and sisters. This fact is a ray of comfort and of hope. Georgetown represents here in the cathedral of San Salvador the sincere solidarity of humane, Christian culture. This culture crosses frontiers and rises above the wordy parleys of diplomacy and of politics. It is placed at the service of equality, freedom, and of the dignity of all human beings.

AN ECHO OF DENUNCIATION AND CALL TO CONVERSION

Finally, I think that the ecclesial and prophetic meaning of this act of homage to humanism would be incomplete were we to forget that powerful segment of humanity that assaults and sacrifices the dignity of the images of God. It does so because it pursues an authentic cult of violence, whether institutionalized or reactionary. Our church's service to, and defense of, human dignity, together with the sorrow and the shame of so many persons and of so many homes abused and left desolate has brought it to utter an anguished cry of denunciation and repudiation. "No to violence" it has cried out impartially against any hand raised against someone else, carrying out an act of violence that stains the world with sin.

But this cry of denunciation and of repudiation has never aroused in the church a passion for vengeance, nor has it aroused ill will. Its call for justice has always been like that of a mother reminding her quarreling children that they are siblings. Its voice has always carried a word of redemption, summoning the guilty to conversion, and offering pardon to the fratricide who repents.

The church's voice has here an echo of that fraternal love that, arising from faith in the truth revealed by God, has inspired its fruitful social teaching. This teaching the church offers as an ingredient—and a much-needed one—for the dialogue that has to take place between government, capital, and labor to the end that bloody violence, repression, and the social ills of our country will be cured and put behind us, and that a solid peace may be built up on the foundations of justice and love.

In its declarations there has also been an echo of the dignity of a church that puts its loyalty to the gospel before the privileges that come with power and wealth, should these get in the way of its testimony and its credibility. But it does not reject the idea of a constructive dialogue with those in power, so long as they display sincerity and effectiveness in a common service to humanity's double vocation: created to live with happiness and dignity in this world, and to enjoy, beyond history, a happy destiny.

CONCLUSION

Mr. President and representatives of the committee of governors of Georgetown University, Doctors Timothy Healy and Robert Mitchell:

In communion with the whole church of the archdiocese of San Salvador and united in ideals with all men and women of good will who are at work in our country for the cause of humanity, and in solidarity with every man and woman whose liberty or whose dignity has been attacked by any kind of violence—I receive with gratitude the high honor of the doctorate of humanities that, through you, the University of Georgetown confers upon me.

May God repay this generous and meaningful gesture by a growth in the Christian reputation of your illustrious alma mater.

A thousand thanks to you, also, my beloved friends, who have organized and taken part in this unforgettable event. With your fraternal understanding and affection you have helped me, too, to understand, and to put into words, the transcendence of this happening that is so important for the life of our church and its pastor.

And thanks to all of my friends. With your loving congratulations and by your presence here, either physically or in spirit, you have expressed your close solidarity with this humble servant of the humanism of the gospel.

I share with all my brothers and sisters this honor that Georgetown has bestowed on us. It is a new voice of the Spirit, which goes on pointing out to us the path that our church must follow.

NOTES

1. Allocution at the end of Vatican II, Dec. 7, 1965.
2. Ibid.
3. "Poverty,"§2.
4. *Populorum Progressio*, §13.
5. Message to the Ambassador of El Salvador, Dec. 15, 1977.
6. *Populorum Progressio*, §20.
7. *Gaudium et Spes*, §15.
8. Address to the United Nations, Oct. 4, 1965.
9. Ibid.

Pastoral Message to
the National Council of Churches

Prepared for Delivery at the Meeting of the Governing Board of the National Council of Churches, New York City, November 8–10, 1979

This occasion is a very extraordinary one in my life as a pastor. I value it as a providential moment of Christian communion with the members of the board of the National Council of Churches, which represents millions of men and women in the United States of America who profess their faith in our Lord, Jesus Christ.

I feel the love of our Lord very close, throbbing in you, which assures us of his presence: "where two or more are gathered in my name. . . ." (Matt. 18:20). And, therefore, I first address myself to him in gratitude and adoration: Thank you, Lord Jesus Christ, because you so wanted to unite persons in your love that you inspired and brought to reality this ecumenical institution. Thank you for the great honor you have given this humble shepherd from the smallest country in Latin America, and for accepting me in this gathering of shepherds so rich in spirit, in wisdom, and in experience. Your presence among us, Lord, gives me the trust and joy your apostles must have felt when they gathered about you to tell of the wonders they had done in your name (Luke 10:17–20).

It is in this spirit I come to you to deliver the "pastoral message" your secretary general, Dr. Claire Randall, so kindly asked of me. With the same feeling of gratitude, allow me to mention here the kindness, friendship, and hospitality of my dear friends Dr. Jorge Lara Braud and Pastor Rubén Lores, who made arrangements for my visit here.

I also believe this the appropriate moment to express my gratitude to the governing board, and through it, to all my brothers and sisters in this great country—bishops and pastors, various Christian communities, and other institutions and persons who, with their many eloquent testimonies of solidarity, have encouraged the pastoral work of our archdiocese and the heroism and patience of the suffering people of El Salvador.

168

One of the most decisive considerations in my acceptance of this invitation, despite the difficult situation in which my country presently finds itself, was the opportunity to be the personal bearer of this expression of gratitude for your support.

There is a Spanish saying, "Love must be paid with love." And that is the purpose of my pastoral message: to repay a debt of love. I have no other reason to be here. With the simplicity of my presence and my word, I should like to let you know more about our church in the archdiocese of San Salvador, its struggle to be faithful to the gospel amid a people valiantly fighting for its freedom.

First, I shall present a brief pastoral vision of Salvadoran reality, in order to enumerate afterward the various ways in which our church contributes to the liberation of our people. I shall conclude by outlining our pastoral ideology.

VIOLENCE

Violence is the outstanding characteristic of my poor country at the present time. Full of anguish, I must agree with the Final document of Puebla: the "muted cry" of persons pleading for a liberation that never came is now "loud and clear, increasing in volume and intensity."[1] It comes from blood-stained and tragic experiences.

At the base of all violence is social injustice, accurately called "structural violence," which is our greatest social evil now. As Puebla says, this is "the most devastating and humiliating kind of scourge," a "situation of inhuman poverty" finding expression in "infant mortality, lack of adequate housing, health problems, starvation salaries, unemployment and underemployment, malnutrition, job uncertainty, compulsory mass migrations, etc."[2]

Together with this structural violence, we have suffered "repressive violence" from the state, which, justifying itself with the ideology of "national security," considers as "subversive" any attempt at liberation of the people. It pretends to justify murder, disappearances, arbitrary imprisonment, acts of terrorism, kidnapings, and acts of torture," all of which show "a complete lack of respect for the dignity of the human person."[3] From January to June of this year alone there have been 406 assassinations and 307 political arrests, all due to this violence.

From these two kinds of violence, oppression and repression, pour forth what Medellín calls "the explosive revolutions of despair," which have claimed at least 95 victims among us in this same period. Side by side with this tragic play of violence, and as the cause of it, there is a scandalous moral deterioration. As Puebla puts it: "[The Latin American countries] are experiencing the heavy burden of economic and institutional crises, and clear symptoms of corruption and violence."[4] Pastoral concern must point out here, painfully, a horrible inventory of infidelities to and betrayals of

Christian and moral values, as much in public administration as in personal affairs. Everywhere we see what the Lord called "the mystery of iniquity."

Something new came to light in El Salvador on October 15. A coup d'etat planned and carried out by young officers of the armed forces, overthrew, without bloodshed, the regime of General Carlos Humberto Romero. But it has not checked the "spiral of violence." The unexpected change brought about by the military was declared a "rupture with the past." A pledge was given to clean up corruption and to change in depth the structures that nourish violence. With this purpose in mind, honest and competent citizens have joined the new government as a guarantee of good and innovating intentions. Never before in the history of our country have we had a government making such promises as the present one.

Unfortunately, despite the hopes of liberation that our church has supported with prudent criticism, repressive actions of security forces have continued to erupt, and leftist groups multiply their violent activities. For the latter the military insurrection is not a real change, but simply a new face for the same repression. Change, they say, will come only through a process of popular insurrection. They are engaged in a so-called prolonged popular rebellion whose final objective is the seizure of power.

On the other hand, the "extreme right," the privileged minority, constitutes the main obstacle to the necessary socio-economic reforms. This minority is highly reactionary when its selfish interests are at stake. Therefore it maintains the oppression, the structural violence; instead of helping a government that proposes the necessary changes, the right continues to press for a government of repressive violence.

This coup d'etat and the platform of the new government bring a breath of hope to the people. In the midst of the crisis there are many positive aspects that allow us to perceive, with a solid basis in reality, that Salvadorans are capable of finding peace, a peace based on justice and attained through rational means, and that it is not necessary to pay in violence and bloodshed the price of our people's liberation. Our people have those great human and Christian values that the church esteems and feels duty-bound to strengthen and to pursue in offering guidance in the spirit of the gospel and the light of faith. Outstanding among these values are the spirit of service, the experience of love, the spirit of solidarity, of responsibility, industry, courage. One of the most basic is the sense of community with which Salvadorans are capable of overcoming selfishness and sterile divisiveness.

COLLABORATION OF THE CHURCH
IN THE PROCESS OF LIBERATION

The church, being the extension of the incarnation and redemption of the Lord Jesus Christ, discovers what must be its specific mission here and now. Its fidelity to the Lord and the cry of its people groaning under oppression and repression orientate its evangelical work in the same direction ratified by the episcopal assembly in Puebla: the preferential option for the poor. This does not mean that our church follows the way of opportunism or demagogy, as many slanderously infer. "We invite all, regardless of class, to accept and take up the cause of the poor as if they were accepting and taking up their own cause, the cause of Christ himself."[5]

With this spirit of service, I formulated in my fourth pastoral letter of August 6 of this year what has been and continues to be the specific contribution of our archdiocese in the liberation process of our people.

Identity as Church

The contribution of our archdiocese is above all a contribution to its identity as church. To be itself is our church's greatest contribution to the nation. The more clearly it identifies itself with the church that Jesus Christ demands in this historical moment, the more effective and original its message and activities will be. In this sense, we understand the words of Pope John Paul II, that the church does not need to become a political body to contribute to the salvation of the world. The church is not a political power. If it fell into this temptation, "the church would lose its fundamental meaning," said John Paul II. Its message of liberation would no longer have any originality and would open itself to monopolization and manipulation by ideological systems and political parties. It would have no more authority to proclaim freedom as in the name of God."[6]

But John Paul II's typification of the church does not make it an alien to the political, social, and economic realities of life. Not to face the world would be a sin against its own identity. In his first encyclical, *Redemptor Hominis,* John Paul II states that "the human being is the first path the church should follow in compliance with its mission." And this is so because the transcendence that should characterize the mission of the church is not a transcendence that sets human nature aside. It is in transcending human nature, but always within human nature, that the church finds and builds the kingdom of God that Jesus promised. And he continues to announce it through the ministrations of his church.

This is my main pastoral concern and this is the spirit that I try to diffuse in my community: to build up our church in the midst of its own conflicts and oppositions. The church does not seek to be in opposition to anyone, and does not want to clash with anyone. It promotes a great affirmation of God and his kingdom; it clashes only with those who oppose God and his kingdom.

Integral Evangelization

In order to be true to its own identity, our church pursues evangelization as its primary specific service. It cannot forget that the Lord sent it to all nations, saying: "Go and preach the gospel." But we understand evangelization in a more complex sense. Since Vatican II, ecclesiastical understanding and documentation on evangelization have been enriched. Pope Paul VI defines evangelization in these terms: "to preach and teach, to be the channel of the gift of grace, to reconcile sinners with God, and to perpetuate Christ's sacrifice in the Mass . . . the memorial of his death and glorious resurrection."[7] In this sense, evangelization becomes a transforming force for all nations.

In our archdiocese, we seek to offer a liberating evangelization—that is to say, one that brings to bear all the transforming force given by our holy Redeemer. In the liberation of our country, we believe the gospel offers an irreplaceable contribution; and thus we seek an integral evangelization, one that does not slight any aspect of the transforming power of the gospel. A dangerous reductionism, a nonintegral proselytism, can come about in two ways: by accentuating only the elements of transcendence, of inner spirituality, and our eternal destiny; or, inversely, by stressing only the immanent elements of the kingdom of God, which certainly has to begin in this world, though it "is not of this world."

Taking into consideration the complexity of the elements of evangelization, and also the complexity of the realities of our country, our church believes that in our national crisis we should emphasize the following aspects of evangelization.

A Solid Doctrinal Guidance

We said in Puebla that we wanted to enlighten our pastoral ministry with the light of the truth that makes us free (John 8:32). And, as in Puebla, I feel that the theological synthesis presented by Pope John Paul II is important for our country: the truth about Christ, the truth about the church, the truth about human nature. The Pope also defended the value of the social doctrine of the church: "When injustices increase and the gap between rich and poor widens distressingly, then the social doctrine of the Church—in a form that is creative and open to the broad areas of the Church's presence—should be a valuable tool for formation and action."[8]

Prophetic Denunciation

This is another element of evangelization that the church cannot do without in a society that lives within structures of injustice, violence, and selfishness. We have done nothing but comply with the fiery words of Pope John Paul II:

> It is necessary that injustice be given its correct designation: the exploitation of some human beings by others, the exploitation of a people by the state, by institutions, by the structures of economic systems, or of regimes that sometimes operate callously. It is necessary to give the correct name to every social injustice, to every act of discrimination or violence inflicted on human beings, whether on persons themselves, or their spirit, or their consciences, or their convictions.[9]

The evangelical stress of this denunciation is not inspired by hate or by revenge but by the love of the Lord who "does not want the death of sinners but their conversion and life."

The Unmasking of Idolatry

It is part of our prophetic function to invoke the greatness of the only Lord to overthrow absolutisms that offend God and destroy human dignity. I have pointed out three principal idolatries:

1) The idolatry of wealth and private property, which inclines persons toward the ideal of "having more" and lessens their interest in "being more." It is this absolutism that supports the structural violence and oppression of our people.

2) The idolatry of power, which under the new label of "national security" has often contributed to strengthening "the totalitarian or authoritarian character of governments based on the use of force, leading to the abuse of power and the violation of human rights."[10]

3) The idolatry of political organizations, which certain popular political groups fall into when they no longer seek the interest of the people who originally inspired them, but rather subordinate the people to the interest of ideologies and organizations. During the last few weeks, this absolutism of radical leftist groups has caused great violence in El Salvador. They want to hinder the stabilization of the new government at any cost, so that their own strategy of popular insurrection may prevail. They refuse any type of dialogue and their only language is violence, which in turn provokes new repressive violence. Many are the dead and wounded, and great is the damage caused by this new game of provocation and repression.

The church feels that it is a part of its evangelical mission to unmask these destructive absolutisms and guide humankind to the one and only Absolute and to human fellowship.

Evangelization and Liberation

To promote integral human liberation is another contribution that, in the name of evangelization, our archdiocese is making to our country. "At the center of the message of which the Church is the trustee and herald, it finds inspiration for acting in favor of brotherhood, justice, and peace; and against all forms of domination, slavery, discrimination, violence, attacks on religious liberty, and aggression against human beings and whatever attacks life."[11]

In my country, as in all of Latin America, no authentic evangelization can be carried out "unless we commit ourselves on the personal level, and in many cases on the structural level as well, to serving and promoting the most dispossessed and downtrodden human groups and social classes, with all the consequences that will entail on the plane of temporal realities."[12]

Therefore, the church would betray its own love for God and its fidelity to the gospel if it should cease to the "the voice of those who do not have a voice,'' advocate of the rights of the poor, counselor and promoter and humanizer of every legitimate struggle to fashion a society based on justice, which prepares the road to the real kingdom of God in history. This demands of the church a greater closeness to the poor, with whom it must identify itself even in their dangers and in their persecution, ready to give the greatest testimony of love, to defend and promote those whom Jesus most loved.

Structural Changes

The church is obliged by its evangelical mission to demand structural changes that favor the kingdom of God and a more just and comradely way of life. Unjust social structures are the roots of all violence and disturbances. How hard and conflicting are the results of this evangelical duty! Those who benefit from obsolete structures react selfishly to any kind of change. And those who advocate violent changes clash impatiently with the gospel of rationality and peace.

Sharing with the People

Another evangelical service of our church is that of accompanying the people, guiding it in its desire for freedom and liberation. This is simply obedience to the command of Jesus to be light, salt, and ferment in society, incarnating itself more deeply in the people's own history, in its anguishes and in its hopes.

This sharing of life and gospel with the people must be adapted differently to the poor and to the privileged classes:

1) The church reminds the poor of their need for conversion. The preferential option for the poor does not justify the evident moral deficiencies that the poor must correct. But without rationalizing their misconduct, they have many human and Christian values that give hope for and stimulate evangelical sharing. Evangelical sharing goes beyond a moralizing and indoctrination of the general public; it encourages social and political organization of the masses, of *campesinos*, factory workers, and others.

2) The church also calls the privileged classes—who have the responsibility of social, economic, and political power—to conversion. The church reminds them of their great responsibility in overcoming disorder and violence, not by means of repression but rather through justice and popular participation. Their privileged situation calls for service to others and not paternalism—"the giving of what is due in justice . . . represented as the offering of a charitable gift."[13]

OUR PASTORAL GUIDELINES

God's will brought me to the chair of the archdiocese of San Salvador on February 22, 1977. My honorable predecessor, Archbishop Luis Chávez y González, passed on to me on that day the rich bequest of a church that was trying to effect the renewal championed by Vatican II and apply it to Latin America as worked out in Medellín. This renovating effort was defined in the archdiocese during the pastoral week of January 1976. Its main themes were: "The priority option for an evangelization at all levels [which] is considered critical, urgent, and necessary. The necessary renewal of all available means in favor of an adequate evangelization without restraints or superficial procedures. The urgent need to select and adequately train pastoral workers, particularly lay persons. The strengthening of Christian communities as a necessary objective that must be kept on our horizon if we want to revitalize the church. And the creation of adequate and dynamic mechanisms that will activate and execute these options."

My first pastoral concern as archbishop was to promote the course of these providential themes. The cruel and bloody trampling of our people's human rights was already on the increase. Our communities were under implacable persecution, particularly evident in the assassination of five of our priests. These circumstances invigorated our impulse to identify with the sorrows of the people and made us seek new ways to defend its rights and transform it into a Christian community. The pastoral options of Puebla for Latin America came to ratify our pastoral guidelines, which can be summarized as follows:

1) *A searching attitude.* The changeable circumstances in our history have made us better understand the meaning of a transcendent, but always pilgrim, church, alert, always seeking to apply the unique and eternal gospel to the historical moment it is living through.

2) *Preferential option for the poor.* The greatest wealth and satisfaction lies in making ours this preference of our Lord Jesus Christ, who identified himself with the cause of the poor. If, due to this option, we have lost honors and privileges, we feel closer to the heart of our people and in greater harmony with the universal church, which has favored us with many testimonies of solidarity. One of these testimonies is my presence here with you in this distinguished assembly. This option for the poor also promotes our evangelical unity as a church and points out the reasons for our failings and the paths of our conversion. We feel that unity in Christ is broken only by those who do not seek for Christ in poverty but in their own welfare.

3) *A common pastoral plan.* It tries to bring together in communion the bishop, responsible for the archdiocese, all the charisma of the Spirit, and the apostolic initiatives of individuals and groups, just as all the waters from separate springs flow toward the river they eventually form.

4) *Pastoral adaptation.* Our effort for pastoral unity is, at the same time, an effort at adaptation, particularly to three types of pastoral ministry that we believe necessary and urgent in our circumstances:

a) Pastoral ministry of the masses—an extensive evangelization and one that cultivates our popular religiosity of the masses.

b) Pastoral ministry of ecclesial communities and small groups, in the sense of being a sign, ferment, salt, and light—an intensive evangelization.

c) Pastoral ministry of accompaniment—personal or group evangelization with a variety of concrete options that Christians can take as demanded by their faith vis-à-vis the urgent changes necessary to make society more human and more Christian.

This is my pastoral message to you, my fellow pastors and Christians. This is the humble contribution I bring to you, not alone, but in communion with my fellow priests, members of religious congregations, and lay persons who form the community of the archdiocese of San Salvador. I thank you once again for your invitation. I pray to the Lord Jesus Christ that this humble voice of a Christian community in Latin America may be of assistance in stimulating the ecumenical efforts of the National Council of Churches to establish in this country, the elder brother of our countries, the kingdom of justice, peace, and love of our Lord Jesus Christ.

NOTES

1. §89.
2. Final Document, §29.
3. Ibid., §1262.
4. Ibid., §508.
5. Puebla, Message to the Peoples of Latin America, §3.
6. *Evangelii Nuntiandi*, §32.
7. Ibid., §14.
8. Opening Address at Puebla, III, 7.
9. *Osservatore Romano*, Feb. 22, 1979.
10. Puebla, Final Document, §49.
11. Opening Address, III, 2.
12. Puebla, Final Document, §327.
13. Vatican II, *Apostolicam Actuositatem*, §8.

The Political Dimension of the Faith from the Perspective of the Option for the Poor

Address by Archbishop Romero on the Occasion
of the Conferral of a Doctorate, Honoris Causa,
by the University of Louvain, Belgium, February 2, 1980

I come from the smallest country in faraway Latin America. I come bringing in my heart, which is that of a Salvadoran Christian and pastor, greetings, gratitude, and the joy of sharing the experiences of life.

I first of all greet with admiration this noble alma mater of Louvain. Never did I imagine the enormous honor of being thus linked with a European center of such academic and cultural prestige, a center where were born so many of the ideas that have contributed to the marvelous effort being made by the church and by society to adapt themselves to the new times in which we live.

Therefore I come also to express my thanks to the University of Louvain, and to the church in Belgium. I want to think of this honorary doctorate as something other than an act of homage to me personally. The enormous disproportion of such a great weight being attributed to my few merits would overwhelm me. Let me rather interpret this generous distinction awarded by the university as an affectionate act of homage to the people of El Salvador and to their church, as an eloquent testimony of support for, and solidarity with, the sufferings of my people and for their noble struggle for liberation, and as a gesture of communion, and of sympathy, with the apostolic work of my archdiocese.

I could not refuse to accept the privilege of this act of homage if, by coming to receive it, I could come to thank the church of Belgium for the invaluable pastoral help it has given to the church of El Salvador. It would not, indeed, have been possible to find a more suitable time and place to say "thank you" than this one, so courteously provided for me by the University of Louvain. So, from the depths of my heart, many thanks to you—bishops, priests, religious, and lay persons—for so generously uniting your lives, your labors, the hardships, and the persecution involved in our pastoral activities.

And in the same spirit of friendship as that in which I expressed my greetings and my gratitude, I want to express the joy I have in coming to share with you, in a fraternal way, my experience as a pastor and as a Salvadoran, and my theological reflection as a teacher of the faith.

In line with the friendly suggestion made by the university, I have the honor of placing this experience and reflection within the series of conferences taking place here upon the theme of the political dimension of the Christian faith.

I shall not try to talk, and you cannot expect me to talk, as would an expert in politics. Nor will I even speculate, as someone might who was an expert, on the theoretical relationship between the faith and politics. No, I am going to speak to you simply as a pastor, as one who, together with his people, has been learning the beautiful but harsh truth that the Christian faith does not cut us off from the world but immerses us in it, that the church is not a fortress set apart from the city. The church follows Jesus who lived, worked, battled and died in the midst of a city, in the *polis*. It is in this sense that I should like to talk about the political dimension of the Christian faith: in the precise sense of the repercussions of the faith on the world, and also of the repercussions that being in the world has on the faith.

A CHURCH AT THE SERVICE OF THE WORLD

We ought to be clear from the start that the Christian faith and the activity of the church have always had socio-political repercussions. By commission or omission, by associating themselves with one or another social group, Christians have always had an influence upon the socio-political makeup of the world in which they lived. The problem is about the "how" of this influence in the socio-political world, whether or not it is in accordance with the faith.

As a first idea, though still a very general one, I want to propose the intuition of Vatican II that lies at the root of every ecclesial movement of today. The essence of the church lies in its mission of service to the world, in its mission to save the world in its totality, and of saving it in history, here and now. The church exists to act in solidarity with the hopes and joys, the anxieties and sorrows, of men and women. Like Jesus, the church was sent "to bring good news to the poor, to heal the contrite of heart . . . to seek and to save what was lost" (Luke 4:18, 19:10).

The World of the Poor

You all know these words of Scripture, given prominence by Vatican II.[1] During the 1960s several of your bishops and theologians helped to throw light on the essence and the mission of the church understood in these terms. My contribution will be to flesh out those beautiful declarations from the standpoint of my own situation, that of a small Latin American country, typical of what today is called the Third World. To put it in one word—in a word that sums it all up and makes it concrete—the world that the church ought to serve is, for us, the world of the poor.

Our Salvadoran world is no abstraction. It is not another example of what is understood by "world" in developed countries such as yours. It is a world made up mostly of men and women who are poor and oppressed. And we say of that world of the poor that it is the key to understanding the Christian faith, to understanding the activity of the church and the political dimension of that faith and that ecclesial activity. It is the poor who tell us what the world is, and what the church's service to the world should be. It is the poor who tell us what the *polis* is, what the city is and what it means for the church really to live in that world.

Allow me, then, briefly to explain from the perspective of the poor among my people, whom I represent, the situation and the activity of our church in the world in which we live, and then to reflect theologically upon the importance that this real world, this culture, this socio-political world, has for the church.

In its pastoral work, our archdiocese in recent years has been moving in a direction that can only be described and only be understood as a turning toward the world of the poor, to their real, concrete world.

Incarnation in the World of the Poor

Just as elsewhere in Latin America, the words of Exodus have, after many years, perhaps centuries, finally resounded in our ears: "The cry of the sons of Israel has come to me, and I have witnessed the way in which the Egyptians oppress them" (Exod. 3:9). These words have given us new eyes to see what has always been the case among us, but which has so often been hidden, even from the view of the church itself. We have learned to see what is the first, basic fact about our world and, as pastors, we have made a judgment about it at Medellín and at Puebla. "That misery, as a collective fact, expresses itself as an injustice which cries to the heavens."[2] At Puebla we declared, "So we brand the situation of inhuman poverty in which millions of Latin Americans live as the most devastating and humiliating kind of scourge. And this situation finds expression in such things as a high rate of infant mortality, lack of adequate housing, health problems, starvation wages, unemployment and underemployment, malnutrition, job uncertainty, compulsory mass migrations, etc."[3] Experiencing these realities, and letting ourselves be affected by them, far from separating us from our faith has sent us back to the world of the poor as to our true home. It has moved us, as a first, basic step, to take the world of the poor upon ourselves.

It is there that we have found the real faces of the poor, about which Puebla speaks.[4] There we have met landworkers without land and without steady employment, without running water or electricity in their homes,

without medical assistance when mothers give birth, and without schools
for their children. There we have met factory workers who have no labor
rights, and who get fired from their jobs if they demand such rights, human
beings who are at the mercy of cold economic calculations. There we have
met the mothers and the wives of those who have disappeared, or who are
political prisoners. There we have met the shantytown dwellers, whose
wretchedness defies imagination, suffering the permanent mockery of the
mansions nearby.

It is within this world devoid of a human face, this contemporary
sacrament of the suffering servant of Yahweh, that the church of my archdiocese has undertaken to incarnate itself. I do not say this in a triumphalis-
tic spirit, for I am well aware how much in this regard remains to be done.
But I say it with immense joy, for we have made the effort not to pass by
afar off, not to circle round the one lying wounded in the roadway, but to
approach him or her as did the good Samaritan.

This coming closer to the world of the poor is what we understand both
by the incarnation and by conversion. The changes that were needed within
the church and in its apostolate, in education, in religious and in priestly
life, in lay movements, which we had not brought about simply by looking
inward upon the church, we are now carrying out by turning ourselves outward toward the world of the poor.

Proclaiming the Good News to the Poor

Our encounter with the poor has regained for us the central truth of the
gospel, through which the word of God urges us to conversion. The church
has to proclaim the good news to the poor. Those who, in this-worldly
terms, have heard bad news, and who have lived out even worse realities,
are now listening through the church to the word of Jesus: "The kingdom
of God is at hand; blessed are you who are poor, for the kingdom of God is
yours." And hence they also have good news to proclaim to the rich: that
they, too, become poor in order to share the benefits of the kingdom with
the poor. Anyone who knows Latin America will be quite clear that there is
no ingenuousness in these words, still less the workings of a soporific drug.
What is to be found in these words is a coming together of the aspiration on
our continent for liberation, and God's offer of love to the poor. This is the
hope that the church offers, and it coincides with the hope, at times dor-
mant and at other times frustrated or manipulated, of the poor of Latin
America.

It is something new among our people that today the poor see in the
church a source of hope and a support for their noble struggle for liberation. The hope that our church encourages is neither naive nor passive. It is
rather a summons from the word of God for the great majority of the people, the poor, that they assume their proper responsibility, that they undertake their own conscientization, that, in a country where it is legally or
practically prohibited (at some periods more so than at others) they set
about organizing themselves. And it is support, sometimes critical support,

for their just causes and demands. The hope that we preach to the poor is intended to give them back their dignity, to encourage them to take charge of their own future. In a word, the church has not only turned toward the poor, it has made of the poor the special beneficiaries of its mission because, as Puebla says, "God takes on their defense and loves them."⁵

Commitment to the Defense of the Poor

The church has not only incarnated itself in the world of the poor, giving them hope; it has also firmly committed itself to their defense. The majority of the poor in our country are oppressed and repressed daily by economic and political structures. The terrible words spoken by the prophets of Israel continue to be verified among us. Among us there are those who sell others for money, who sell a poor person for a pair of sandals; those who, in their mansions, pile up violence and plunder; those who crush the poor; those who make the kingdom of violence come closer as they lie upon their beds of ivory; those who join house to house, and field to field, until they occupy the whole land, and are the only ones there.

Amos and Isaiah are not just voices from distant centuries; their writings are not merely texts that we reverently read in the liturgy. They are everyday realities. Day by day we live out the cruelty and ferocity they excoriate. We live them out when there come to us the mothers and the wives of those who have been arrested or who have disappeared, when mutilated bodies turn up in secret cemeteries, when those who fight for justice and peace are assassinated. Daily we live out in our archdiocese what Puebla so vigorously denounced: "There are the anxieties based on systematic or selective repression; it is accompanied by accusations, violations of privacy, improper pressures, tortures, and exiles. There are the anxieties produced in many families by the disappearance of their loved ones, about whom they cannot get any news. There is the total insecurity bound up with arrest and detention without judicial consent. There are the anxieties felt in the face of a system of justice that has been suborned or cowed."⁶

In this situation of conflict and antagonism, in which just a few persons control economic and political power, the church has placed itself at the side of the poor and has undertaken their defense. The church cannot do otherwise, for it remembers that Jesus had pity on the multitude. But by defending the poor it has entered into serious conflict with the powerful who belong to the monied oligarchies and with the political and military authorities of the state.

Persecuted for Serving the Poor

This defense of the poor in a world deep in conflict has occasioned something new in the recent history of our church: persecution. You know the more important facts. In less than three years over fifty priests have been attacked, threatened, calumniated. Six are already martyrs—they were murdered. Some have been tortured and others expelled. Nuns have also been persecuted. The archdiocesan radio station and educational institutions that are Catholic or of a Christian inspiration have been attacked, threatened, intimidated, even bombed. Several parish communities have been raided.

If all this has happened to persons who are the most evident representatives of the church, you can guess what has happened to ordinary Christians, to the *campesinos,* catechists, lay ministers, and to the ecclesial base communities. There have been threats, arrests, tortures, murders, numbering in the hundreds and thousands. As always, even in persecution, it has been the poor among the Christians who have suffered most.

It is, then, an indisputable fact that, over the last three years, our church has been persecuted. But it is important to note why it has been persecuted. Not any and every priest has been persecuted, not any and every institution has been attacked. That part of the church has been attacked and persecuted that put itself on the side of the people and went to the people's defense.

Here again we find the same key to understanding the persecution of the church: the poor. Once again it is the poor who bring us to understand what has really happened. That is why the church has understood the persecution from the perspective of the poor. Persecution has been occasioned by the defense of the poor. It amounts to nothing other than the church's taking upon itself the lot of the poor.

Real persecution has been directed against the poor, the body of Christ in history today. They, like Jesus, are the crucified, the persecuted servant of Yahweh. They are the ones who make up in their own bodies that which is lacking in the passion of Christ. And for that reason when the church has organized and united itself around the hopes and the anxieties of the poor it has incurred the same fate as that of Jesus and of the poor: persecution.

The Political Dimension of the Faith

This has been a brief sketch of the situation, and of the stance, of the church in El Salvador. The political dimension of the faith is nothing other than the church's response to the demands made upon it by the de facto socio-political world in which it exists. What we have rediscovered is that this demand is a fundamental one for the faith, and that the church cannot ignore it. That is not to say that the church should regard itself as a political institution entering into competition with other political institutions, or that it has its own political processes. Nor, much less, is it to say that our church seeks political leadership. I am talking of something more profound, something more in keeping with the gospel. I am talking about an authentic option for the poor, of becoming incarnate in their world, of proclaiming the good news to them, of giving them hope, of encouraging them to engage in a liberating praxis, of defending their cause and of sharing their fate.

The church's option for the poor explains the political dimension of the faith in its fundamentals and in its basic outline. Because the church has opted for the truly poor, not for the fictitiously poor, because it has opted for those who really are oppressed and repressed, the church lives in a political world, and it fulfills itself as church also through politics. It cannot be otherwise if the church, like Jesus, is to turn itself toward the poor.

Making the Faith Real in the World of the Poor

The course taken by the archdiocese has clearly issued from its faith conviction. The transcendence of the gospel has guided us in our judgment and in our action. We have judged the social and political situation from the standpoint of the faith. But it is also true, to look at it another way, that the faith itself has been deepened, that hidden riches of the gospel have been opened, precisely by taking up this stance toward socio-political reality such as it is.

Now I should just like to put forward some short reflections on several fundamental aspects of the faith that we have seen enriched through this real incarnation in the socio-political world.

A Clearer Awareness of Sin

In the first place, we have a better knowledge of what sin is. We know that offending God is death for humans. We know that such a sin really is mortal, not only in the sense of the interior death of the person who commits the sin, but also because of the real, objective death the sin produces. Let us remind ourselves of a fundamental datum of our Christian faith: sin killed the Son of God, and sin is what goes on killing the children of God.

We see that basic truth of the Christian faith daily in the situation in our country. It is impossible to offend God without offending one's brother or sister. And the worst offense against God, the worst form of secularism, as one of our Salvadoran theologians has said, is:

> to turn children of God, temples of the Holy Spirit, the body of Christ in history, into victims of oppression and injustice, into slaves to economic greed, into fodder for political repression. The worst of these forms of secularism is the denial of grace by the objectivization of this world as an operative presence of the powers of evil, the visible presence of the denial of God.[7]

It is not a matter of sheer routine that I insist once again on the existence in our country of structures of sin. They are sin because they produce the fruits of sin: the deaths of Salvadorans—the swift death brought by repression or the long, drawn out, but no less real, death from structural oppression. That is why we have denounced what in our country has become the idolatry of wealth, of the absolute right, within the capitalist system, of private property, of political power in national security regimes, in the name of which personal security is itself institutionalized.

No matter how tragic it may appear, the church through its entrance into the real socio-political world has learned how to recognize, and how to deepen its understanding of, the essence of sin. The fundamental essence of sin, in our world, is revealed in the death of Salvadorans.

Greater Clarity on the Incarnation and Redemption

In the second place we now have a better understanding of what the incarnation means, what it means to say that Jesus really took human flesh and made himself one with his brothers and sisters in suffering, in tears and laments, in surrender. I am not speaking of a universal incarnation. This is impossible. I am speaking of an incarnation that is preferential and partial: incarnation in the world of the poor. From that perspective the church will become a church for everybody. It will offer a service to the powerful, too, through the apostolate of conversion—but not the other way around, as has so often been the case in the past.

The world of the poor, with its very concrete social and political characteristics, teaches us where the church can incarnate itself in such a way that it will avoid the false universalism that inclines the church to associate itself with the powerful. The world of the poor teaches us what the nature of Christian love is, a love that certainly seeks peace but also unmasks false pacifism—the pacifism of resignation and inactivity. It is a love that should certainly be freely offered, but that seeks to be effective in history. The world of the poor teaches us that the sublimity of Christian love ought to be mediated through the overriding necessity of justice for the majority. It ought not to turn away from honorable conflict. The world of the poor teaches us that liberation will arrive only when the poor are not simply on the receiving end of handouts from governments or from the church, but when they themselves are the masters of, and protagonists in, their own struggle and liberation, thereby unmasking the root of false paternalism, including ecclesiastical paternalism.

The real world of the poor also teaches us about Christian hope. The church preaches a new heaven and a new earth. It knows, moreover, that no socio-political system can be exchanged for the final fullness that is given by God. But it has also learned that transcendent hope must be preserved by signs of hope in history, no matter how simple they may apparently be— such as those proclaimed by the Trito-Isaiah when he says "they will build houses and inhabit them, plant vineyards and eat their fruit" (Isa. 65:21). What in this is an authentically Christian hope—not reduced, as is so often said disparagingly, to what is merely of this world or purely human—is being learned daily through contact with those who have no houses and no vineyards, those who build for others to inhabit and work so that others may eat the fruits.

A Deeper Faith in God and in His Christ

In the third place, incarnation in the socio-political world is the locus for deepening faith in God and in his Christ. We believe in Jesus who came to bring the fullness of life, and we believe in a living God who gives life to men and women and wants them truly to live. These radical truths of the faith become really true and truly radical when the church enters into the heart of the life and death of its people. Then there is put before the faith of the church, as it is put before the faith of every individual, the most fundamental choice: to be in favor of life or to be in favor of death. We see, with great clarity, that here neutrality is impossible. Either we serve the life of Salvadorans, or we are accomplices in their death. And here what is most fundamental about the faith is given expression in history: either we believe in a God of life, or we serve the idols of death.

In the name of Jesus we want, and we work for, life in its fullness, a life that is not reduced to the frantic search for basic material needs, nor one reduced to the sphere of the socio-political. We know perfectly well that the superabundant fullness of life is to be achieved only in the kingdom of the Father. In human history this fullness is achieved through a worthy service of that kingdom, and total surrender to the Father. But we see with equal clarity that in the name of Jesus it would be sheer illusion, it would be an irony, and, at bottom, it would be the most profound blasphemy, to forget and to ignore the basic levels of life, the life that begins with bread, a roof, a job.

With the Apostle John we believe that Jesus is "the Word who is life" (1 John 1:1), and that God reveals himself wherever this life is to be found. Where the poor begin to really live, where the poor begin to free themselves, where persons are able to sit around a common table to share with one another—the God of life is there. When the church inserts itself into the socio-political world it does so in order to work with it so that from such cooperation life may be given to the poor. In doing so, therefore, it is not distancing itself from its mission, nor is it doing something of secondary importance or something incidental to its mission. It is giving testimony to its faith in God; it is being the instrument of the Spirit, the Lord and giver of life.

This faith in the God of life is the explanation for what lies deepest in the Christian mystery. To give life to the poor one has to give of one's own life, even to give one's life itself. The greatest sign of faith in a God of life is the witness of those who are ready to give up their own life. "A man can have no greater love than to lay down his life for his friends" (John 15:13). And we see this daily in our country. Many Salvadorans, many Christians, are ready to give their lives so that the poor may have life. They are following Jesus and showing their faith in him. Living within the real world just as Jesus did, like him accused and threatened, like him laying down their lives, they are giving witness to the Word of life.

Our story, then, is a very old one. It is Jesus' story that we, in all modesty, are trying to follow. As church, we are not political experts, nor do we want to manipulate politics through its own internal mechanisms. But entrance into the socio-political world, into the world where the lives and deaths of the great mass of the population are decided upon, is necessary and urgent if we are to preserve, not only in word but in deed, faith in a God of life, and follow the lead of Jesus.

CONCLUSION

In conclusion, I should like to sum up what is central to the things I have been saying. In the ecclesial life of our archdiocese the political dimension of the faith—or, if one prefers, the relationship between faith and politics—has not been discovered by purely theoretical reflection, reflection made before the church has acted. Such reflection is important—but not decisive. Such reflection becomes important *and* decisive when it does indeed reflect the real life of the church. The honor of putting my pastoral experience into words in this university setting has obliged me today to undertake theological reflection. But it is rather in the actual practice of service to the poor that the political dimension of the faith is to be found, and correctly found. In such practice one can discover the relationship between the two, and what distinguishes them. It is the faith that provides the first impulse to incarnate oneself in the socio-political world of the poor, and gives encouragement to actions that lead to liberation and are also socio-political. And in their own turn that praxis and that incarnation make concrete the basic aspects of the faith.

In what I have here laid out, I have sketched only a broad outline of this double movement. Naturally, there are many more topics to be discussed. I might have talked about the relationship between the faith and political ideologies—in particular Marxism. I could have dwelt upon the question of violence and its legitimacy—a burning issue for us. Such topics are frequent subjects for reflection, and we face them without preconceptions and without fear. But we face them to the extent that they become real problems, and we are learning to provide solutions within the same process.

In the short period it has fallen to me to guide the archdiocese, there have been four different governments with distinctive political programs. Over these years other political forces, revolutionary and democratic, have been growing and developing. So the church has had to go on making judgments about politics from within a changing scene. At the present time the outlook is ambiguous. On the one hand all the projects emanating from the government are collapsing, and the possibility of popular liberation is growing.

But rather than listing for you all the fluctuations in the politics of El Salvador, I have chosen to explain what lies at the root of the church's stance in our explosive socio-political world. I have tried to make clear to you the ultimate criterion, one which is theological and historical, for the church's involvement in the world of the poor. In accordance with its own specific nature the church will go on supporting one or another political program to the extent that it operates in favor of the poor among the people.

I believe that this is the way to maintain the church's identity and transcendence. We enter into the real socio-political development of our people. We judge it from the point of view of the poor. We encourage all liberation movements that really lead to justice and peace for the majority of the people. We think this is the way to preserve the transcendence and the identity of the church, because in this way we preserve our faith in God.

Early Christians used to say *Gloria Dei, vivens homo* ("the glory of God is the living person"). We could make this more concrete by saying *Gloria Dei, vivens pauper* ("the glory of God is the living poor person"). From the perspective of the transcendence of the gospel, I believe we can determine what the life of the poor truly is. And I also believe that by putting ourselves alongside the poor and trying to bring life to them we shall come to know the eternal truth of the gospel.

NOTES

1. *Lumen Gentium*, §8.

2. "Justice," §1.

3. Final Document, §29.

4. See ibid., §§31–39.

5. Ibid., §1142.

6. Ibid., §42.

7. I. Ellacuría, "Entre Medellín y Puebla," *Estudios Centroamericanos*, March 1978, n. 353, p. 123.

Letter to President Carter

February 17, 1980

Archbishop Romero read the letter to Jimmy Carter in his homily of February 17 for the people's approval, which they indicated by their applause. The following day, he noted in his diary in regard to the letter: "It is prompted by the proximate danger that military aid signifies for El Salvador and especially by the new notion of special warfare, which consists in eliminating in murderous fashion all the endeavors of the people's organizations under the pretext of fighting communism or terrorism. This type of warfare means to do away with not only the men directly responsible but with their whole families, which in this view are all poisoned by these terroristic ideas and must be eliminated. The danger is serious, and the letter is designed to beg the president of the United States not to provide military aid, which would mean great harm to our people, because it would be destined to snuff out many lives."

San Salvador
February 17, 1980

His Excellency
The President of the United States
Mr. Jimmy Carter

Dear Mr. President:

In the last few days, news has appeared in the national press that worries me greatly. According to the reports, your government is studying the possibility of economic and military support and assistance to the present government junta.

Because you are a Christian and because you have shown that you want to defend human rights, I venture to set forth for you my pastoral point of view in regard to this news and to make a specific request of you.

I am very concerned by the news that the government of the United States is planning to further El Salvador's arms race by sending military equipment and advisers to "train three Salvadoran batallions in logistics, communications, and intelligence." If this information from the newspapers is correct, instead of favoring greater justice and peace in El Salvador, your government's contribution will undoubtedly sharpen the injustice and the repression inflicted on the organized people, whose struggle has often been for respect for their most basic human rights.

The present government junta and, especially, the armed forces and security forces have unfortunately not demonstrated their capacity to resolve in practice the nation's serious political and structural problems. For the most part, they have resorted to repressive violence, producing a total of deaths and injuries much greater than under the previous military regime, whose systematic violation of human rights was reported by the Inter-American Commission on Human Rights.

The brutal form in which the security forces recently evicted and murdered the occupiers of the headquarters of the Christian Democratic Party even though the junta and the party apparently did not authorize the operation is an indication that the junta and the Christian Democrats do not govern the country, but that political power is in the hands of unscrupulous military officers who know only how to repress the people and favor the interests of the Salvadoran oligarchy.

If it is true that last November "a group of six Americans was in El Salvador . . . providing $200,000 in gas masks and flak jackets and teaching how to use them against demonstrators," you ought to be informed that it is evident that since then the security forces, with increased personal protection and efficiency, have even more violently repressed the people, using deadly weapons.

For this reason, given that as a Salvadoran and archbishop of the archdiocese of San Salvador, I have an obligation to see that faith and justice reign in my country, I ask you, if you truly want to defend human rights:

—to forbid that military aid be given to the Salvadoran government;

—to guarantee that your government will not intervene directly or indirectly, with military, economic, diplomatic, or other pressures, in determining the destiny of the Salvadoran people.

—In these moments, we are living through a grave economic and political crisis in our country, but it is certain that increasingly the people are awakening and organizing and have begun to prepare themselves to manage and be responsible for the future of El Salvador, as the only ones capable of surmounting the crisis.

It would be unjust and deplorable for foreign powers to intervene and frustrate the Salvadoran people, to repress them and keep them from deciding autonomously the economic and political course that our nation should follow. It would be to violate a right that the Latin American bishops, meeting at Puebla, recognized publicly when we spoke of "the legitimate self-determination of our peoples, which allows them to organize according to their own spirit and the course of their history and to cooperate in a new international order'' (Puebla, 505).

I hope that your religious sentiments and your feelings for the defense of human rights will move you to accept my petition, thus avoiding greater bloodshed in this suffering country.

Sincerely,

Oscar A. Romero
Archbishop

Last Homily of Archbishop Romero

March 24, 1980

Archbishop Romero celebrated Mass for the first anniversary of the death of Sara Meardi de Pinto, the mother of Jorge Pinto, publisher and editor of El Independiente, *a weekly newspaper that was one of the few voices for justice and human rights in El Salvador. The Mass began about 6 P.M. in the chapel of the Divine Providence cancer hospital, in San Salvador. The gospel reading was John 12:23-26:*

"The hour has come for the Son of Man to be glorified . . . . Unless the grain of wheat falls to the earth and dies, it remains only a grain. But if it dies, it bears much fruit. Those who love their own life will lose it; those who hate their own life in this world will keep it for life eternal. Whoever wants to serve me must follow me, so that my servant may be with me where I am."

Because of the manifold relationship I have had with the editor of the newspaper *El Independiente*, I am able to share to some extent his feelings on the anniversary of his mother's death. Above all, I can appreciate her noble spirit, how she put all of her educated upbringing, all her graciousness, at the service of a cause that is so important now: our people's true liberation.

My dear brothers and sisters, I think we should not only pray this evening for the eternal rest of our dear Doña Sarita, but above all we should take to ourselves her message, one that every Christian ought to want to live intensely. Many do not understand; they think Christianity should not be involved in such things. But, to the contrary, you have just heard in Christ's gospel that one must not love oneself so much as to avoid getting involved in the risks of life that history demands of us, and that those who try to fend off the danger will lose their lives, while those who out of love for Christ give themselves to the service of others will live, like the grain of wheat that dies, but only apparently. If it did not die, it would remain alone. The harvest comes about only because it dies, allowing itself to be sacrificed in the earth and destroyed. Only by undoing itself does it produce the harvest.

Now in eternity, Doña Sarita gives us the same wonderful message that Vatican II gives us in the following passage, which I have chosen on her behalf:

> We do not know the time for the consummation of the earth and of humanity. Nor do we know how all things will be transformed. As deformed by sin, the shape of this world will pass away. But we are taught that God is preparing a new dwelling place and a new earth where justice will abide, and whose blessedness will answer and surpass all the longings for peace which spring up in the human heart.
>
> Then, with death overcome, the sons of God will be raised up in Christ. What was sown in weakness and corruption will be clothed with incorruptibility. While charity and its fruits endure, all that creation which God made on man's account will be unchained from the bondage of vanity.
>
> Therefore, while we are warned that it profits a man nothing if he gain the whole world and lose himself, the expectation of a new earth must not weaken but rather stimulate our concern for cultivating this one. For here grows the body of a new human family, a body which even now is able to give some kind of foreshadowing of the new age.
>
> Earthly progress must be carefully distinguished from the growth of Christ's kingdom. Nevertheless, to the extent that the former can contribute to the better ordering of human society, it is of vital concern to the kingdom of God.
>
> For after we have obeyed the Lord, and in His Spirit nurtured on earth the values of human dignity, brotherhood and freedom, and indeed all the good fruits of our nature and enterprise, we will find them again, but freed of stain, burnished and transfigured. This will be so when Christ hands over to the Father a kingdom eternal and universal: "a kingdom of truth and life, of holiness and grace, of justice, love, and peace." On this earth that kingdom is already present in mystery. When the Lord returns, it will be brought into full flower [*Gaudium et Spes,* 39].

This is the hope that inspires us Christians. We know that every effort to better society, especially when injustice and sin are so ingrained, is an effort that God blesses, that God wants, that God demands of us. Doña Sarita was that kind of generous person, and her attitude was embodied in her son Jorge and in all those who work for these ideals. Of course, we must try to purify these ideals, Christianize them, clothe them with the hope of what lies beyond. That makes them stronger, because it gives us the assurance that all that we cultivate on earth, if we nourish it with Christian hope, will never be a failure. We will find it in a purer form in that kingdom where our merit will be in the labor we have done here on earth.

As we celebrate this anniversary, I think we do not aspire in vain in these times of hope and struggle. We remember with gratitude this generous woman who was able to sympathize with the concerns of her husband and her son and of all those who work for a better world, and who added her own grain of wheat through her suffering. I have no doubt this will guarantee that her heavenly reward will be in proportion to her sacrifice and to her sympathy—self-sacrifice and sympathy that many lack at this moment in El Salvador.

Dear brothers and sisters, let us all view these matters at this historic moment with that hope, that spirit of giving and of sacrifice. Let us all do what we can. We can all do something, at least have a sense of understanding and sympathy. The holy woman we remember today could not do many things directly perhaps, but she did encourage those who can work, sympathized with their struggle, and above all prayed. Even after her death, she sends a message from eternity that it is worthwhile to labor, because all those longings for justice, peace, and well-being that we experience on earth become realized for us if we enlighten them with Christian hope. We know that no one can go on forever, but those who have put into their work a sense of very great faith, of love of God, of hope among human beings, find it all results in the splendors of a crown that is the sure reward of those who labor thus, cultivating truth, justice, love, and goodness on the earth. Such labor does not remain here below, but purified by God's Spirit, is harvested for our reward.

This holy mass, now, this Eucharist, is just such an act of faith. To Christian faith at this moment the voice of diatribe appears changed for the body of the Lord, who offered himself for the redemption of the world, and in this chalice the wine is transformed into the blood that was the price of salvation. May this body immolated and this blood sacrificed for humans nourish us also, so that we may give our body and our blood to suffering and to pain—like Christ, not for self, but to bring about justice and peace for our people.

Let us join together, then, intimately in faith and hope at this moment of prayer for Doña Sarita and ourselves.

[At this moment, a shot rang out in the chapel and Archbishop Romero fell mortally wounded. He died within minutes, on arriving at a nearby hospital emergency room.]

Index

Compiled by James Sullivan